Reading Miscue Inventory
Alternative Procedures

Reading Miscue Inventory
Alternative Procedures

Yetta M. Goodman
Dorothy J. Watson
Carolyn L. Burke

RICHARD C. OWEN PUBLISHERS, INC.
New York

Library of Congress Cataloging-in-Publication Data

Goodman, Yetta M., 1931–
Reading miscue inventory.

Bibliography: p.
Includes index.
1. Miscue analysis. 2. Reading. I. Watson, Dorothy J. (Dorothy Jo), 1930– II. Burke, Carolyn L. III. Title.
LB1050.33.G66 1987 428.4 86-28604
ISBN 0–913461–80–6

RICHARD C. OWEN PUBLISHERS, INC.
Rockefeller Center
Box 819
New York, New York 10185

PRINTED IN THE UNITED STATES OF AMERICA

In Honor and Memory
of
BARRY SHERMAN

Contents

Preface

In the original *Reading Miscue Inventory* we stated our conviction that teachers will more readily make changes in their reading curriculum when they have an effective procedure that provides "a window on the reading process" at the same time that it helps them to observe and understand the reading of their students. This is still the main benefit of learning to do miscue analysis. For reading specialists, special educators, reading researchers, and classroom teachers, knowing miscue analysis well develops an understanding concerning the reading process that guides all subsequent decisions about the teaching or exploration of reading.

Once reading professionals allow their understandings to be informed by students' miscues, new concerns about reading and learning to read must be addressed. For example, when reading about and studying the complexity of Frank's substitutions of *for* for *from* in two or three of his stories, it becomes obvious that he substitutes one for the other in some grammatical settings, and not others, and that he substitutes when there are certain relationships being expressed, but not others. Through such analysis, researchers learn a great deal about language and how readers use it. They realize how different text structures affect miscues (and therefore the reading process) in various ways. Teachers begin to understand that simplistic remediation will not help Frank and may even cause further complications. Instead, Frank's knowledge and use of the syntactic and semantic complexities of his language is understood. His strength as a language user is celebrated. Reading research and the teaching of reading can never be the same once they are informed by the power of the miscue analysis of a reader.

In addition to helping our understanding of how reading works, miscue analysis supplies more information about a single reader than any other instrument available. John omits the word *oxygen* each time it appears in the published text of the story he reads. During the retelling, as he is trying to express why "the men were getting so sleepy," John shows that he had been comprehending the text throughout his reading when he explodes with "Oxygen . . . that's the word I didn't know . . . oxygen." The miscue analysis of John's reading shows how he transacts with the text and how this transaction builds his comprehension. Reading specialists and classroom teachers who know how to analyze such processing while students read become aware that students like John are actively involved in their reading. Then they find ways to support such strengths. When Alta reads *then* for *when* throughout a story, but reads *whistle* and *white* without problems, her special education teacher has more to think about than the simple notion that Alta has problems with a *th, wh* confusion.

Those who know us are aware of our enthusiasm and conviction about the power of miscue analysis. Although miscue analysis is complicated and time consuming, its use allows the individual to take charge. Miscue analysis is based on theoretical notions that are informed by linguistic, psycholinguistic, and sociolinguistic knowledge. It also is informed by a view of science: Miscue analysis is a tool that provides users with the power to inquire into their own questions and to solve their own problems in order to come to their own conclusions. It is an open-ended heuristic instrument that helps teachers and researchers become part of the knowledge explosion that is taking place in the field of literacy learning today. We believe that the results of miscue analysis will allow its users to want to know more about reading and the reader.

Recently I returned from a conference on the East Coast of the United States where over a thousand teachers and other school personnel came together to consider issues related to whole language teaching and learning. In a few weeks I will participate in a conference in the Southwest where teachers and administrators will explore how to immerse their students in writing and how to integrate reading and writing in every aspect of the curriculum.

Little did we realize when we introduced the ideas behind the RMI to 25 teachers in a school district near San Diego in 1970 that two decades later we would be part of a movement of professional educators and researchers who are committed to understanding why readers do what they do, to understanding that what students do when they read reflects their knowledge about language and the world, and to realizing that the more they understand about the processes of reading and learning to read the more they are able to facilitate and support the growth of literacy.

I don't mean to imply that miscue analysis alone has been responsible for this historic movement toward teachers taking ownership of their professional responsibilities in the classroom. However, I do believe that miscue analysis has been an important impetus to allow educators to view the process of learning to read in new ways and in paving the way for teachers and researchers to raise questions about the relationship between the teaching of reading and learning to read.

To the large number of friends of miscue analysis who have been asking when we will have a new publication available, we can finally say *here it is.* In the years since the first publication of the *Reading Miscue Inventory* we have adapted and expanded many of the original ideas and have promised to publish our new ideas and insights. However, *Reading Miscue Inventory: Alternative Procedures* is not simply a revision. Much has happened to our own thinking over the years. Colleagues who have followed our work are aware of the interim forms that we shared during these years, and even those have been changed or amended. We wish it were possible to list the many graduate students, professors of reading, and English/language arts teachers and special educators who raised questions, criticized, and wondered with us whether one particular procedure was better than another, whether a particular wording would clarify or make things more ambiguous. But so many have contributed to the integration of arguments, discussions, and collaborations that we have decided to just say thanks. Those who read this and know your influence on our work should realize how much we appreciate our continued discussions and interactions.

Dorothy, Carol, and I invite those of you who use miscue analysis to continue the dialogue that led to this new *RMI.* We invite your comments, your reactions, and your questions. We will respond.

Yetta

Yetta M. Goodman
University of Arizona
College of Education
Tucson, AZ 85721

Part I

Miscue Analysis and the Reading Process

The importance of miscue analysis for various professionals concerned with reading, reading instruction, and reading research is discussed in Chapter 1 along with historical information about the development of various miscue analysis procedures. The chapter ends with a recommendation for self-monitoring the reading process and an introduction of Betsy, whose oral reading is used as an exemplar for miscue analysis throughout this book. Chapter 2 provides an overview of the model of reading developed by K. Goodman, which is the basis for the theory underlying the analysis of miscues.

1

Observing the Reading Process

Have you ever heard a student read an entire story, article or chapter without any interruption? For teachers and researchers, such an experience adds a new dimension to the term *language learning*.

Have you ever wondered:

Why readers say *daddy* for *father* or *day* for *morning?*

Why readers are able to read a word or phrase on Tuesday and are unable to read it on Thursday?

Why readers have difficulty with a word or phrase in one part of the text and no problem with it in another part of the same text?

Why readers read certain segments of a text slowly and deliberately, then move quickly through other segments of the same text, leaving out words or phrases that don't seem to change the author's intended meaning?

Why readers omit or substitute one word for another throughout a text and then when they talk about what they've read use the word as it appeared in the text?

Why readers can read a whole story with dramatic expression but not understand what they have read?

Miscue analysis is a tool that allows people who want to know more about reading to investigate why such phenomena occur. Listening to students read uninterrupted texts provides a "window on the reading process" (K. Goodman, 1973b, p5). Those who look through the "window" at the reading process have a way to describe, explain, and evaluate a reader's control or ownership of the process. Miscue analysis not only reveals degrees of reading proficiency; more important, it provides teacher/researchers with knowledge about the reading process itself.

Miscue analysis is to reading what radiology is to the examination of the human body. It includes a number of procedures to view what readers do when they read in order to understand the reading process, just as radiology uses X-rays and sonograms to achieve an understanding of the inner workings of the skeleton and organs. Miscue analysis evaluates reading problems at the same time as it provides a view of the knowledge readers bring to their reading and the strategies they use to solve their problems. Miscue analysis shows how readers use various systems of language and a variety of strategies to construct meaning. Medical practitioners and researchers who are specialists in radiology are much better able to comprehend and interpret X-rays, sonograms, and other procedures that provide various views of the human body than physicians who are not radiology specialists. In the same way, the more knowledge and experience teacher/researchers have about language, reading, and miscue analysis, the greater will be their ability to understand and evaluate reading, the reading process, and reading materials.

Those who study miscue analysis simultaneously increase their knowledge about reading and other language processes, as well as their knowledge about the reader. Those who understand and use miscue analysis a great deal will not only be able to analyze miscues formally, but they will also be able to use miscue analysis techniques whenever they listen to anyone read. Once professionals concerned with reading have developed miscue analysis techniques they will never again listen to readers in the way they did in the past.

Purposes of Miscue Analysis

The most important use of miscue analysis is to help teacher/researchers gain insight into the reading process. Miscue analysis differs significantly from all other commonly used diagnostic and evaluative instruments in that the resulting analysis of reading proficiency is qualitative as well as quantitative.

When a diagnostic instrument results only in quantitative analysis, all errors have equal weight because exactness is the goal; deviations are considered random and irrational, and the reader is expected to "attack" written material in a prescribed manner. Because quantitative analysis examines surface behavior, strategies such as self-correction and regressions, which are in fact necessary for proficient reading, are often treated as problematic instead. Qualitative analysis, on the other hand, evaluates why miscues are made and assumes that they derive from the language and thought that the reader brings to the written material in the attempt to construct meaning from reading. Such analysis allows the teacher/researcher to interpret and understand what miscues reveal about the reading process.

A second purpose of miscue analysis is to analyze the oral reading of individual students. Such analysis provides a great deal of specific information about a student's reading ability, allowing teachers in regular classrooms or special education programs to plan reading programs and instructional strategies that build on strengths rather than on weaknesses. At the same time, it allows researchers to inquire into the linguistic knowledge and strategy use of readers of diverse populations.

In addition to building a view of the reading process and evaluating a student's reading, another purpose of miscue analysis is to help teacher/researchers evaluate reading material. Such evaluation provides an objective basis for determining whether a given selection should be used in a reading program and for determining its suitability for use by students. The text itself can also be examined to evaluate its cohesion and coherence, the complexity of its grammatical structures, and the density and level of familiarity of the new concepts it presents.

The Quest for Understanding Reading

Miscue analysis was originally developed by K. Goodman for the purpose of understanding the reading process. After two decades of miscue research, K. Goodman has concluded that there is a single reading process that readers adapt depending on the value they place on their reading, the function that a particular piece of reading serves, and their proficiency as readers (Gollasch, 1982).

The Goodman Taxonomy of Reading Miscues

The Goodman Reading Model was developed by analyzing the degree to which unexpected responses or *miscues* change, disrupt, or enhance the meaning of a written text. K. Goodman initiated the use of the term miscue in reading in order to eliminate the pejorative connotations of words such as *error* and *mistake* and to underscore the belief that all reading is cued by language and personal experience and is not simply random, uncontrolled behavior. On the basis of his research, he developed the Goodman Taxonomy of Reading Miscues (Goodman, 1973b) to evaluate, categorize, and explain the miscue phenomena he found to be prevalent in *every* reader. The taxonomy, which has gone through a dozen revisions since its original development, evaluates each of the reader's consecutive miscues through a series of questions designed to gain the greatest amount of information about the causes of miscues and their influences on readers' comprehension. These questions are concerned with linguistic qualities of each miscue and the strategies readers use in relation to their miscues. Some of the questions are:

Do miscues result in sentences that are semantically and syntactically acceptable?
Do miscues cause grammatical transformations?
To what degree do miscues retain the grammatical function of text items?
To what degree do miscues retain a semantic relationship to the text item?
To what degree do miscues retain graphic and phonological similarity to text items?
In what ways do readers use strategies such as self-correcting and predicting?

K. Goodman, in collaboration with many students and colleagues, has designed and conducted a large number of miscue studies to answer these and related questions. An extensive number and broad range of complete stories and articles have been used with readers of varying abilities, ethnic backgrounds, types of physical and learning problems, and languages and English dialects. The Goodman Taxonomy has been used to evaluate the reading of hundreds of subjects, from children in the first grade to adults both in college and in basic literacy programs (Marek, Goodman, and Babcock, 1985).

K. Goodman continues testing and adapting his theory and model of the reading process, adjusting the taxonomy to take new findings into account (K. Goodman, 1984). The Goodman Taxonomy, with its complex system of questions, reflects current knowledge and theory in linguistics, psycholinguistics, and sociolinguistics (see Appendix D).

The Reading Miscue Inventory

While working with K. Goodman during his early research, Y. Goodman and Burke (1972) became interested in bringing the impact of miscue analysis to teachers working with readers in classrooms and clinics. The miscue analysis to be used to organize reading curricula and plan individual instructional strategies for students was developed with the help of teachers, special educators, and reading specialists. The original Reading Miscue Inventory (Y. Goodman and Burke,

1972), therefore, included questions from the Goodman Taxonomy that provided information about readers and language that helped teachers use and understand miscue analysis. The project through which the inventory was developed became an exemplary dissemination project for the State of California (Psycholinguistic Approach to Reading, 1974).

The original Reading Miscue Inventory (RMI) includes nine questions and has been used for many years for preservice and inservice classes, for the evaluation of students' reading and as a research instrument (see Appendix D). The RMI has been used to analyze the readings of thousands of primary and secondary school students and adult readers with varying abilities in both regular and special education programs (Marek, Goodman, and Babcock, 1985).

Many teacher/researchers who have used miscue analysis over the years have asked for simpler and less time-consuming procedures than the original RMI. Some modified it to suit their own purposes (Long, 1985).

Alternative Miscue Analysis Procedures

Over more than 15 years, adaptations have been made to the categories and procedures of the RMI during research and work with preservice and inservice teachers. Miscue analysis procedures have been modified to save time and to accommodate changes in setting, material, purpose, and audience. These adapted procedures have become options for those using miscue analysis. Four of these options are presented in detail in Chapters 5 and 6.

Procedure I, the most complex and time-consuming option, provides the greatest amount of information about reading and the reading process. It reveals the strategies readers use in monitoring a text in ways that are not as apparent in the other procedures. This procedure allows teacher/researchers to observe how readers use their prediction and correction strategies as each miscue is analyzed separately in relation to other miscues. Because this procedure provides the greatest insights into the reading process, it is recommended for:

Teacher education courses with a major focus on miscue analysis
Evaluation of students with perplexing problems in reading
Most research purposes

Each subsequent procedure is less time-consuming, and the knowledge obtained becomes more general. Procedures II and III are similar in that each evaluates all the miscues within one sentence at the same time. Procedure II results in forms that may be placed in a student's record-keeping folder. Procedure III is organized in such a way that the miscue marking and coding are done directly on the typescript, and separate forms are not used. A great deal of information about a student's reading is obtainable using Procedures II and III, and they are recommended for classroom teachers who want to refer students for special services. Researchers may find these procedures useful for answering certain questions about reading. Procedure III is also useful for workshops, seminars, or teacher education courses that devote only part of the time to miscue analysis.

Procedure IV is an informal procedure developed for use with readers during individual reading conferences. Teachers who become proficient in miscue analysis find themselves using the processes of Procedure IV intuitively whenever they listen to a reader. This procedure basically deals with a single question and monitors the reader's comprehending process. Teacher/researchers are strongly cautioned *not* to use Procedure IV before they acquire proficiency with the other procedures.

Although some of the procedures are simpler than others, none of them can be accomplished without an understanding of the major concepts of miscue analysis. Research indicates that use of overly simplified miscue analysis forms does not help teachers develop their own reading model, nor does it help them understand the issues concerned with the evaluation of individual readers (Long, 1985). Therefore, we recommend that those new to miscue analysis become thoroughly familiar with the more complex procedures before trying the less time-consuming ones. When teacher/researchers are familiar with all the procedures, they will be in a good position to decide which will best suit their purposes.

The concepts involved in miscue analysis are often new and difficult for teacher/researchers who have not had to take into account linguistic knowledge and the qualitative influences of miscues on texts and on readers' comprehension. There is no simple road to understanding complex ideas. The ideas and concepts about reading, linguistics, psycholinguistics, and sociolinguistics that teacher/researchers stand to gain from developing ability in the use of miscue analysis will be well worth their efforts.

The process of learning to do miscue analysis builds and extends many concepts about language that are needed to understand both the reading process and miscue analysis itself. The knowledge about language that is necessary for miscue analysis is provided here when appropriate, but the procedures developed for the book do not require sophisticated linguistic knowledge.

Audiences for Miscue Analysis

Miscue analysis serves a variety of purposes for a number of different groups of people.

Teachers, Special Educators, and Reading Specialists

For most professionals working with readers, the major purpose of miscue analysis is to analyze the oral reading of individual students in order to plan specific reading programs for each and to organize reading programs for the classroom or small groups of problem readers. Miscue analysis gives teachers in both regular and special education classrooms a great deal of specific information about student reading. Not only does miscue analysis allow teachers to see a reader's problems; more important, it provides evidence of the reader's strengths.*

As teachers become more aware of what happens during reading, they can involve students in developing awareness of the reading process. Thus the reader, too, will be able to make use of miscue analysis for purposes of self-evaluation (see Part Three).

Each miscue analysis procedure allows teachers to determine the quality and variety of the reader's miscues through a series of questions. These questions focus on the effect each miscue has on the meaning of what is being read. Answers to the questions enable the teacher to analyze the reader's use of available language cues and background information, as well as to examine and evaluate the relationship

*Since reading specialists and those who work with variously designated populations such as the hearing impaired or learning disabled are essentially *teachers* with additional study in reading theory, more in-depth understanding of special populations, and more years of working directly with students, the term *teacher* will usually be used to refer to both specialists and regular classroom teachers.

between the language of the reader and the language of the author. They help the teacher understand how the reader's thoughts and language are brought to the reading task; how the reader's experiences aid in the interpretation of an author's meaning; and how the reader builds or constructs meaning. The retelling adds information about the reader's search for meaning and supports explanations about many of the reader's miscues.

Because miscue analysis examines the way in which the reader's language, thought, and experiences function in reading, it helps the teacher to:

Determine the varying causes of miscues
Highlight the strengths of high-quality miscues
Pinpoint specific and repetitive problems
Distinguish these problems from difficulties caused by the syntactic complexity or conceptual load of the reading material

The miscue data is usually compiled on a Coding Form showing the interrelationship of all these factors, and is used to construct a profile of the reader. The Reader Profile indicates the student's use of various reading strategies and the student's patterns of reading strengths and weaknesses. The profile can be compared with other profiles throughout a school year as well as with those made from year to year. In this way, an accurate and current picture of growth in reading proficiency is obtained and maintained. The information gathered becomes the basis for formulating a reading program that will provide the reader with supportive and broadening reading experiences.

Researchers

For researchers, miscue analysis provides ways to inquire into specific aspects of the reading process as well as to explore issues about how reading works, how readers interpret and respond while reading, and what readers' transactions with the text reveal about textual organization.

Initially miscue analysis was used to develop a model of how people read. Researchers interested in model-building can test their own models of reading through the use of miscue analysis. For this purpose, a researcher might use the Goodman Taxonomy of Reading Miscues (Allen and Watson, 1976).

The following questions and others raised earlier suggest many research issues that continue to be explored through miscue analysis:

How does a reader's oral language (specific dialect features) affect reading?
What are the patterns of miscues at different age levels?
What are developmental trends in the use of reading strategies and the control of language cueing systems?
How do text features affect the patterns of miscues?
Do biliterate readers produce different kinds of miscues in the reading of their first and second languages?
In what ways are miscues different in silent and oral reading?

Researchers interested in these or other similar reading research questions should select the miscue procedure that serves them best.

Sadoski and Page (1984), among others, have related issues of reliability and validity to cloze procedures as well as other measures of reading. These issues are important to researchers such as Gollasch (1980) and Woodley (1983) who are concerned with the experimental research paradigm.

Much of miscue analysis is on a continuum closer to naturalistic research than to experimental studies. Therefore, it is helpful to consider concepts raised by Lincoln and Guba (1985) that support the various basic beliefs and knowledge claims of naturalistic researchers (pp. 289–331). Lincoln and Guba show how naturalistic researchers are as concerned with the trustworthiness of data as researchers who work with other paradigms that yield credible findings and interpretations. They suggest that researchers must become thoroughly familiar with the participants and culture being studied through in-depth and persistent observation. Such researchers become sensitive to qualities that are pervasive in the research setting and are able to sort out irrelevancies. Lincoln and Guba also make a case for careful observation over long periods of time and comparisons of data through the use of multiple and different sources. Miscue analysis, which provides for prolonged and careful observation of different readers using the same kind of material or using different materials with the same readers over periods of time, lends itself to such careful research.

Material Developers

Miscue analysis procedures are valuable for those involved in developing and publishing reading materials by providing ways to determine suitability for student use. Miscue analysis supplies a unique basis for determining whether a given selection can be used in a reading program or for particular readers. It was used in this way in the development of the Scott Foresman Reading Unlimited and Reading Systems from 1970 to 1975 (Smith and Lindberg, 1979).

Miscue analysis has been used both formally and informally to study the readability of texts (Smith and Lindberg, 1979; Altwerger and Goodman, 1981; K. Goodman and Gespass, 1983). The advantage miscue analysis offers readability research is that both the reader and the text are considered as factors in determining text difficulty.

A teacher who uses the same material repeatedly for miscue analysis becomes aware of the areas of the text in which many readers make the same or similar miscues. A linguistic analysis of such areas will reveal the kinds of structures that are difficult to predict. This helps teachers understand that certain text constructions cause problems for many readers, and gives them ways to help readers deal with such problems. It also provides the knowledge necessary to make decisions about the kinds of structures to be avoided in writing texts.

Building a Personal Model of Reading

The most significant outcome of understanding miscue analysis is the ability to build a personal model of the reading process. Few people who learn to use miscue analysis do not change their views of reading. One issue related to building a personal model of reading through learning about and using miscue analysis has to do with the explicit knowledge about language that develops through the use of these procedures. This is especially significant for reading instruction.

When young children come to school, they have a great deal of knowlege about the language spoken in their home communities. They know how to use language successfully in order to get what they want and to accomplish the things they need to do. Such language knowledge is quite sophisticated. For example, all English-speaking children know subject-verb-object relationships, or they could never successfully construct a sentence such as *Mary hit Johnny.* Children know that third person singular verbs have an *s* on the end, and they know how to construct the past tense appropriately by adding *ed.* Without such knowledge, children could never produce sentences such as, *Hey, teacher, he gots my ball* or *I runned all the way to the fence.* Child language development scholars are impressed with the knowledge that kids as young as 2 years old must have that they often characterize children as linguistic geniuses.

However, all of this knowledge is intuitive; it is not explicit or conscious. In other words, children know such rules and patterns and have an organizational system, called a schema by some psychologists (Gruber and Voneche, 1977), that allows the knowledge and rules to be used and developed even though children cannot talk about what the language rules are or discuss how they learned them.

The reading strategies used during reading, described in Chapter 2, show that all readers of all ages operate with intuitive knowledge about reading. Readers know intuitively, but not necessarily consciously, the rules that help them sample, predict, self-correct, and construct meaning as they read. Many readers of this text may never before have thought about these ideas, nor are they able to explain them to others; nevertheless they use the reading strategies and are considered proficient readers.

However, when students of a particular subject begin to examine why certain kinds of events happen and what makes them happen, they develop conscious knowledge about the particular phenomena they are studying. The ability to talk and think consciously about language is called by some metalinguistic knowledge (Yaden and Templeton, 1986), while others say that this ability provides evidence of overt linguistic or language knowledge (Halliday, 1975).

Miscue analysis allows teacher/researchers to become consciously aware of the process of reading—to develop metalinguistic knowledge about reading. Those working in the field of reading should be as knowledgeable about reading as possible. Professionals must know the significance of a miscue when a reader makes one. If teacher/researchers do not understand this important concept, they may treat miscues as unnecessary phenomena that must be eliminated. Once teacher/researchers understand, through examination of the reading process, that miscues reflect the reader's development, the reader's language system, and the reader's interpretations of meaning and context, then miscues can become a window through which much can be discovered about the individual reader as well as about the reading process.

Discovering How People Read

Both miscue analysis and its underlying theory grew out of listening to people read and trying to understand why they do what they do while reading. That is why this book on miscue analysis stays close to reality because it allows professionals to look at themselves read and to examine how others read. In this way, we continuously relate theory to reality and reality to theory. Our intention is to help you to utilize miscue analysis to revalue both the reader and the reading process.

Soon you will meet Betsy, who provides many examples to help us explore the reading process. Before exploring Betsy's reading, however, you should participate in an activity that will allow you to monitor your own reading. Read the unmarked copy of *The Man Who Kept House* in Appendix C. This is the same story Betsy read. If you have already read the story, read another complete story or article, such as a short chapter from a text being used for a class or a complete article from the morning newspaper.

After reading silently, write down everything you remember. This experiment works best if at least two or three people read the same text. Then, without looking at the story, discuss the text with the other readers; note similarities and differences among the responses of the members of the group. During the discussion, consider what caused the similarities and differences and what each person knows that may have influenced the responses. Now compare the responses with the original text. You may want to list some generalizations about the processes of reading and retelling on the basis of this experience. As you continue to use this book, refer to this activity, comparing what you and other adult readers did with what Betsy did, and continue to add to or change your developing list of generalizations about the reading process.

Observing the Reader

We introduce Betsy at this time because she will be the reader used to explain the various miscue analysis procedures and the application of the procedures for use in research and curriculum development. Betsy is typical of students in classrooms, reading clinics, and reading research studies. The readers of this text will become well acquainted with her.

Betsy was 9 years old, in the 2nd month of third grade, and lived in Toronto, Canada, when Ms. Blau, her regular classroom teacher, taped her reading *The Man Who Kept House.* According to standardized tests and other school records, she showed little progress in reading development at the end of first grade and therefore was retained for a year. Betsy's standardized test scores, at the time of this taping, indicated that she was reading at a second-grade level.

This student was selected for miscue analysis because although she had been making slow progress in reading, Ms. Blau believed she had untapped potential. Ms. Blau knew that Betsy was bright, alert, interested in listening to stories read in class, not interested in reading on her own, and moving even further away from active personal involvement with print. Ms. Blau was searching for information about Betsy that would help her plan a reading program that would be effective.

By studying Betsy's reading and retelling of *The Man Who Kept House,* her reading strengths as well as her problems will become evident. Specifically, the language cueing systems Betsy controls and the reading strategies she uses will be revealed through the miscue analysis procedures. Such information will be used to suggest a reading program for Betsy and show how a program can be developed for other readers.

Betsy Reads

This section includes the conversation between Betsy and Ms. Blau before the reading; Betsy's typescript, including her marked miscues; and other notations, followed by her retelling of the story. The procedures Ms. Blau followed to gather this information will be explained in depth in Part Two.

Directions Before Reading Betsy and Ms. Blau are seated comfortably at a table. They have chatted informally for a few minutes and Ms. Blau has tested the tape recorder to see that it is functioning properly. (The teacher's remarks are marked T and Betsy's are marked B.)

T: Betsy, this is the story I want you to read. Have you ever read or heard this story before? (Encourages Betsy to leaf through the pages to see how long the story is and to be sure she has not previously read or heard it.)

B: No.

T: Good. I'd like you to read the story aloud. I'll record your reading. As you are reading try to think about what you are reading and when you are finished I'll take the book from you and ask you to tell me everything you can remember about the story.

Betsy, when you're reading and come to something that you don't know . . . anything that gives you trouble . . . do whatever you would do if you were reading all by yourself . . . as if I weren't here. Do you have any questions?

B: No. (Betsy reads the story without interruptions from her teacher.)

Betsy's Marked Typescript (The way the typescript is organized and marked is explained in Chapter 3.)

Name: Betsy Date: November 3
Grade/Age: Grade Three Teacher: Mrs. Blau
Reference: The Man Who Kept House

The Man Who Kept House

0101 Once upon a time there was a woodman
0102 who thought that no one worked as hard as
0103 he did. One evening when he came home
0104 from work, he said to his wife, "What do you
0105 do all day while I am away cutting wood?"
0106 "I keep house," replied the wife, "and
0107 keeping house is hard work."
0108 "Hard work!" said the husband. "You don't
0109 know what hard work is! You should try
0110 cutting wood!"
0111 "I'd be glad to," said the wife.
0112 "Why don't you do my work some day? I'll

0113 stay home and keep house," said the woodman.

0114 "If you stay home to do my work, you'll

0115 have to make butter, carry water from the

0116 well, wash the clothes, clean the house, and

0117 look after the baby," said the wife.

0118 "I can do all that," replied the husband.

0119 "We'll do it tomorrow!"

0201 So the next morning the wife went off to

0202 the forest. The husband stayed home and

0203 began to do his wife's work.

0204 He began to make some butter. As he put

0205 the cream into the churn, he said, "This is

0206 not going to be hard work. All I have to do

0207 is sit here and move this stick up and down.

0208 Soon the cream will turn into butter."

0209 Just then the woodman heard the baby

0210 crying. He looked around, but he could not

0211 see her. She was not in the house. Quickly,

0212 he ran outside to look for her. He found the

0213 baby at the far end of the garden and

0214 brought her back to the house.

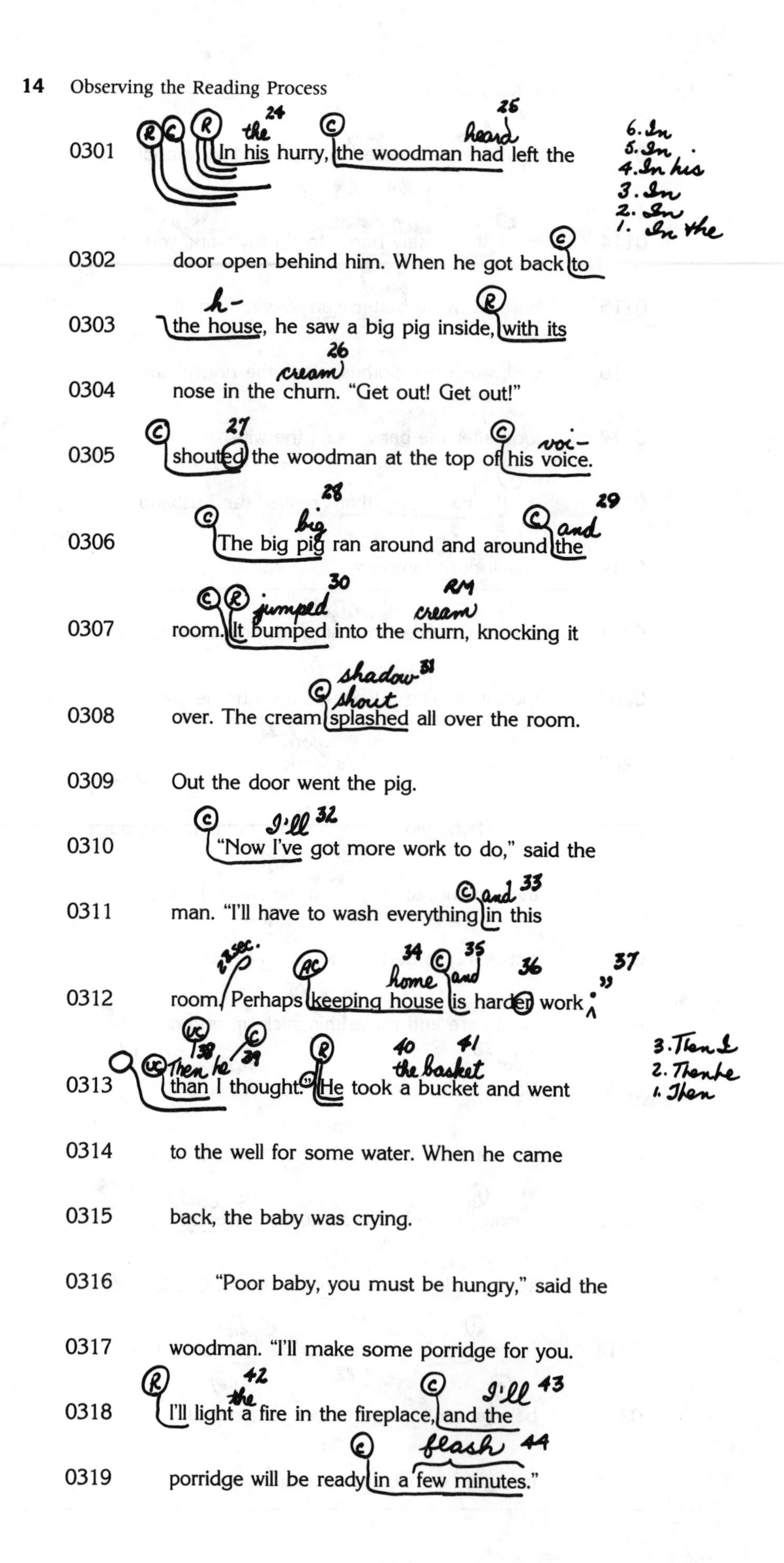

0301 In his hurry, the woodman had left the

0302 door open behind him. When he got back to

0303 the house, he saw a big pig inside, with its

0304 nose in the churn. "Get out! Get out!"

0305 shouted the woodman at the top of his voice.

0306 The big pig ran around and around the

0307 room. It bumped into the churn, knocking it

0308 over. The cream splashed all over the room.

0309 Out the door went the pig.

0310 "Now I've got more work to do," said the

0311 man. "I'll have to wash everything in this

0312 room. Perhaps keeping house is harder work

0313 than I thought." He took a bucket and went

0314 to the well for some water. When he came

0315 back, the baby was crying.

0316 "Poor baby, you must be hungry," said the

0317 woodman. "I'll make some porridge for you.

0318 I'll light a fire in the fireplace, and the

0319 porridge will be ready in a few minutes."

0320 Just as the husband was putting the

0321 water into the big pot, he heard the cow

0401 mooing outside the door. "I guess the cow is

0402 hungry, too," he thought. "No one has given

0403 her any grass to eat or any water to drink

0404 today."

0405 The man left the porridge to cook on the

0406 fire and hurried outside. He gave the cow

0407 some water.

0408 "I haven't time to find any grass for you

0409 now," he said to the cow. "I'll put you up

0410 on the roof. You'll find something to eat

0411 up there."

0412 The man put the cow on top of the house.

0413 Then he was afraid that she would fall off

0414 the roof and hurt herself. So he put one

0415 end of a rope around the cow's neck. He

0416 dropped the other end down the chimney.

0501 Then he climbed down from the roof and

0502 went into the house. He pulled the end of the

0503 rope out of the fireplace and put it around

0504 his left leg.

0505 "Now I can finish making this porridge,"

0506 said the woodman, "and the cow will

0507 be safe."

0508 But the man spoke too soon, for just then

0509 the cow fell off the roof. She pulled him up

0510 the chimney by the rope. There he hung,

0511 upside down over the porridge pot. As for the

0512 cow, she hung between the roof and the

0513 ground, and there she had to stay.

0514 It was not very long before the woodman's

0515 wife came home. As she came near the

0516 house, she could hear the cow mooing, the

0601 baby crying, and her husband shouting for

0602 help. She hurried up the path. She cut the

0603 rope from the cow's neck. As she did so,

0604 the cow fell down to the ground, and the

0605 husband dropped head first down the chimney.

0606 When the wife went into the house, she

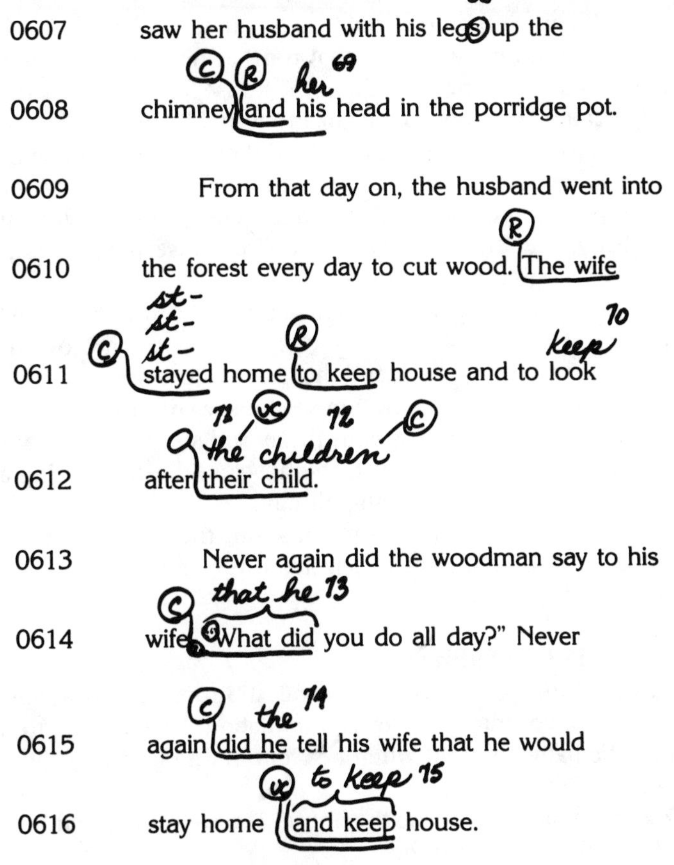

0607 saw her husband with his legs up the
0608 chimney and his head in the porridge pot.
0609 From that day on, the husband went into
0610 the forest every day to cut wood. The wife
0611 stayed home to keep house and to look
0612 after their child.
0613 Never again did the woodman say to his
0614 wife, "What did you do all day?" Never
0615 again did he tell his wife that he would
0616 stay home and keep house.

Betsy's Unaided Retelling

T: Betsy, you did a nice job. Thank you. Now, would you close the book and in your own words tell me the story? (Betsy hands the book to Ms. Blau.)

B: Um, it was about this woodman, when he . . . he thought that he had harder work to do than his wife, so he went home and he told his wife, "What have you been doing all day?" And then his wife told him, and he thought that it was easy work. And so . . . so his wife . . . so his wife, she said, "Well, so you have to keep . . ." No, the husband says that, "You have to go to the woods and cut . . . and have to go out in the forest and cut wood and I'll stay home."

And the next day they did that. And the wife left home with a ax. And the husband was sitting down and he poured some buttermilk and um . . . in the jar. And, he um . . . heard the baby crying. So he looked all around in the room, and he didn't see the baby. So he went out to . . . to um . . . to get the baby. And so he didn't shut the door behind him, and so he, when he came back to, from the baby . . . he found the baby, then he came back with her.

And then he saw a pig, a big pig. He saw a big pig inside the house. So he told him to get out and the pig started racing around and he um . . .he . . . he um . . . he bumped into the buttermilk and then the buttermilk fell down and then the pig went out. Then the woodman said that he was going to have to clean all the . . . wash everything in the house.

And then the . . . the baby started crying again. And then the man said that, "You must be hungry. I'll make some porridge for you." So he lit the fire and he put the porridge on it. And then he heard the cow mooing. And then he went out . . . he went outside and said, "You must . . . um nobody, you must . . . you haven't had any milk or anything like . . . or anything to eat." So he said, "I'll put you on the roof." So he put the . . . he put him on the roof and he was . . . and he was scared that um . . . he was scared that . . . that the cow would fall out of the . . . off into the house from . . . He was scared that the cow might fall off the roof. So he got a rope and he tied it on the cow's neck. And he put the rope down the chimney and then he climbed down from the roof, and then he went back into the house again and um . . . and then he tied . . . then he took the rope and he tied it on his left leg. And then he got the porridge for the baby. And the cow fell over onto the house and the man was upside down . . . was hanging upside down.

And then his wife was coming down the forest and she heard her husband yelling, "Help." And so then she . . . so she saw the cow and then she cut the rope from the cow's neck and then . . . and then she ran inside the house. Then when she went inside the house she saw her husband with one leg up the chimney and his head was in the porridge.

And then from then on the husband did the cutting and he never said, "What have you been doing all day?"

T: Betsy, you remembered so much about the story! What a good job. Is there anything else you want to tell about the story?

B: No.

Betsy's Aided Retelling

T: Now, I'd like to ask you a few questions. You told about a lot of ways the woodman got into trouble. You told about how he had to um . . . go out and find the baby and that when he went out he forgot to shut the door. Did that cause a problem?

B: Yes, a big pig went inside the house. The woodman told him to get out and the pig started racing around.

T: What happened then . . . you know . . . when the pig started racing around?

B: He . . . he um . . . he bumped into the buttermilk and then the buttermilk fell down and then the pig went out. Then the woodman said that he was going to have to clean all the . . . wash everything in the house.

T: How did the woodman feel about that?

B: Probably didn't like it much.

T: Betsy, if you were telling a friend what this story was about, what would you say . . . in just a few words?

B: I'd say it was about a woodman who thought he had a harder job than his wife had, and he didn't, and so he stopped saying it.

T: Why do you think the author wanted to write this story?

B: He just wanted to tell a story.

T: About anything in particular?

B: Well, maybe about how people shouldn't brag about all they have to do.

T: What about those people who brag?

B: Well, they get in trouble and other people prove that they work just as hard as they do.

T: Betsy, did you like the story?

B: Yes.

T: What part did you like best?

B: I liked it all.

T: Did you think any part was special?

B: Uh uh (no).

T: Did you think any part was funny, or silly, or . . .

B: No.

T: Betsy, who did you like best the woodman or his wife?
B: The wife because she had to work too hard and she had to live with the old man.
T: What do you think that woodman was like?
B: Well, he was grumpy and he griped a lot about everything he had to do.
T: Do you have anything more to say about him?
B: No—Yeah. When he said he would take care of the house he really tried to take care of everything—the baby and the water and the cow—everything.
T: Do you think the wife had any trouble with the woodman's job?
B: No—well, maybe a little blister, but she did it okay.

2

A Holistic View of Reading: Theoretical Understandings

Theoretical Assumptions

The model of the reading process presented in this chapter, explained through the use of examples produced by Betsy and other readers, grows out of miscue analysis research and is the basis for the whole language curriculum used to plan reading instruction (see Part Three). First, however, we want to explore four basic assumptions about language, thinking, and learners:

Reading is an active process
Reading is a language process
Readers have knowledge about language
Authors have knowledge about language

Reading: An Active Process

To understand a holistic view of reading, we need to consider that both the reader and the author are equally *active in constructing or building meaning*. The text or the written material is the medium through which the reader and the author *transact*. The concept of transaction in the reading process, as elaborated by Rosenblatt (1978), suggests that when a reader and an author, by way of the written text, transact, significant changes take place.

Reading changes readers; they know more when they finish reading than when they started, and they know more about the reading process when they come to the end of what they are reading than they did at the beginning. In other words, readers add new knowledge to knowledge they already have, which often means changing or accommodating their old knowledge to be consistent with the new knowledge. At the same time, they adjust or develop their reading strategies to meet any new demands made of them by the text. The text has also been changed by the reader. This change is not only reflected in miscues but also in the underlining or marginal notes some readers make.

Text has potential for all readers. The degree to which a reader taps its potential depends partly on how the reader *changes* the text. A book or story read a second or third time or at different points during a reader's life calls forth different meanings and understandings. The term *transaction* suggests the dynamic nature of reading. It emphasizes that the reader is as active and creative in the process of reading as the writer is in the process of writing. Writing changes authors as well; however, since the focus of this book is on reading, we will not elaborate on the change that takes place in authors.

Reading: A Language Process

Another important assumption related to the transaction involving reader, writer, and text is that *reading is a language process.* Although this statement seems obvious, it needs to be explored because many instructional reading programs, testing materials, and models of reading fail to treat reading as language. Reading involves the communication of ideas, beliefs, thoughts, and emotions through shared syntactic and semantic systems in the same way that oral language does. The image of readers having a long-distance conversation with an author brings to light the many features that oral and written language have in common. The most obvious similarity is the use of similar syntactic forms to express meaning. For alphabetic languages such as English, a relationship exists between the graphic system of the written language and the phonological system of the oral language. A comparison of the published text *The Man Who Kept House* with Betsy's retelling of the story provides examples of some of the similarities between oral and written language.

The grammar, for the most part, is similarly organized. In Betsy's retelling, most of her clauses start with noun phrases and are followed by verb phrases, which is how the author writes the story. Betsy says, for example, *it was, he thought, he went,* and *he told his wife* early in her retelling. The author uses similar constructions on the first page of the story: *there was, who thought, he came, he said to his wife.* A good deal of the vocabulary Betsy uses is similar to the author's. Betsy refers to the main character as *husband* and *woodman* in the same way the author does. The overall organization of the story Betsy relates is similar to the one in the published text. Betsy tells about the chracters and the setting. She knows the story has a beginning, a sequence of events, and an end.

However, important differences exist between oral and written language that stem from the various purposes for which each is used and the ways in which each is used. Oral language often serves informal purposes such as phone conversations and coffee klatches, but can also be used formally, such as in structured interviews or lectures. Written language, although more formal than oral language when used for essays, scientific reports, and historical documents, can also be informal, as reflected in personal letters, notes, and shopping lists.

In Betsy's retelling she uses *um,* connects many of her clauses with *and* or *and then,* starts a thought and repeats it or changes it to correct an idea she is trying to relate. These are rarely part of written language, even in written dialogue. In the aided retelling, Betsy uses turn-taking well, waiting until Ms. Blau finishes a question or comment before she responds. Turn-taking, so common to oral conversation, is rarely a part of written language unless the author is representing oral dialogue or the text is a play. On the other hand, the written story has features that Betsy does not use in oral language. The author uses language that conveys the style of the folktale genre, such as *keeping house* or the sentence starting on line 511 and ending on line 513 . . . *As for the cow, she hung . . . and there she had to stay.* Only if Betsy were an accomplished story teller would she use such language in her oral retelling; she would probably never use such language in oral conversation with her friends or even in more serious discussions with her teacher.

These differences do not mean that oral language is language and written language is a secondary representation of the oral form. Rather, the differences and similarities between written and oral language suggest that they are parallel systems, each with unique forms and purposes.

Readers Have Knowledge About Language

All students have important knowledge about language by the time they come to school is a third important assumption. When we say that children have knowledge about language, we do not mean that they can give definitions of grammatical terminology (a noun is the name of an object) or make statements about phonological theory (this is a back vowel and this is a schwa). Instead, we mean that they have an intuitive knowledge—a knowledge inside their heads, which they use to produce the sounds, words, and sentences of their language in order to communicate with others—to produce language and to comprehend it.

Oral Language

Betsy has been speaking a dialect of Canadian English for nine years. She knows the sounds of her language and how the sounds are used. When she reads *"Get out! Get out!" shouted the woodman* . . . (line 304), she reveals that she is Canadian from Toronto by the vowels she uses. When she reads *Poor baby* . . . (line 316), she also provides evidence of her dialect as she pronounces *poor* to rhyme with *sir* and not with *pour* as other English speakers might. Her reading of this sentence reveals that she also knows how to use intonation to show empathy, as she stresses the word *poor* and elongates the medial vowel. Betsy, like all children, knew a great deal about the sounds of her language long before she came to school.

Children also come to school knowing about the organizational structure of their language: how words, phrases, and sentences are put together. In other words, they know its grammar or syntax. Children as young as 18 months begin to develop a fully functioning and rule-governed system. Even though it does not yet reflect the rules of adult speech, children's language becomes consistent and systematic, serving as the means for communicating with others. Betsy's retelling provides a good deal of evidence about her knowledge and control over the syntax of English.

As children mature, their language system becomes more complex. By school age, children's language closely approximates the dialect of the adults in their family and community. Because the adult speech which children hear is structurally close to their own, and because it is learned in functional settings, children find it highly predictable. Speakers of different dialects (variations of a language, discussed in Chapter 4) can usually communicate with each other because the similarities between dialects far outweigh their differences. Each language consists of highly similar, mutually intelligible but distinct speech communities. Everyone, therefore, is a speaker of a dialect.

English language users who hear or read *The_______ was chewing on a bone* know intuitively that only a limited group of nouns such as *dog, cat, lion* or *woman* are possible in the slot, either alone or with appropriate adjectives preceding them. Words such as *yellow, happen, walking,* or *quickly* would be rejected because of the speakers' or readers' intuitive knowledge of syntax. On line 104, Betsy predicts what a husband might say after he comes home from work when she reads *He said to his wife, "I want you."* She then slows down in her reading considerably as she reads the next three words, *do all day,* followed by a long pause. She seems to know that *I want you* is an acceptable structure with what comes before it, especially with the word *said* cueing a declarative sentence rather than an interrogative one. On the other hand, her slowed-down reading and long pause, which leads to her rereading to the beginning of the quotation mark in order to self-correct, indicates that she is well aware that the structure she produced didn't sound quite like an English sentence. Examination of the syntactic acceptability of Betsy's and other readers' miscues shows how readers bring their knowledge of the syntax of their oral language system to their reading.

In addition to knowing the sounds and grammar of their language, students also know how to use language to make sense out of the world and to communicate. They know that language can help them get things done; understand the world; transmit information to others; and gain information from others. Students know how to use language, including vocabulary, to talk about their world, their families, their communities, their values, and their experiences.

Reading is most predictable when the language of the written text and the ideas expressed are similar to the oral language and conceptual knowledge of the readers. Teachers from the United States who have listened to Betsy are often surprised that she read the word *porridge* easily. When the teachers learn that many Canadians use the word *porridge* to refer to hot cereal, especially oatmeal, and that Betsy eats hot cereal often and calls it *porridge,* they understand why she comprehends the word. On the other hand, Betsy's lack of experience with the language and activities related to making butter in old-fashioned churns, putting cows to graze on the roofs of sod houses, or keeping house can help to explain some of her difficulty with reading about these concepts.

Written Language

Readers bring much to their reading: knowledge of their language or languages; ideas about written language; such as how it works and what it is used for; and concepts based on their backgrounds and experiences as individuals, and as members of a family and a community. Being a member of a community and possessing knowledge about the world and language reflecting the community form the basis of an individual's expectations and beliefs about reading and its importance. This social knowledge is well embedded in students and influences their attitudes about reading and learning to read.

Young children, years before they come to school, have learned a lot about written language, which they make use of when they read or write. They have encountered a large variety of written language in their first five years of life before they become part of the literate community of the classroom. They've handled books, magazines, newspapers, and letters, and they've been read to. They are very knowledgeable about the advertising for the food and drink they love; signs that control people's driving and walking in streets; signs that tell people the names of stores, games, or television programs. They often have had a great deal of experience with the writing of their own names and the names of family members. Every experience that people have in relation to written language helps them begin to see themselves as readers and writers. The kinds of things that are read in the home, the way reading is used, the importance of reading, and the control that readers believe they have over their reading are all part of their knowledge about reading.

In addition to knowledge about written language and developing attitudes about reading, students know what reading is used for. They know that some people get information from reading newspapers or books; that many people get pleasure from reading; that people need to read to get on buses, to buy things in markets, and to participate in religious or patriotic activities. All the functions that readers see reading used for are also part of their knowledge about reading and will influence their own reading. Betsy has heard many stories read by Ms. Blau and the teachers she had during her earlier years in school. In this school, a language policy states that teachers are to read stories to their children daily. Betsy's retelling of *The Man Who Kept House,* in which she maintained the familiar structure of a story, no doubt reflects her experiences of being read to.

Authors Have Knowledge About Language

Authors have the same kinds of knowledge that readers do. They have knowledge about their language, their culture, their community. They have backgrounds and experiences that influence what they believe about the world, and this influences their writing. They have beliefs about their own ability to read and write and the abilities of those who will read their writing. Authors are sometimes in a position of authority that influences how they present their information and how they view what the reader will gain from their presentations. The authority of the author, or the reader's beliefs about the authority of the author, will also influence the way in which the reader reads.

The text is produced by the author through a creative act and is understood by the readers as a creative act. In order for communication to occur between readers and authors, certain social conventions are developed and maintained, such as how sentences should be structured, how stories and conversations are organized, and what direction written language should take. These conventions grow and change over years of history and tradition. The more a reader is familiar with the social conventions shared and used by the author, the more the organization of the published text can be taken for granted and not distract from the main purpose of reading—constructing a meaning for the text. *The Man Who Kept House* follows a number of conventions chosen both by the author and the editors responsible for the publishing of the text. The length of the story and the way it is organized on the page represent conventions that publishers of basal readers have decided best fit the particular grade level for which a basal is written. Three pictures in the original story are among text features chosen by someone on the editorial staff. The language of the text was chosen by the author, who wanted to portray the conventions of a folktale.

Of course, not all texts are organized in the same way. Each kind of text has its own organization that makes it recognizable to a reader. Readers expect letters to start and end in certain ways that are different from the ways in which stories or newspaper articles begin and end. Authors know what readers expect and they use this knowledge as they write.

In the next section, as we present a holistic model of the reading process, it is important to keep in mind the view of reading as an active language process that is influenced by the knowledge that readers and authors have about language.

A Holistic Model of Reading

In order to understand the model of reading that is the basis of the miscue analysis and curriculum development presented in the following chapters, it is necessary to explore the language cueing systems and the reading strategies that interrelate constantly as reading takes place.

Language Cueing Systems

Language cueing systems are the sources of information readers use in their transactions with the text as they seek to comprehend. Three language cueing systems operate during reading—graphophonic, syntactic, and semantic systems. The interrelationships of these three linguistic systems with the social-cultural context in which they occur is the pragmatic system, which must also be considered. The following sections provide additional information about each.

The Graphophonic System

The graphophonic system is the set of relationships between the sounds and the written forms of the language. In alphabetic writing systems, this includes the conventions of the spelling (orthographic) system and how it is organized in the text, the sound (phonological) system of the oral language, and the complex relationships between the two. The English spelling system and some aspects of the system of punctuation are part of the graphophonic system. Because of its long history as well as influences from many languages, the English spelling system is complex, with more than one spelling pattern often relating to the same sounds. Horn (1929) discovered that 50 different sounds are represented by the letter *a*. Although English is spelled in a more regular fashion than is commonly believed, the regularities are not simple, and even proficient spellers have difficulty with certain patterns of the English spelling system. Use of double consonants, changes made to words when endings are added to change tense or grammatical function, and ways to represent long vowel sounds are all examples of complex aspects of English spelling. In addition, the spelling system of English is complicated by conventions of abbreviation and punctuation. At any rate, proficient spelling is not necessarily the mark of a proficient reader. There are many good readers who are not necessarily good spellers. Since readers only sample the graphophonic system and then make predictions on the basis of their sampling, they do not have to have control over the spelling system to be good readers. For example, we do know how Betsy would have spelled *porridge* if she had written her retelling.

No written language system can in any perfect way represent the oral system. The writing system has symbols (letters, words, punctuation marks, phrases, etc.) representing objects or ideas about objects. Oral language also has symbols (phonemes, morphemes, etc.) that represent ideas and their objects. In fact, the thoughts we have about objects are also symbolic representations of those objects. Each symbolic system—written language, oral language, and thought—represents our perceptions in different ways. Oral pronunciation changes over time, and people who speak and read the same language use variations of the language that represent regional, social class, racial, and ethnic dialect differences. But regardless of how speakers say *out, poor, marry,* or *caught,* the spelling stays the same. The standardization of spelling allows for flexibility in reading. Regardless of the ways in which the reader's dialect differs from the author's, both make use of the same spelling system. That is, we can all read English even though we pronounce it differently. In fact, there are three different pronounciations of *poor* among the three authors of this book. All of us, however, including Betsy, comprehend the various concepts of *poor.*

Although the sounds of vowels and consonants change over time, the spelling that has become standardized usually stays the same. Patterns such as the *kn* in *knife* and *knot* and the *ght* in *light* and *flight* are examples.

Oral language also includes words and phrases that seem to run together when they are spoken but usually appear as individual words in written language. Examples include *going to (gonna) don't you (doncha),* and *could have (coulduv).*

Besty's oral retelling reveals many such words and phrases. However, because of the conventions of written language, these are not represented in her retelling transcript.

In addition to the spelling system, the graphophonic system provides other cues. Punctuation provides cues to readers that have little relationship to the oral system. Although some apostrophes represent contracted forms such as *don't* for *do not,* other apostrophes represent meaning relationships, such as the possessive *s* in *Patty's hat.* Speakers, contrary to popular belief, do not always stop at periods and take breaths at commas. Although periods and commas reflect phrase, clause, and sentence boundaries, no orthographic markers exist in the written language that can actually serve as intonational cues for the pitch, and junctures of oral language. Authors must find other ways of providing such clues.

The lengths and graphic shapes of words and letters also provide cues that readers use. If you examine Betsy's word substitutions, you will find few observed responses that are more than one letter longer or shorter than the word in the text. However, note that none of the graphophonic cues operate apart from the other systems. For example, readers use the knowledge that short words usually are single syllables. At the same time they also know that such words are function words, such as prepositions and conjunctions, depending on the context. Readers use all of these cues selectively.

The first one or two letters of a word are usually the most important graphic cues for readers. Initial letters, followed by final letters and word length, often provide readers with enough information to predict a word. This produces successful reading when the reader is also making selective and effective use of the syntactic and semantic cues. The following examples indicate how this process operates.

> The people followed the minister into the ch_____.
> Trudging down the r_____d, the group sang to keep up their sp_____.
> The sheep j_____ed.

Proficient readers resort to an intensive graphophonic analysis of a word only when the use of the syntactic and semantic systems does not yield enough information to support selective use of the graphophonic system.

The questions concerning graphic and sound similarity in the discussion of miscue analysis procedures in Part Two examine and evaluate aspects of the reader's use of the graphophonic system.

The Syntactic System

The syntactic system refers to the interrelationships of words, sentences, and paragraphs within a coherent text. It includes word order, tense, number, and gender. The word *grammar,* often substituted for the word *syntax,* can actually refer to all the structural rules of a language. However, too often teachers think of grammar in terms of correct forms of language. In talking about the syntactic system, correctness is not an issue. The way humans organize the sentences of a language in relation to other sentences—whether for purposes of reading, writing, speaking, or listening—is its syntax. Speakers of English know where to put the subjects and objects in sentences, which pronouns to use in relation to those subjects and objects, and where adjectives occur in relation to nouns. It is this system that writers use in producing a text and that readers use in comprehending.

The typical syntactic organization for most sentences in English is a noun phrase followed by a verb phrase. Once readers perceive the noun phrase (NP), they operate on the assumption that a verb phrase (VP) follows.

The scared cat / ran up the tree.

NP VP

This pattern is so predictable that sentences that fail to produce such simple structures are often where miscues occur:

M0413 Then he was afraid that she would fall off

M0414 the roof and hurt herself. So he put one

Betsy provides an example as she anticipates the end of a sentence at the end of line 413 with falling intonation on the word *off.* She then intones *the roof* as if it were the beginning of a new sentence, predicting, therefore, that a verb would follow. This sentence and her miscues caused too complex a setting for her to be able to produce the expected response, even though she made attempts to self-correct.

Betsy's prediction of *the* instead of *he* on line 615 provides another example to show how readers predict syntactic structures appropriately. Many readers produce such miscues.

M0615 again did he tell his wife that he would

In a story in which a reference needs to be made to a previously identified character, the author may choose to use a pronoun instead of repeating the noun or noun phrase. In such settings, readers make use of similar options. In line 615 the author, in referring to the husband, chose to use the pronoun *he.* Studies have shown that pronouns are usually used unless it clarifies aspects of the story to use the noun phrase (K. Goodman and Gespass, 1983). However, Betsy may have decided that at the end of a folk tale the noun phrase should be repeated to provide emphasis to the moral statements concluding the story, and therefore predicted the noun phrase *the woodman.* In this case, however, she self-corrected before she produced the noun.

The question we ask in miscue analysis about syntactic acceptability examines the reader's use of and control over the syntactic system of language.

The Semantic System

The semantic system refers to the system of meanings in a language. Everything the language user knows about the world and about language comes together to make up the semantic system of language. Meanings are strongly related to the cultural group to which a language user belongs, and therefore semantics is strongly influenced by all kinds of cultural concerns and beliefs. Betsy's knowledge of common roles of husbands and wives in families and the chores that need to be done around a house help her understand a good deal about *The Man Who Kept House* even though the story is about a time and place very different from the world in which she lives. She could, because of her own personal experiences, add to her knowledge about what it means to keep house.

The semantic system is at the heart of reading. We evaluate the reader's use of the semantic system with questions about semantic acceptability and meaning change.

The Pragmatic System

Language always occurs in a particular context. The three systems of language depend on the context in which they occur for their rules and their relationship to each other. The ways in which we use language to express and understand meanings is very complex and relates to how language is used in social settings or to the pragmatic system of language and meaning. We do not believe that language can exist outside of a context. In some contexts, people will pronounce words differently, use different dialects, or use a second language. In some contexts, some people may take greater control of the situation even to the point of directing the conversation. Parents use language differently than their children. And when these parents address their own parents, their language will not be the same as when they are talking to their kids. Teachers use language differently than their students. And when the same teachers sit in graduate seminars, their language changes to adapt to the new context and to the relationships between themselves, other students, and the professor.

The knowledge people have about how and when to adapt and change their language to fit the constraints of a social context is not always conscious. People provide evidence that they are responding to pragmatic rules every time they talk. The complex of systems underlying how language is used and therefore revealing what it actually means in a particular contextual setting is called pragmatics.

Pragmatics is important in written as well as in oral language. Certain written texts are organized in particular ways. Shopping lists and menus are organized differently, using different kinds of paper, page organization, writing or print styles, and language styles. Fiction and nonfiction have different text characteristics that are reflected in vocabulary, syntax, and style. Cartoons may be used in both fiction and nonfiction texts but will be used for different purposes. Students can recognize social studies textbooks as different from novels almost as soon as they open them.

Understanding the constraints of the pragmatic system on written texts is especially important to those concerned with holistic views of reading. Students respond differently when they read standardized tests, worksheets, and picture storybooks. If performance on a test is used by the school in grading and promotion, this fact becomes part of the pragmatics and will influence performance in complex ways. Teaching reading by using only one type of format does not help readers deal with the pragmatics of other types. Helping kids handle materials that focus on simple, present-day narratives does not necessarily help them handle folk tales, poetry, or scientific writing. Each type of material has its own system of organization and its own system of pragmatics, although each shares common semantic, syntactic, and graphophonic features with the others. For readers to be able to handle each kind of material, they have to come to understand how the various systems are organized within particular contexts.

The questions about semantic acceptability and meaning change take pragmatic considerations into account. Let's consider Betsy's miscues of *bread* for *butter* on line 115 and *buttermilk* for *butter* on line 208 as examples. Both miscues fit the pragmatic constraints of the story. It is as possible to make bread within the story context as it is to make butter. And buttermilk is part of the process of turning cream into butter. Readers are usually so knowledgeable about the pragmatic constraints of a story that it is rare to find miscues that do not fit pragmatically. Perhaps if Betsy had said *bagels* for *butter* in the first instance and *peanut butter* for *butter* in the second, it would be harder to decide whether the miscues fit the pragmatic sense of the story. Often the arguments that people who code miscues have about the acceptability of miscues involve pragmatic issues.

Each of the language cueing systems has its function and its place in relation to the other systems. While they can be separated for the purposes of discussion, research, or definition, they cannot stand alone or be isolated from the others during actual use. They must all be available for comprehension to occur. This is one of the most important principles of a holistic view of reading. *All four language systems must be intact and interacting whenever reading occurs.*

Reading Strategies

When people read, they are actively involved. As they transact with a written text in their long-distance conversation with the author, they are engaged in a wide variety of plans, or *reading strategies,* building or creating their own meaning or comprehension. Readers bring their knowledge of the world and of language to their reading in a way similar to that in which authors bring their knowledge of the world and of language to their writing. It is in this transaction that readers at all ages and of all materials use the same overall reading strategies:

Initiating and sampling strategies
Predicting strategies
Confirming strategies

Each of these strategies is activated whenever readers make sense of a written text and construct their meaning of the text. (In Figure 1 the angles of the lines represent the strategies which are always available and interrelated.)

Initiating and Sampling

Readers activate their reading strategies as soon as they recognize that there is something they want to read. When Betsy was asked to read *The Man Who Kept*

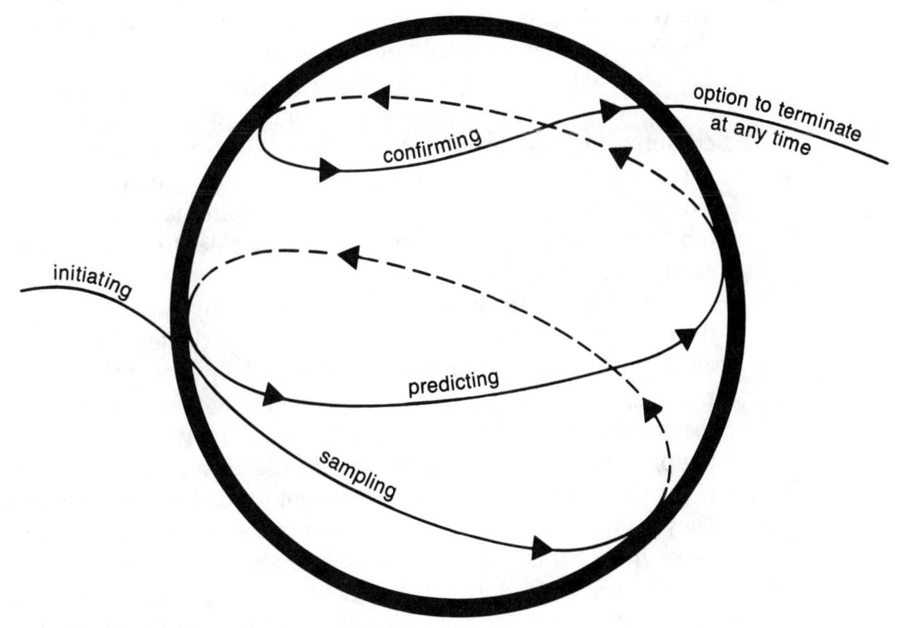

Figure 1 Reading Strategies.

House, she knew how, when, and where to *initiate* her reading. She read the title of the story and looked at the upper left-hand corner of the page in order to *sample* the print. As she was reading, it was obvious that she knew the print provided the principal information, although she also *sampled* the pictures. When readers open a book they ignore much of the title page as well as information about publication and libraries because they know this is not necessarily intended for them.

Through our research we learned that no readers read word-for-word, even though some readers read in a slow and halting manner. The speed with which reading is accomplished adds to the evidence that no exact replication of the text is possible. The silent reading speed of even moderately skilled elementary school children is so rapid that it transcends the physical ability of the human eye to focus on each printed letter and of the mind to be consciously aware of each word. Instead of focusing on individual graphic items, readers *sample* or select. *Sampling* is not unique to reading; it occurs as part of all perceptual processes (Neisser, 1976). Conversation, for example, flows so rapidly that listeners sample from the available oral information.

The following reveals Betsy's *sampling* strategies:

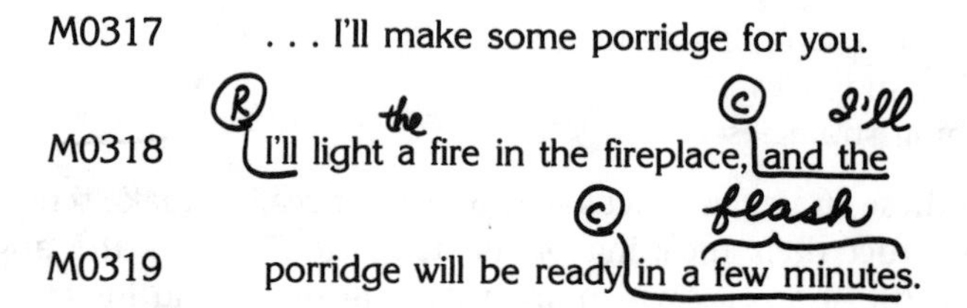

Betsy knows from the story that the woodman now has more work to do because of the mess made by the pig. He has already admitted that keeping house is hard work. She picks up the *I'll* + verb pattern in *I'll make* (line 317) and *I'll light* (line 318). She is aware from her knowledge of syntax, as soon as she samples the conjunction *and,* that conjunctions usually combine two equal clauses, so she knows it is logical for the second clause on line 318 to start in the same way as the first one. She has sampled both the graphophonic and syntactic systems to predict *I'll* at the end of the line. In line 319, she has sampled the end of the sentence enough to know that a preposition phrase will occur, and also to pick up the initial consonant in *few,* to predict *in a flash.* A more secure reader may not even have corrected this miscue, since it resulted in a semantically acceptable structure. However, Betsy is aware because of her continual use of sampling that the line is too long to match her prediction, so she decides to regress to sample the print once again, and self-corrects.

As soon as readers recognize that reading is necessary, they begin to sample the print to make inferences or guesses about the text in order to predict the text at all linguistic levels. Another example may help here. When readers open a morning newspaper, they know that they are not going to read it all. They may look through the newspaper quickly for cues about their favorite sections and pick up features of the print that let them know where to focus a greater amount of attention. Even when they come to an article they want to read, they continue to sample the print. They sample aspects of the graphophonic, syntactic, and semantic systems in order to predict what the text is going to be about. The brain does not process everything that the senses feed into it. It seeks information, directing the eyes where to look and what to look for. Without selectivity toward information, the brain would be overloaded; it cannot take in every aspect of information provided on a page of printed text. Try to monitor your own reading to verify these ideas.

Predicting
At the same time that readers sample information, they begin to *predict* on the basis of knowledge they already have. Predictions are also often based on inferences that readers make on the basis of what they know. Using examples from Betsy will help us review her sampling strategies, and at the same time examine her *predicting* strategies.

M0103 . . . One evening when he came home

M0104 from work, he said to his wife, "What do you

M0105 do all day while I am away cutting wood?"

As Betsy reads about the woodman, she is bringing her knowledge about common male and female relationships to her reading. She also knows that the author used *he said* before the question in the dialogue. Because of this information from her own knowledge of the world and her knowledge of the syntactic and semantic system of language, Betsy predicts that the dialogue will be a statement. Her sampling of the written text has provided her with enough graphophonic and syntactic clues from the beginning of the dialogue for her to predict a subject-verb-object structure—*I want you.* In sampling the print for the next line of written text, her oral reading slows down as she begins to wonder about her prediction and reads *do all day.* She then has a 23-second pause while she considers which strategies to use (discussed later under confirming strategies).

Betsy's prediction of *when* substituted for *while* and *always* for *away* in the last clause of the sentence shows: (a) her sampling of the graphophonic cues in the initial consonants of the two words; (b) her use of the syntactic system, since the substituted words perform the same grammatical function as the expected responses; and (c) her use of semantic cues because the miscues show related concepts of time and place.

Confirming
Making inferences or guessing involves risk taking because doing so may result in inappropriate predictions. Nevertheless, inferencing and guessing are absolutely necessary for reading to occur. As shown in Betsy's examples, readers make inferences about all the language cueing systems. On the basis of inferences and continuous sampling of the text, the reader is able to make a prediction. If the prediction is appropriate to the meaning that has been built up in the reading (as in the *when* and *always* examples), readers *confirm* their predictions and continue to read. However, if the readers' predictions are not *confirmed* by the subsequent text, readers *disconfirm* and then pursue a variety of options to continue to make sense of the text.

When Betsy reads *I want you* for *what do you,* she makes a good guess that this is what the husband would say one evening when he came home from work. However, as she continues reading she realizes that the sentence doesn't sound like an English sentence *(I want you do all day)*, nor does it make much sense. She therefore *disconfirms* her prediction by sampling the text again and then self-*correcting*. Betsy could have chosen another strategy once she decided to disconfirm her prediction.

Some readers do not always sample the text again, depending on the environment in which the problem occurs. Readers sometimes decide to stop for a few moments, think through possibilities, reorganize, modify the meaning of the text that is being built, and then continue reading. This is a strategy that readers of mysteries know well. If the reader has predicted that one character is the culprit and later finds new clues that point to another character, the reader does not need to reread the text. Instead, simply rethinking all the possibilities is all that is necessary before the reader continues with the adventure. In other situations, readers may decide that additional information is necessary before modification is possible; so they will read on, sampling the text for more information, hoping for clarification.

This may have occurred to Betsy in lines 312 and 313:

M0312 . . . Perhaps keeping house is harder work

M0313 than I thought. . . .

In this situation she disconfirmed and attempted to self-correct, but there were too many complexities and her strategies were not working, so she chose to keep going in order to maintain the overall meaning of the story rather than work out this particular section.

Of course, readers may at any time choose to stop reading because they decide that the material is too boring, too simple, or too difficult; that their mind is wandering; or that additional background is necessary before further reading is possible. Our research shows that readers seldom choose these options. In the context of instructional settings, readers rarely stop reading and say, "This is too

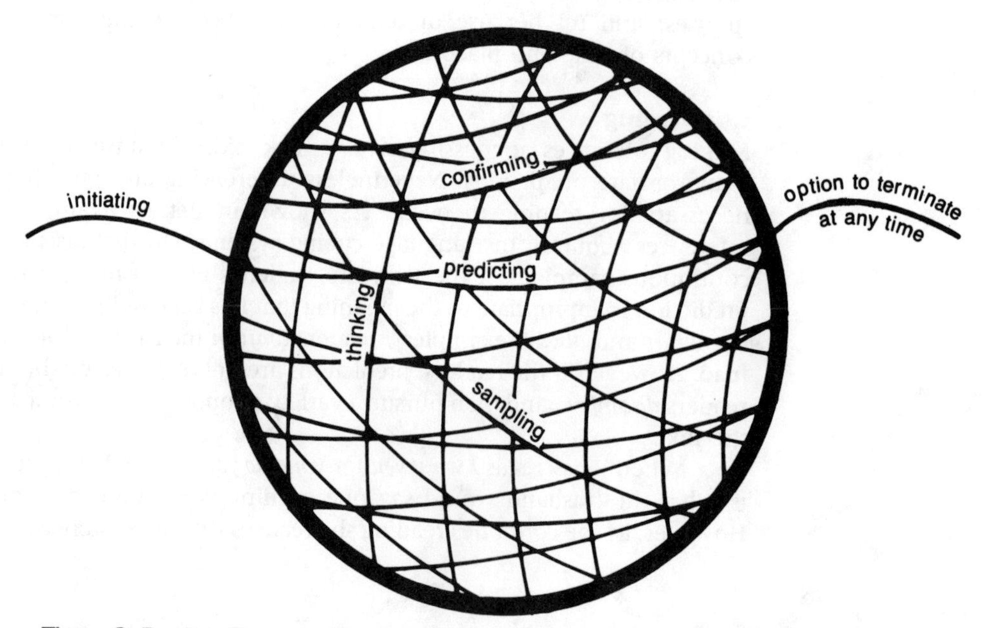

Figure 2 Reading Strategies in operation.

difficult" or "I find this boring." It may be that in certain school environments readers are willing to "read" when they are not comprehending.

The reading strategies we have just described interact continually with the four language systems as shown in Figure 2. Once the decision to read has been made, readers sample, predict, and confirm as they make use of their knowledge of the graphophonic, syntactic, semantic, and pragmatic cueing systems in a cyclical fashion, each interacting with the other. They put their perceptual systems to work in order to process the print. Their reading strategies direct the eyes in informed ways. The knowledge that the brain uses to inform the eye that starts the process depends on perceptual information, which in turn depends on optical input. The perceptual cycle organizes the material being perceived in such a way that it is recognized as a particular type of reading. These perceptions in turn activate the semantic system, which is influenced and dependent on syntactic information. Each follows the others but at the same time precedes them, always moving toward constructing a text and making meaning. Each cycle is tentative and partial, melting into the next. Inference and prediction make it possible to leap toward meaning without fully completing the cycles, even though most readers actually believe they see every part of the text (K. Goodman, 1984).

With this reading model in mind, we now move to the miscue analysis procedures that were responsible for the development of this model.

Part II

Procedures for Miscue Analysis

The procedures discussed in Chapters 3 and 4 hold for all miscue analyses, while Chapters 5 and 6 present specific suggestions for each of the four miscue analysis procedures.

Chapter 3 includes information concerning the collection of the data during the reading experience, how to organize the reading and retelling experiences, and an explanation of the miscue marking system. Chapter 4 presents the questions used for miscue analysis and the general rationale underlying each of the questions. For each of the alternative procedures presented in Chapters 5 and 6, the following information is provided: (a) how miscues are selected for coding; (b) which questions are used and how they are related to each procedure; (c) how to score the retelling; (d) which forms to use for both miscue coding and retelling; and (e) how to calculate the statistical information.

3

General Procedures for Data Collection

All miscue procedures include the collection and examination of a single and complete oral reading experience followed by a retelling. Miscues made during that experience are an important part of the data collection. A miscue is defined as an observed response (the OR), that does not match what the person listening to the reading expects to hear (the ER). What teacher/researchers consider to be a miscue depends on their view of the reading process. A developing concept of miscue will emerge as the procedures of miscue analysis are explored.

In addition to describing miscue analysis procedures, the following sections provide the rationale for the procedures so that users can understand the theoretical considerations on which decisions are based, and, as a result, can build their own theoretical rationale whenever they adapt any of the procedures.

This data collection chapter includes information concerning: the selection of students for miscue analysis and the selection of appropriate material for them to read; the preparation of the materials to be used during the reading and the retelling; and the sequence of the miscue analysis session, including the retelling.

Selecting Students

The selection of students for miscue analysis depends on the teacher/researcher's particular interests and needs.

Teachers using miscue analysis for the first time should choose a reader who appears to have persistent problems and who will provide enough miscues for an in-depth analysis. An extremely troubled reader, however, may produce too many complex miscues that are so difficult that a new user of miscue analysis may become overwhelmed. Such students can be evaluated after some experience with miscue analysis.

Researchers should become very familiar with all aspects of miscue analysis before they select their subjects according to the purposes of their research.

Selecting Materials

Unless there is a good rationale for using reading material that is known to the readers, the material selected for miscue analysis should be unfamiliar and unpracticed. While the selection should be new to the reader, it must include concepts that are known to the readers, and it must be written in language that supports readers in their understanding of new information.

The material should be difficult enough to challenge readers' strategies, but not so difficult that they are unable to continue independently. A *minimum* of 25 miscues is needed to give an in-depth, well-rounded description of a reader's strategies; therefore, one selection identified as one grade level above the student's assigned reading level and one or two alternative selections of varying difficulty should be available to choose from during the reading session. The recommendation to select a passage one grade level above students' reading scores comes from miscue analysis research that suggests that the majority of standardized test scores *underrepresent* students' abilities to handle authentic reading material.

An entire cohesive text (story, poem, article, chapter, etc.) that is both of interest to the student and well written should be selected. The choice of the material is based on the goals of the teacher/researcher, and may include fiction or nonfiction, stories from trade books or basal readers, and selections from content-area textbooks, journals, or newspapers. Fiction should have a story line and plot and, if appropriate, a recognizable theme. Nonfiction should develop at least one concept thoroughly or fully describe an act or event. Teacher/researchers sometimes write stories specifically for individual readers.

Although the length of the material used for miscue analysis depends on the age of the reader and the purpose of the teacher/researcher, the passage should rarely be shorter than 500 words. It is important to keep in mind that as the text gets longer, other aspects of the analysis (preparation of material, data gathering, and analysis) will also take longer.

Instructional materials for young children are typically short; therefore, if such material is selected, it may be necessary to ask children to read two or three related selections. Longer stories found in trade books are usually more suitable for readers than stories found in instructional reading material, especially at the early grades. A study by Menosky (1971) indicates that the quality of miscues changes after the reader passes the first 200 words of text. Semantic and syntactic acceptability scores increase as the graphic and phonemic similarity of miscues to expected responses decreases. In other words, as readers become familiar with the text, they produce more miscues that reflect an accumulating knowledge of the text, or they self-correct more of the miscues that don't make sense. At the same time, readers seem to be more efficient in the selection of cues concerned with letter-to-sound relationships. Interested teacher/researchers may want to examine the patterns of miscues at the beginnings of reading selections to discover how flexibly readers change strategies in relation to different portions of the text. Because of such findings in miscue studies, longer passages are encouraged for miscue analysis. In addition, it is recommended that for evaluation purposes the coding begin with the miscues that occur after the first few paragraphs of the material.

Researchers planning to use a passage extensively may want to test the suitability of the material by presenting it first to a small group of students who are similar to those in the research population.

Building a Set of Reading Materials

Teacher/researchers may want to collect a permanent file of the actual books, magazines, or photocopied passages that span a diverse range of materials, difficulty, and interests. The original Reading Miscue Inventory (RMI) included readings that accompanied the RMI manual. Although some people found the readings helpful, others developed their own set of materials to relate to the particular readers they were working with. Those who found the readings useful are encouraged to photocopy and continue using them. In the following sections, criteria are suggested for teacher/researchers to use in compiling a set of their own materials.

Once a set of materials has been collected, repeated use will provide information on which to base decisions concerning the readability of a particular written text. In this way, over a period of time, the set of materials will more closely fit the specific needs of the students and teacher/researchers. Materials that do not seem to be interesting to students and are too dificult to read should be discarded. Materials that show potential for interesting miscues and that students say they enjoy should be retained for the miscue readings collection.

Readability means the ease or difficulty with which a reader constructs meaning. By using the same material over a period of time, it becomes obvious which miscues are caused by the complexity of the text. When a large number of readers regardless of background and ability miscue at the same point, the miscue can often be attributed to a feature or features of the text. Miscues that occur for small numbers of readers provide information about the background and knowledge of those particular readers.

Sometimes good stories of appropriate length can be found in content-area textbooks, in trade books, and in old basal readers. Often, especially for adult readers, relevant articles from daily newspapers or magazines can become part of the materials collection. Selections that are used repeatedly for miscue analysis may be removed from the original material and made into booklets. Bibliographic references and comments concerning the text should be noted on the materials. After preparing typescripts of suitable materials, several copies can be duplicated and made available for continual use. The passages for reading and the typescripts should be kept apart from instructional materials and used for miscue analysis purposes only; this helps ensure that the materials have not previously been read by the students. With a large enough and appropriate set of materials, it is possible to offer students a choice of three or four reading selections for their reading.

Although the influence of self-selection of reading materials on miscues needs to be researched, encouraging students to choose their own readings has proved to be successful, especially for individual reading conferences. Readers bring to the conference the trade book they are currently reading. A segment of the conference is set aside for students to begin reading from the point in the text that they have just completed.

Text Analysis and Miscue Patterns

Research in miscue analysis has examined the points in written texts where large numbers of readers make miscues and the influences the text or the background of the reader have on these miscues (Altwerger and K. Goodman, 1981). Such information helps teacher/researchers understand the complexity of text features that may affect readers, and helps them select materials both for miscue analysis and for classroom instruction. Written texts with particular problems need not be avoided in miscue analysis, especially if they fit the purposes of the analysis. The idea is not to simplify texts or avoid their use but to know how different students respond to different kinds of texts so that all students become flexible in reading a wide variety of text materials.

Aspects to consider in selecting material include: (a) the predictability of the language and the overall structure of the text; (b) the concept load of the content or subject matter; and (c) the relevance of the material to the reader.

Predictable Language and Structure

Language that is predictable for the reader mades a book easy to read. Examples of predictable language include song lyrics, nursery rhymes, or children's books with repeated sequences, such as the *Great Big Enormous Turnip* (Tolstoy, 1971) or *Brown Bear, Brown Bear* (Martin, 1983). A set of such materials is good to have available, especially for readers who have doubts about their own abilities. Such texts help them revalue themselves as readers (K. Goodman, 1986; Rhodes, 1981). To determine whether the language of the text will be predictable it is necessary to become knowledgeable about the oral language of the students being evaluated and their experiences with written language. To make decisions about language predictability, it is necessary to consider syntactic structure, the language of the community (dialect features), and the familiarity the student has with the language of the particular genre.

A number of features of text format also need to be considered in relation to the issue of predictability:

The unique style of a particular author
Unpredictable beginnings
Breaks in the traditional sequence of events
Information in the text that is irrelevent to the rest of the text

These all add to difficulty in predicting and therefore make the material under question more difficult to read. Unusual punctuation or print style may also cause materials to be unpredictable. For example, in a basal reader for early elementary grades, the last sentence of a story is: *they laughed and LAUGHED.* Many of the readers had no problem predicting the first occurrence of *laughed* in the sentence because of the previous story line. However, these children had minimal experience with texts in different type styles, and the second *LAUGHED* printed in all capital letters caused a number of miscues.

Concept Load and Relevance

The amount of new knowledge for the reader also needs to be taken into consideration in the selection of material. Teacher/researchers must know what their students know and what their interests are. Brainstorming activities in social studies and science, open-ended discussions, individual conferences, and interest inventories are ways of finding out about the backgrounds of students. Such activities will reveal the need for a variety of material of different genres and content. The need for relevance is closely related to the issue of concept load. Material becomes easier for readers when aspects of the story or article are important to their personal lives. Material can be collected and organized considering the different interests, ages, and ethnic or racial backgrounds of the students.

A general rule of thumb in selecting material is to strike a balance among these factors. If the language or the format of the material is not highly predictable, then the information should be well known to the readers and relevant to their lives. If, on the other hand, the material represents a great deal of new knowledge, then the language and the format should be familiar and predictable.

The materials used will differ, of course, for teachers and researchers. Teachers will want a set of materials that show readers' strengths and development over time. This point relates to instruction as well as evaluation and will be elaborated in Part Three. Researchers will choose materials depending on the questions they are trying to answer. Additional miscue research on the role of readability, taking into consideration predictable language and structure, concept load, and relevance, adds exciting and necessary knowledge to understanding the reading process.

Preparing the Typescript

In order to approximate an authentic setting, the student is asked to read directly from the original source (science text, trade book, magazine, etc.). If it is impossible to provide the original text, the reproduced passage must be highly legible and free of blurs. Good black and white copies are often acceptable, but ditto machine copies usually are not.

For Miscue Analysis Procedures I, II, and III (see Chapters 5 and 6), a *typescript* of the passage is prepared. The typescript is used by the teacher/researcher to follow along as students read, as well as to record miscues, verbal asides, and any significant nonverbal actions. During the reading, the student may say or do something that raises questions in the mind of the observer about the reader's understanding. These questions can be jotted in the margin of the typescript and referred to during the retelling. In Procedure III, the coding as well as the marking is done directly on the typescript. On the last page of the typescript, student information (name, age, grade, school, etc.) and text information (source of passage, presumed reading level, etc.) are noted (see typescripts in Chapter 1 and Appendix B).

The original passage and the typescript should look as much alike as possible. Specifically, the line length, spelling, punctuation, and any special markings should be identical. This allows the observer to make decisions about the influence of the format itself on the miscue. There must be sufficient space between the lines of print (usually triple space) to clearly record miscues. The last line of each page of the original passage is indicated on the typescript by a solid horizontal line. The subsequent page of the original text is typed on the typescript below the solid line (see *The Man Who Kept House* typescript in Chapter 1). If the original passage is printed in two or more columns, a dotted horizontal line is used to show the separation between the last line of one column and the beginning of the next (see *The Beat of My Heart* typescript in Appendix B).

For repeatedly used materials, expecially for research or computer purposes, the line and page numbers of the original text are typed along the left margin of the typescript. The first two digits identify the text page, and the second two digits identify the line of print (as shown in the following excerpt). Such numbering provides an address for the coding sheet and for computer entries. It also facilitates quick identification of the miscue during coding, analysis, and discussion. An alternative is simply to number the lines consecutively, starting with number one.

The Man Who Kept House

0101	Once upon a time there was a woodman
0102	who thought that no one worked as hard as
0103	he did. One evening when he came home
. . .	(The last line on page 1 of the original text follows.)
0119	"We'll do it tomorrow!"
0201	So the next morning the wife went off to
0202	the forest. The husband stayed home and

Data Collection Session

Before the Taping

An audio tape recorder in good working condition, suitable reading selections, typescripts of the selections, retelling guides, *pencils* for marking miscues, and a comfortable setting for the student and the teacher/researcher are needed. For the first three procedures, the whole of the reading experience must be preserved and kept on tape long enough for the miscues to be marked on the typescript, for markings to be rechecked, and for the retelling to be transcribed. Many teacher/researchers will find it helpful to keep the tapes for documenting development in readers, as a basic data base for continuing research, or for use as demonstration protocols for preservice and inservice teacher education. Some, depending on their interests and needs, may want to videotape the reading and retelling.

Before taping, the physical requirements (quiet location, suitable table and chairs, proper lighting, and convenient electric outlets) are checked, and all materials are collected. Everything possible should be done to assure a good recording of the reading and retelling; for example, the microphone is placed on a stand or on a folded cloth with the microphone head toward the reader and away from sources of background noise, and the student's voice is checked on the recorder before the taping proceeds.

The reader and the observer sit comfortably, either side by side or across from each other. We have found that marking miscues or making notes on the typescript does not distract students as they read. Most students glance once or twice at the observer and then become involved in their reading. If students are bothered by the observer's marking and note taking, these actions are discontinued until it is obvious that the readers are involved and paying no attention to the observer.

Although teacher/researchers mark miscues as the student is reading, they should not expect to be able to mark them all, especially if they are new to miscue marking; if the student is reading at a fast rate; or if a great many regressions and complex miscues are being made. Observers should focus on marking miscues that they may want to ask questions about during the directed retelling.

The atmosphere during the data collection session is informal and friendly. The teacher/researcher may want to chat briefly with the student or give the Reading Inverview (discussed in Part Three) before the reading.

Most teacher/researchers briefly tell students why they are being asked to read and exactly what is expected of them during the procedure. They encourage readers to leaf through the passage to see how long it is, and they ask students if they have read or heard the story before. Depending on the student and the purpose of the miscue analysis, it is sometimes helpful, especially with insecure students, to tell them the title of the story or article they are going to read ("I'm going to ask you to read a story called *The Man Who Kept House,*" or "This article is about baseball, which I know is one of your favorite sports"). If this is done, the title should not be visible to the reader. This gives the student a bit of background knowledge with which to start reading.

Observers then ask students to read aloud, and if necessary they remind students that they are being recorded. The students are encouraged to read as if they were reading alone. They are told that they will not receive help or be given suggestions about what to do as they are reading. Students must also know before they begin reading that when they are finished they will be asked to retell and to discuss the story. Students should know that they are to be concerned with understanding what they are reading.

Ms. Blau's comments and directions given before Betsy's reading provide examples of the retelling procedure. Ms. Blau makes sure Betsy has not previously read the story; she tells Betsy that she is tape-recording the reading, but doesn't go into unnecessary detail; and she lets Betsy see how long the story is, thus assuring her that the session won't last too long. She also reminds Betsy that she is to use her own strategies: "When you are reading and come to something that gives you trouble, do whatever you would do if you were reading all by yourself—as if I weren't here." Betsy is also given a chance to ask questions before she begins reading.

Stopping the Reader

Once students begin reading, they should be stopped *only* under two conditions:

1. They are making very few miscues. Readers are to be given challenging material with which they are expected to miscue. If the student doesn't generate enough miscues for analysis, the data will be insufficient to compile a representative profile of the student's reading.
2. They are unable to continue independently. Only if readers seem to be *extremely* uncomfortable and are having a *very* difficult time should they be asked to stop. Surface features such as slow, choppy, and hesitant reading do not provide enough evidence to conclude that readers *cannot* read independently. In fact, miscue analysis often provides the opportunity for such readers to surprise teacher/researchers with their reading ability.

In the unlikely event that it is necessary to stop the reader, the teacher/researcher should thank the student, ask for a retelling of the material, and then decide whether another selection is needed and what the new selection should be. Such a retelling will indicate whether students are gaining meaning from the experience or simply giving an oral performance with little or no understanding of the passage. If the reader cannot handle the text independently, and if the retelling reflects the reader's inability to read with understanding, a more predictable selection should be chosen.

If readers are generating very few miscues and the retelling is good, it may be necessary to provide a less predictable passage. If such is the case, the readers should be told that they are being given a more challenging passage. Some proficient readers have miscue patterns that are quite stable across materials. For these students, changing passages may not cause them to produce more miscues; rather, a longer text should be provided in order to gain the minimum number of miscues for analysis.

During the Reading

If students stop reading and look to the observer for help, they should be reminded to do whatever they do when they are reading alone. If they have not moved ahead after 60 seconds, the observer may ask the readers to tell what they do when they are reading alone and come to something they don't know. They should be assured that any strategy they adopt is acceptable.

Reading time usually runs from 15 to 30 minutes, depending on the age and proficiency of the reader and the length and complexity of the written material. When the reading is completed, the observer takes the material from the student, thanks the reader, and begins the retelling procedure.

Readers' Presentations: Retellings and Other Reader Responses

Responding to a story by retelling, illustrating, or dramatizing it, by relating its events and themes to past experiences through discussion, or by setting the story to music or dance provides powerful opportunities for readers to relive, rehearse, modify, and integrate their interpretations of the author's messages into their own reality—in other words, the opportunity to enhance the construction of meaning. Such responses also provide teachers and researchers with insights into the depth and breadth of the reader's understanding of a story.

Smith, Goodman, and Meredith (1978) discuss education as "coming to know through the symbolic transformation and representation of experience" (p. 96). For Smith, Goodman, and Meredith, this educational process involves three phases of mental activity: perceiving, ideating, and presenting. Reading as a comprehending process also involves *perceiving* new information and *ideating* on the perceptions of the new experience. Reading provides the opportunity for *perceiving* new information as readers relate the experiences they live through during reading to what they already know. As readers think through what they are reading and wonder about it, whether consciously or intuitively, they are *ideating*. This process suggests the need for readers to have time for reflecting on their reading. In addition, the construction of meaning is enhanced as readers are involved in *presenting* what they have perceived and ideated in ways that are interesting to the readers and compatible with the reading material.

Presenting one's reflections, concepts, theories, and generalizations to oneself or to others is a way of confirming new knowledge and of testing it against an audience, even if the audience consists of only the reader. Although a variety of retelling procedures will be recommended, an oral retelling is commonly a part of miscue analysis. The type of presentational form a teacher/researcher selects should depend on the reader, the reading material, and the purposes of the reading experience.

Oral Retelling Procedures

(Re)telling a story is an authentic and familiar presentational form that is relatively unconstraining and during which the reader can take charge. When the reader does need encouragement or help, an oral retelling allows the teacher a way of offering aid without being intrusive. As revealing as retelling a story can be, however, it can *never* represent a reader's total understanding of a text; readers' retelling scores must always be considered along with their comprehending patterns and other presentational responses. Even all of these together do not reflect total comprehension of the text.

Before the Reading

It is a good idea to have a written outline of the selection available in order to follow the reader's retelling and to collect anecdotal information about the retelling. If a score is needed for purposes of comparison, the retelling guide will provide a stable means of organization. Different scoring procedures and retelling formats are suggested later for each procedure. Constructing an outline as a guide for the student's retelling necessitates thorough reading and understanding of the selection by the teacher/researcher. Such familiarity with the text not only provides information about the passage but also helps ensure appropriate questioning during the student's retelling. It makes it easier to monitor the reader's response as the story is read and retold and to identify aspects of the story that may prove interesting and useful to explore with readers.

Although the retelling guide is carefully constructed, it is important to be flexible with its use and to keep in mind that there are a variety of appropriate ways for readers to present their understanding of a story or article. At no time are the words in the retelling guide considered the only appropriate responses to events, themes, or generalizations. If, as we've said, reading is constructing meaning, then teacher/researchers should view retellings as new stories, often organized in forms that differ from the published text and with understandings that differ from those of the teacher/researchers. (Harste and Carey, 1979; Y. Goodman, 1982; Kalmbach, 1986).

The teacher/researcher prepares the retelling guide by carefully analyzing the selection in order to become familiar with and to determine all its features (characterization, setting, events, plot, theme, concepts, organization, and stylistics). Many users find that one of the best ways of becoming acquainted with a text is by writing and then analyzing their own retelling, and discussing it with others who have gone through the same procedure. After studying the material, the user lists the events, facts, and so on, reflecting, within reason, the author's organization. It is not necessary to use the exact language of the text in listing events or specific information.

With a narrative passage, attention may be focused on characters and characterization, noting physical appearance, attitudes, feelings, behavior, relationships to other characters, personality, and morals. Uniquely important aspects of narration, such as setting, inferential information, as well as plot and theme statements, should also be noted on the retelling guide.

In preparing an outline for expository passages, the information may be organized around specific information, generalizations, and major concepts. Specific information includes facts, events, details, truths, incidents, and conditions. Generalizations are drawn from the examination of the interrelationships of specific principles, items, or facts as they relate directly to the topic of the passage. Major concepts involve universal views or positions abstracted from generalizations. Concepts may be applied to diverse topics and across fields of study. Some scholars use a similar hierarchy of categories: subordinate concepts, concepts, and superordinate concepts.

After using the selection and retelling guide with a few students, teacher/researchers may want to reorganize the outline keeping in mind the students' responses. Students often focus on aspects of the text that may be viewed from different vantage points, overlooked, or considered unimportant by adults.

As described in the data collection section, readers should be made aware before they start reading that they will be asked to retell the story or article after their reading.

Unaided Retelling

Begin the retelling on a positive note, even if the reading performance is lacking: "John, thanks for reading. You finished the entire story!" Ms. Blau began, "Betsy, you did a nice job. Thank you." (See Betsy's Unaided Retelling in Chapter 1.)

Once the reader begins to retell the story, the teacher/researcher should sit back and listen carefully, taking notes or checking off items on the retelling outline, appropriate to the procedure, as the reader responds. Don't rush; allow students to reflect, retract, repeat; that is, to tell the story in any way that makes sense to them. Don't ask students to start at the beginning; rather let them decide on their own where they want to begin and how they will proceed with the retelling. This decision provides insight into how the reader believes a story should be organized for a retelling.

Encourage readers by showing interest, but avoid asking information-giving questions or shaking your head *yes* or *no*. Information-giving questions may suggest elements to the reader that they really did not know by themselves. For example, if the reader has not mentioned the baby in the story and the teacher/reserarcher says, "How do you think the baby felt?" the reader has been given information by the interviewer, not from the transaction with the text. Questions that do not give information, such as, "Can you tell me more?" "Is there anything you want to add?" or "What else do you remember?" are suitable if the reader appears to be finished and the teacher/researcher wants to be sure there is nothing more to be added. This is also a good time to develop the ability to use silence as a way to get students talking again. A pause of 40 or 50 seconds sometimes seems too long, but often students begin relating additional information without additional probing questions.

Often a student's retelling can be surprising; Betsy's is one such example. It's understandable that Betsy didn't have much more to add when she was invited to tell more about the story. Such is not always the case. Occasionally, students have a difficult time getting the retelling started. If this happens, be patient and make sure your directions are clear. When you think that you have waited long enough for a response, you may ask the readers to close their eyes and think about the story. Urge them to tell about anything or anyone that was of special interest. Keep probing without providing specific information from the story or article.

When the readers have related as much as they want to share, move to the aided retelling.

Aided Retelling

Drawing on the information given by the reader during the unaided retelling, ask open-ended questions that will stimulate the reader's continued retelling. In your questioning and discussion, always use the reader's pronunciation of names, places, or events. For example, if Betsy called the *woodman* the *worker* throughout the story, Ms. Blau would have used Betsy's term, *worker*, in the retelling pro-

cedure, unless Betsy used both terms during the retelling. By the same token, when readers substitute nonwords for real words, the reader's nonword should be used during any discussion of the retelling. For example, Betsy substituted *$gorun** for *ground;* therefore, Ms. Blau would use *$gorun* when any reference to *ground* is made unless Betsy corrects or provides another term for it in her retelling.

Questioning Strategies

Following are examples of open-ended questions:

Tell more about *(character mentioned by reader)*
After *(character mentioned by reader)* or *(event mentioned by reader)*, what happened?
Why do you think *(character mentioned by reader)* did that?
Why do you think *(event mentioned by reader)* happened?
When appropriate, follow the reader's responses with: Why do you think so? or What in the story made you think so?

Questions that help readers relate plot and theme are sometimes difficult to formulate. If students are familiar with the terms for the concepts of plot, theme, moral, characterizations, and so on, don't hesitate to use those labels in your questioning. If that is not the case, the following questions may be helpful:

Now that you have told me so much about the story, will you tell what the story was about in just a few sentences?
If someone stopped you at the most exciting point in the story, what question would you ask about the end of the story? (If the reader has mentioned such a moment, you might ask, at the appropriate point, for the plot question.)
What question(s) were you wondering about as you were reading the story?
Why do you think the author wrote this story?
Do you think the author was trying to teach something in this story?
Does this story remind you of any other story? In what way?
What problem was the story concerned with?

To get information about characters, character development, and setting, ask direct questions using these terms if you believe the reader understands them, and if you can do so without providing information. If you think the reader will not understand questions such as, "What is the setting of the story" or "Tell me more about the other characters in the story," the following may be suitable:

Where did the story take place?
Tell me about anyone else in the story that you haven't already mentioned.
Describe (*character named by reader*) at the beginning of the story and describe (him/her) at the end of the story.

To get at subtleties, follow up on any aspect of the reading or retelling in which the student appears to be especially interested. For example:

Was there something in the story that made you feel good? happy? sad?
Was there anything funny?
Did anything seem strange, unusual, or scary?
Did anything make you feel uncertain or uneasy?
Tell about the part of the story that made you want to laugh or cry.

To encourage readers to evaluate and judge, consider the following:

Did you like the story? Why?

*Nonwords are preceded by a $ in miscue analysis procedure.

Is there anything you would have changed in the story, such as the ending?
Did you think *(character mentioned by student)* was right or wrong when (he/she) *(event mentioned by subject)?*

The following questions are directed toward revealing the reader's awareness of cultural relevancy:

Was there anything in the story that didn't make sense to you?
Did the people in the story act or talk like people you know? In what ways?
Do you think *(mentioned cultural group)* people act or talk like the people in the story? How?
Do you feel *(specified setting)* is the way it is described in the story?

In the event that important details, characters, or entire segments of the text have been omitted in the retelling, ask open-ended questions that might help students remember. These questions should be asked when you are reasonably certain students have the information, but for some reason have not included it in the retelling. The following are examples of such cued questions:

You told me about the time Freddie got in trouble because he tinkered with the alarm clock, and the time he turned his sister's doll green. Were there any other times that his parents really got angry at him?
You mentioned Andre, his father, and his grandfather. Were there any other important people in that story?

Retelling Related Directly to the Reading Event

When the aided retelling is completed, the teacher/researcher may have reason to ask questions specifically related to the readers' processing of the text. It may, for example, be useful to learn why readers used a particular reading strategy, or to learn about the influence of their background knowledge and the influence of the text itself; in other words, this is the opportune time to ask readers why they did what they did. For example, if readers persistently substitute one word for another until a certain point when they self-correct, the teacher/researcher may ask what prompted the correction. Return the book to the reader and ask, for example:

Is there anything at all you would like to ask me about this story?
Were there any *(concepts, ideas, sentences, words)* that gave you trouble?
Why did you leave this word out?
You said *(reader's word, nonword or phrase)* here. What do you think that means?
Have you ever heard this word before?
Did you know what this was before you began the story, or did you learn it as you read the story?
Where were the easiest and hardest parts of the story? Explain.
Remember when you said *(character named by reader)* used a *(nonword)?* Can you explain?
Did you understand the story from the very beginning?
Were there times when you weren't understanding the story? Show me. Tell me about those times.
Were there times when your mind wandered? When?
Did the pictures help or bother you? How?

Techniques for conducting good retellings develop with experience and it is important to critique your retelling procedures carefully because they influence the retelling score as well as help readers realize they know more about their reading than they thought. Be as patient with yourself as you are with students. The hints given in the box, along with lots of experience, will help you develop proficiency in conducting retellings.

REMINDERS FOR GOOD RETELLING PROCEDURES

1. Get to know the reader.
2. Become familiar with the story.
3. Avoid giving the reader information from the text.
4. Include in questions and comments only information introduced by the reader.
5. Don't rush yourself or the reader. Think through your questions and patiently wait for the reader's reply.
6. Make your directions and questions very clear and avoid giving more than one question at a time.
7. Don't take "I don't know" for an answer. Rephrase questions to get the information another way. At the same time, don't exhaust the reader with too great a focus on any one topic.
8. Let students develop a topic and reach their own conclusions before changing the subject.
9. Ask open-ended questions. Questions that can be answered with *yes* or *no* or with single words often limit the reader's presentation potential.
10. Retain any nonwords or name changes given by the reader.

Other Presentational Forms

Presentations about reading experiences can and should take a variety of forms. It is important to note that most research and instruction related to ways of sharing reading experiences have focused on oral retellings. A great contribution could be made to the field of comprehension by exploring other forms of presentations.

Written Retellings

Readers can be asked to write retellings. Some students may be able to relate more in their writing than in their oral retellings, although this is not often the case. Written retellings provide the opportunity for small groups or whole classes to retell stories without the teacher being involved in an individual conference. Teachers need to use a variety of presentational techniques, avoiding the "book report," which is an overused form.

Other Symbolic Presentations

Siegel (1984) describes a sketching activity through which readers explore their comprehension of text. The sketching provides an instructional experience that engages students in successful instances of language use. The lessons are based on the assumption that asking students to draw their interpretations of what they have read will enable them to take a new perspective. In "Sketch-to-Stretch" activities, the students are encouraged to see that it is possible to adopt either a "scientific stance" (read in order to gain facts) or an "aesthetic stance" (read in order to live or feel the experience) toward the text (Rosenblatt, 1978). Siegel suggests that sketching is a learning strategy in which children use art to think about what they read.

The movement across symbolic systems (from written language to an art form) allows the student to take alternate perspectives and to highlight meanings that may not be explored when only one system is used (Siegel, 1984).

Certainly art, music, and dance all have such potential. Not only can teachers experiment with varieties of forms for instructional purposes, but there are many questions about how different kinds of presentational forms may influence a reader's comprehension as well as show that some students have better comprehension given different forms of presentation.

It is necessary to explore various kinds of presentational responses to expository materials such as science, math, and social studies. Tierney, Bridge, and Cera (1979) conclude that people often retell expository material as narrative. It is possible that readers do this because they control narrative, and retelling is a narrative form. Even when people retell a true experience that happened to them, they are presenting a personal narrative.

For retellings that are in keeping with expository genre, it would be helpful to provide opportunities for students to participate in presentations that fit the genre being read. For example, students may:

construct products to show how they follow written directions
cook to show their comprehension of recipes
record observations to indicate that science experiments have been understood
produce time lines, maps, or graphic designs to show that sequences or layouts have been followed

Marking the Miscues on the Typescript

The typescript is the means by which the reading is permanently preserved and the record from which the miscues are analyzed and described. Therefore, all differences between what the teacher/researcher expects to hear—the expected response (ER)—and the reader's miscues—the observed response (OR)—must be recorded on the typescript as accurately and efficiently as possible.

As the student reads, the teacher/researcher tapes the reading and marks some miscues on the typescript. Later, the observer listens to the tape as often as needed in order to verify, revise, and record all the reader's miscues on the typescript. A second typescript is often convenient, but not necessary, providing a cleaner and neater copy of the markings. It is advisable to do all markings in pencil; erasing is to be expected.

In miscue analysis studies by K. Goodman and his colleagues, all miscue markings are done by a second researcher without reference to the original marked typescript and are arbitrated whenever necessary by a third listener. If researchers are well trained in miscue analysis, interrater reliability is always high. Researchers need a second listener to provide reliability to their marking and coding of miscues. Teachers may use second listeners more selectively, depending on their confidence in doing miscue analysis.

The Marking System

For ease in marking and later in reading the miscues, it is expedient to use standard symbols and standard marking procedures.

The markings that represent phenomena that occur in oral reading—substitutions (including reversals), omissions, insertions, and repetitions—are illustrated in the examples that follow. For purposes of clarity, the examples are sometimes presented as if only a single miscue occurred in the sentence. In many reading situations, however, multiple miscues occur. The number of the miscue occasionally is added to examples for purposes of clarification.

All the examples used in this book are from Betsy's and Gordon's reading or from the readings of other real readers; none of the miscues are fabricated. Betsy's examples are preceded by M (for *The Man Who Kept House*). Since it is helpful to have additional miscues to use as examples and to refer to, especially from an expository text, a marked typescript of *Beat of my Heart* read by Gordon is given in the appendix. Since no single reader makes all the miscues needed to explain miscue analysis in one written text, we added a few representative miscues to Gordon's transcript from other readers of *Beat of my Heart*. Examples from *Beat of my Heart* are preceded with a B. Each letter is followed by the page and line number of the appropriate story. When the miscue examples are from students reading other stories, no letter or line number precedes the text examples. In the examples, the lines from the text are in print and the miscues are written as they would appear on a typescript.

Substitutions

Substitution miscues are indicated by writing the miscue above the appropriate text.

1. Text Item Substitutions

couldn't
MO210–211 . . . He looked around, but he could not see her.

There
Where is Sven?

mysterious whispering
I heard a musical whistle near my ear . . .

flash
This brought a fresh flood of tears from Anita.

P strong
st-
B0209 the heartbeat is strongest

In the last example, Gordon produces a partial attempt (explained later) and then a word substitution (P indicates pause).

2. Substitutions That Are Complex Miscues In some instances miscues occur together and it is not possible to determine word-for-word relationships. When this situation occurs, the miscue is written over the entire sequence and a bracket is placed above the text sequence to clarify the relationship between the observed and expected responses. For coding purposes, the whole complex miscue is counted as one miscue. Sometimes it does not become apparent until the coding that a complex miscue has occurred. This often results in the renumbering of all the miscues. The criteria to use to decide what constitutes a complex miscue will be discussed later.

this is a
"No," said the voice.

and
M0107 keeping house is hard work."

anything
. . . nothing has any weight in space.

Kitten Jones would not have changed her white
another thing
fur coat for anything.

3. Substitutions Often Called Reversals Two possible markings can be used to show whether letters, words, or other linguistic features have been reversed: either a transpositional symbol that clearly shows what was transposed, or writing the OR above the text using the procedures for substitutions.

B0710–7111 . . . but the two best ones are the easiest to do.

or

best two
B0710–7111 . . . but the two best ones are the easiest to do.

down looking
I sat looking down at Andrew.

Where can I see this baby brother of yours?

Was something wrong with Papa?

saw
Outside he was someone else.

4. Substitutions Involving Bound Morphemes Insertions or omissions of bound morphemes (i.e., prefixes, suffixes) are always coded as word-for-word *substitutions*. However, for ease of marking, they may be marked in different ways, as follows. Inserted bound morphemes may be written in, or the entire word substitution may be written above the ER. Deleted bound morphemes may be circled, or the word substitution written above the ER.

M0113	. . . and keep^ing house	or	. . . and keep house . . . (Keeping)
B0109	. . . heart beat(ing)	or	. . . heart beating. (beat)
B0220	. . . friend('s) heart.	or	. . . friend's heart. (friend)

B0324 . . . a minute. or . . . a minute.

B0505 on the inside . . . or on the inside . . .

Omissions

Omissions are indicated by circling the text item.

B0726-727 On and on your heart beats year in and year out.

M0613 Never again did the woodman say to his

614 wife, "What did you do all day?"

He worked at home every afternoon.

With these reservations out of the way . . .

The student, in the last example, read: *With these re-* . . . (5-second pause) . . . *out of the way*.

In this example, the partial *re-* was not corrected; therefore, it is coded as an omission of *reservations*. Partials are coded as omissions because the reader does not provide enough information for the coder to infer about the linguistic knowledge the reader is using in order to answer the questions for analysis.

Insertions

An insertion mark or caret (∧) is made to indicate the insertion and then the OR is written in.

M0415–416 He dropped the other end down the chimney.

B0321 First listen

B0718 The other way

719 to take care of your heart

When the chair rocked the boy fell.

Repetitions

The terms *repetitions* and *regressions* are used synonomously to mean the overt rereading of a portion of the text. Regressions provide evidence of strategies readers use to solve their problems. To mark regressions, a line is drawn from where the reader begins to regress, to the left under the text portion repeated, and up in front of the first word that is repeated—culminating in a circle. The reader's purpose for regressing is indicated by the letter selected and written inside the circle. Each time the reader regresses an additional line is added.

A large number of regressions show either: (a) the anticipation of a problem in the text, usually to the right of where the reader seems to be focusing; or (b) reflection on what strategies need to be used as the reader slows down before or during the rereading. Another large group of regressions relate to the reader's use of self-correction strategies, which do not always result in the expected response.

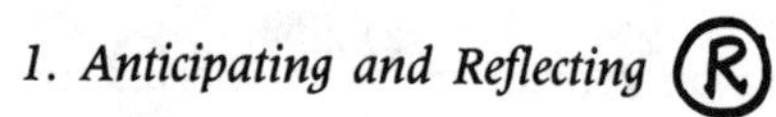

1. Anticipating and Reflecting Ⓡ

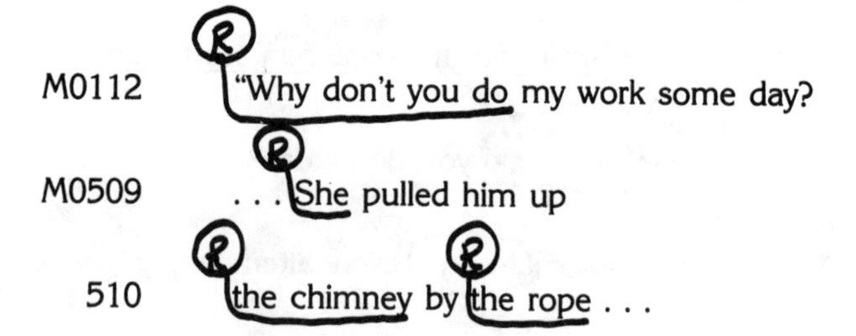

M0112 "Why don't you do my work some day?
M0509 . . . She pulled him up
510 the chimney by the rope . . .

Some repetitions extend beyond a single line:

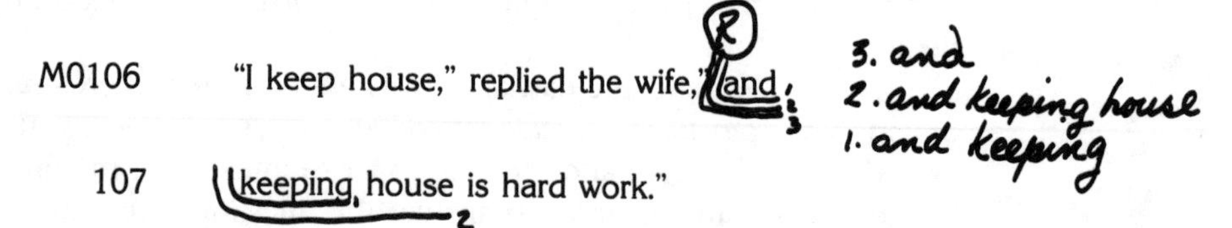

M0106 "I keep house," replied the wife, "and
107 keeping house is hard work."
3. and
2. and keeping house
1. and keeping

Betsy read: . . . *and keeping . . . and keeping house . . . and . . . and keeping house . . .* then continued reading.

This is an example of a great deal of miscue activity that should be written in the margin of the typescript in order to help the observer with subsequent readings and coding of Betsy's text. Note that the number of repetition lines under a repeated text item will be one less than the number of times the reader actually read the item. Because the final reading continues into the text, it is not a repetition and therefore should not be underlined.

2. Repeating and Correcting the Miscue Ⓒ

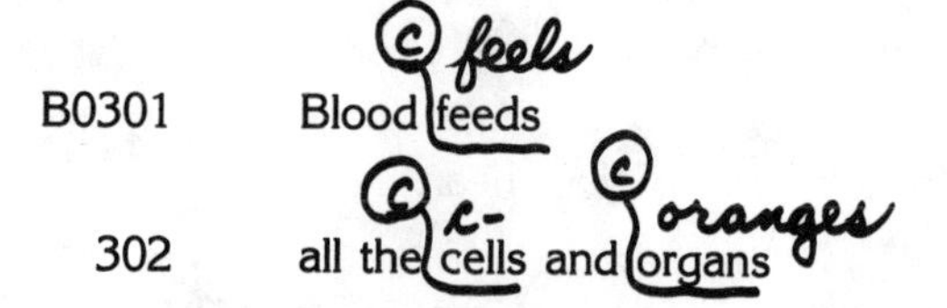

Gordon corrected each of the above miscues almost immediately.

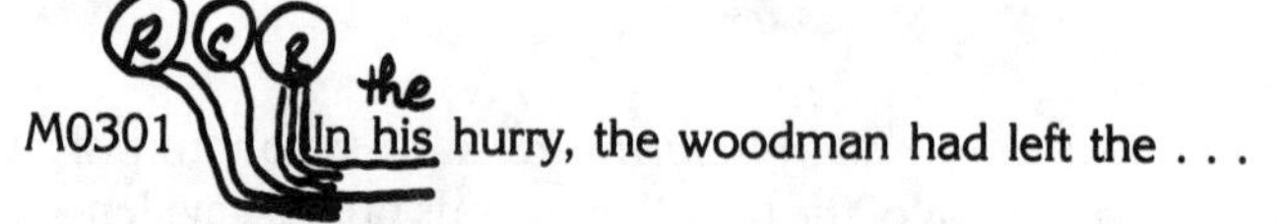

M0301 In his hurry, the woodman had left the . . .
the

Betsy read: *In the . . . In . . . In . . . In his . . . In . . . In . . .* then continued reading.

B0727 Year in and year out.

3. Repeating and Abandoning a Correct Form 

She ran into the store.

The student read: *She ran into* . . . He then regressed, abandoned the correct response, and read: . . . *in the store.*

She was always comparing.

The student read: *She was always comparing* . . . He then regressed, abandoned the correct response, and read: . . . *complaining.*

He left home to make his fortune.

The student read: *He left home to make his fortune* . . . She then regressed, abandoned the correct response, and read: . . . *his future.*

4. Repeating and Unsuccessfully Attempting to Correct 

B0508 This is called your pulse.

Gordon read: *Then* . . . *That is called your pulse.*

In this example, he makes multiple miscue attempts without producing the ER by regressing after reading *then* for *this* and unsuccessfully attempting to correct by reading *that.*

The fish swam . . .

The student read: *The frog* . . . *the frog* . . . *the frog swam* . . . The reader repeated the same observed response twice.

The frog swam . . .

The student read: *The* . . . *fern* . . . *Fred swam* . . .

He had heard a lot.

The student read: *He had head* . . . *hid a lot.*

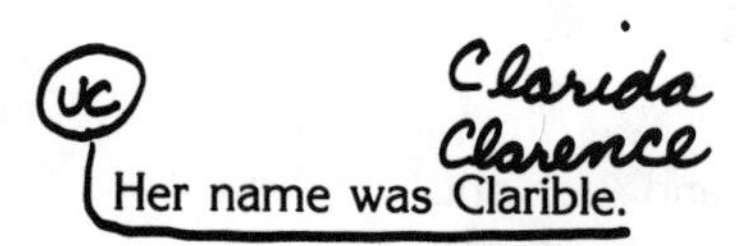

The student read: *Her name was Clarence . . . Her name was Clarida.*

5. Repeating That Affects More Than One Miscue

B0408–9 . . . the heart is a sensitive machine . . .

Gordon read: *the heart is sense . . . is a sense machine.*

A circle without a marking in it at the end of the regression line indicates that two or more things happened during the repetition. Gordon corrected the omission of *a*, but did not correct *sense* for *sensitive*. Therefore, it is necessary to leave the circle empty and make individual markings in a circle at each miscue.

M0313 than I thought . . .

Betsy read: *Then . . . Then he . . . Then I thought . . .*

The first UC is marked because Betsy did not correct *then* for *than* when she made her first one-word regression. After she read *then he*, she made a two-word regression. Again, she did not correct *then* for *than*, but she did correct *he* for *I*.

M0114 "If you stay home to do my work, . . .

Betsy read: *If you start house to do . . . If you start home to . . .* then continued reading. In her rereading, Betsy does not correct *start* for *stay*, but corrects *house* for *home*.

Additional Markings

1. Partials When a reader attempts, but does not produce an entire word, the partial attempt is written above the ER and is followed with a dash. The reader's intonation is used to help the observer decide whether the OR is a complete word or only a partial rendition of the ER.

M0206 . . . All I have to do

M0405 The man left the porridge . . .

B0609 Exercise helps your heart

The readers in these examples regressed and corrected their partial attempts. Therefore these partials are marked on the typescript as corrected but are not coded on the coding form.

©roll-
B0218 or a rolled-up piece . . .

Although *roll* can be a complete word, Gordon read it with the rising, abrupt intonation that indicates a partial rendition of a word. It is therefore followed with a dash and, because it was corrected, is not coded. If *roll* had been read with intonation that indicated a complete word, it would be written as a word and coded as a substitution.

2. *Nonword Substitutions* When a reader produces a miscue that is not recognizable as a known word in the language of the reader, the miscue is identified as a nonword substitution. In marking nonwords, retain as much of the original spelling of the ER as possible. For example, if a nonword that sounds like *fu-hon-ma* is substituted for the word *phenomena,* the OR written above the ER should be spelled *phuhonma.* This provides information about the graphophonic cues the reader is using. If there is any doubt that the nonword can be read, make a notation in the margin of the typescript about its pronunciation. Nonwords are preceded by a dollar sign ($) to indicate that a spelling was invented to reflect the reader's pronunciation.

$gorun
M0512–513 . . . between the roof and the ground . . .

$liver
B0310 to your liver . . . Marginal note: Rhymes with diver.

Her usually restless tail hung straight down, not
$twigching
twitching at all.

$distroubles
If it bothers you to think of it as baby sitting . . .

3. *Dialect and Other Language Variations* ⓓ The dialect of students is reflected phonologically, syntactically, and semantically in their reading. While syntactic and semantic reflections of dialect are always marked and coded, a reader's phonological variations are marked only if the teacher/researcher has a particular interest in this phenomenon. In such cases, the variation should be spelled as close to the way it sounds as possible and should retain as much of the ER spelling as possible—for example, *mus* for *must, aks* for *ask* and *libary* for *library.* All ORs influenced by dialect should be indicated with a circled *d.*

likeⓓ
. . . just about everybody likes babies.

Howⓓ
How're you doing?

headlights ⓓ
I switched off the headlamps of the car . . .

done ⓓ
He did this experiment

4. Misarticulations The misarticulation category is closely related to dialect and includes child language forms that usually diminish with age, although even adult readers can produce misarticulations on words such as *tachistoscope* and *strategy*. Since these are present in the readers' oral language, they are not non-words. However, the dollar sign used for nonwords is used to indicate that the spelling represents the reader's pronunciation. Unless there is a special interest in this information, misarticulations are marked on the typescript but not coded.

$pecific ⓐ
He had a specific place in mind.

$pasghetti ⓐ
The spaghetti was delicious.

5. Intonation Shifts Intonation shifts are marked only if the shifts change the meaning or the grammatical structure of the ER. Intonation shifts within the word are noted by the use of an accent mark immediately following the stressed syllable. Intonation shifts at the clause level are noted above the ER and in the margin if necessary. Intonation shifts within and between sentences are indicated through the insertion, substitution, or omission of appropriate punctuation and capitaliza-tion.

récord
He will record her voice.

cóntented
That is one contented cow!

pro'ject
We want the 'project to succeed.

After the cut in his allowance. The noun "cut" is changed to the verb "cut".

M0413 . . . she would fall off .

414 The
the roof and hurt herself . . .

anyway The
Dog was almost right. Anyway, the fall had . . .

This example was read by the student as if it were punctuated: *Dog was almost right, anyway. The fall had . . .*

6. *Split Syllables* When a reader separates words into identifiable syllables, resulting in unnatural pronunciation, the deviations are indicated with a slash.

M0109–110 You should try cut|ting wood!

The lit|tle girl yelled her head off.

7. *Pauses* Ⓟ Pauses (usually more than 5 seconds) are indicated as follows. If it is of interest to the teacher/researcher, the length of the pause may be noted.

M0204–205 As he put the cream into the Ⓟ 23 sec. churn . . .

M0320 Just as the Ⓟ 16 sec. husband . . .

All miscues are *marked* on the typescript. However, miscues are coded or analyzed in different ways depending on which of the four procedures is selected. (A summary of miscue markings is available in a condensed form in Appendix A.)

4

General Procedures for Analyzing Miscues

The Questions

At the heart of miscue analysis are questions that are asked about each miscue and about patterns of miscues in relationship to each other. These questions evaluate the relationship between miscues and

Linguistic systems of the text and of the reader
Language of the reader and the author
Concepts of the reader and the author
Reader's use of sampling, predicting, and confirming strategies

It is important to keep in mind that teacher/researchers who are involved in analyzing or evaluating miscues bring their own language, concepts, and knowledge about language and cognition to the interpretation of miscue analysis and that this interpretation influences the analysis and evaluation of miscues. What is in the text is always an interpretation based on expectations by the reader, anyone listening to the reader, or anyone evaluating or examining reading. For this reason, it is best to avoid the common-sense notion that what the reader was supposed to have read was printed in the text.

Such responses can best be demonstrated by an example of a dialect feature. A reader might say something for the word *picture* that sounds like *pitcher*. Speakers of English who have these two words as homophones in their dialect and say *pitcher* for both the container that holds liquid as well as for a piece of art will expect a reader to say it the same way and assume it is an acceptable response. Speakers of English who say something that sounds like *pick-chure* for a piece of art and *pitcher* only for the pouring container might expect the reader to say pick-chure and decide to mark the item as a miscue.

As discussed earlier, it is because of such expectations that what teacher/researchers believe a reader should produce is called the expected response (ER)

and what teacher/researchers believe the reader actually produces is called the *observed response* (OR).

The variety of questions used in miscue analysis reveal the complexity of the reading process. The specific questions selected by teacher/researchers depend on their purposes and the issues, features, or strategies in which they are interested. A teacher may need to know whether a particular student is self-correcting appropriately, while a researcher may want to discover the types of linguistic structures that readers self-correct.

The questions selected from the Goodman Taxonomy and the original Reading Miscue Inventory (RMI) for inclusion here are the most significant for classroom instruction, reader evaluation, and reading research, and for the understanding of the reading process. A rationale is discussed for each question to explain its significance. As mentioned earlier, the decisions about which questions to present in this manual come from the miscue analysis of thousands of readers, more than 20 years of miscue analysis used in research, and experience with preservice and inservice teacher education courses.

Some of the questions selected for the miscue analysis presented in this text will be used in all four procedures described in the next chapter, some will be used in only some of the procedures, and some will be recommended for limited use depending on the needs of the teacher/researchers.

The question areas to be discussed in depth include:

Syntactic Acceptability
Semantic Acceptability
Meaning Change
Correction
Graphic Similarity
Sound Similarity

Other questions will also be suggested to provide additional options in using miscue analysis. The questions are asked about each miscue in such a way that the effect of the interaction of all the language cueing systems and the reading strategies within the reading process can be observed. Such interrelationships are involved in most miscues. Rarely does a miscue involve only a single system of language or an isolated reading strategy. Examination of the language and strategies used and integrated by readers gives teacher/researchers the opportunity to determine which reading strategies and language systems are being used, how proficiently they are being used, and the ways in which they are being used.

Syntactic Acceptability and Semantic Acceptability

The questions that relate to syntactic and semantic acceptability reveal how proficiently a reader uses prediction and confirmation strategies. Although all readers produce miscues, the degree to which their miscues result in structures that sound like language (syntactic acceptability) and make sense within the story context (semantic acceptability) reveals their reading proficiency. Proficient readers tend to produce miscues that are semantically and syntactically acceptable within the context of the written text. When they do produce unacceptable miscues, they make use of their confirming strategies. What this means is that proficient readers tend to self-correct miscues that disrupt meaning. Less proficient readers are not so consistent in their patterns and may produce acceptable sentences less than half of the time (K. Goodman and Burke, 1973). The ability to produce semantically and syntactically acceptable structures or, if the structures are unacceptable, to correct them, provides evidence of a reader's predicting and confirming strategies.

Syntactic Acceptability

Words in a sentence have both a syntactic and a semantic organization. A sentence can have an acceptable syntactic structure without having acceptable meaning.*

It is syntactically acceptable to read *the plants ate the ripe grapes* because the sentence has a subject and a verb with an object in the appropriate English order. In addition, the determiners *the* (rather than *a*) are used appropriately because the nouns are plural. The sentence would not be considered semantically acceptable, however, unless the author is telling a story about a herbivorous plant. Even a nonsense structure can assume syntactic acceptability, as in *the flugs glatted the slusy eberts*. Readers do produce such English nonsense words, though seldom a whole nonsense sentence. The structure of the previous nonsense sentence makes it obvious *the flugs* are some kind of things (a plural noun phrase serving as subject of the clause) that did something called *glatted* (serving as the verb of the clause) to something called *the slusy eberts* (another plural noun phrase serving as the object of the clause). Another way to test that this sentence is syntactically acceptable is to see whether a native speaker of the language can answer questions about the sentence, such as *who glatted the slusy eberts?* or *what did the flugs do to the slusy eberts?*

The syntactic structure for such declarative sentences can be described as determiner, noun + plural marker, verb + past tense, determiner, adjective, noun + plural marker, and can be used to produce any number of semantically acceptable sentences:

The cars hit the rusty barrels.
The men moved some heavy tractors.
The magicians tricked the surprised children.

When the syntactic acceptability question is asked about a structure the reader produces, it reveals the degree to which the sentence sounds like language. It reveals the success with which the reader is controlling the structure of sentences as well as the relationship of the sentences to the structure of the whole text. Miscues can produce syntactically acceptable sentences that are structurally different from the expected text but still retain acceptability within the whole text.

For example, in the last sentence of *The Man Who Kept House,* Betsy changed the conjoined verb phrases *stay home and keep house* to a verb phrase followed by an infinitive, *stay home to keep house.* Although Betsy changed the syntax of the sentence, she still produced a sentence that was syntactically acceptable in the story. In answering the question about syntactic acceptability, the teacher/researcher needs to consider the following possibilities, keeping in mind the examples in the previous discussion: "Did the reader produce a syntactically acceptable sentence?" or "Does this sound like an English nonsense sentence?" or "Does it sound like language?"

Semantic Acceptability

The semantic acceptability question focuses on the success with which the reader is producing understandable structures. Just as readers have an intuitive feel for the structure of language, they have an intuitive feel for possible meaning relationships. The semantic system of language is the most significant language cueing system because it cues the meaning relationships in a language. Miscues can result

*In this text, we will use syntax and grammar synonymously although linguists have different concepts for the two. In the questions and discussions, we will usually use the term *syntax* because many people think of grammar as a set of prescriptive rules about how language is supposed to be spoken or written—a notion we reject.

in semantically acceptable sentences that differ from the text meaning but are still fully acceptable within the story.

For example, Betsy reads *he took the basket and went to the well for some water* for *he took a bucket and went . . .* For many of the readers of this text, *basket* and *bucket* may mean different things and therefore the meaning of the text may be changed. However, since there are any number of types of baskets that can hold water, this miscue produces a semantically acceptable sentence in the context of this story. To determine the degree of semantic acceptability, the teacher/researcher asks, "Does this sentence fit into the story as a whole?"

Syntactic structures create a pattern within which appropriately ordered words, phrases, and clauses support meaning. Semantic acceptability, therefore, is dependent on and limited by syntactic acceptability. For this reason, for the purposes of miscue analysis, semantic acceptability is judged after syntactic acceptability, and a sentence is always considered to be semantically unacceptable if it is syntactically unacceptable. However, once the sentence is considered to be syntactically acceptable, then it can be evaluated as either semantically acceptable or unacceptable.

Readers sometimes produce sentences that are acceptable on the sentence level but are not acceptable within the context of the whole story or article. For example, in reading *The Man Who Kept House,* a reader may have produced the sentence: *So the next month the wife went off to the forest* for *So the next morning the wife went off to the forest* (lines 201 to 202). The miscue of *month* for *morning,* the substitution of a noun for a noun, produces a sentence that is syntactically acceptable within the whole story. However, it would be considered semantically acceptable only on the sentence level, not in the context of the total story, because the previous sentence is *"We'll do it tomorrow!"* In order to be fully acceptable in the entire text, the sentence must fit the pragmatic considerations or have acceptability within the total social context of the written selection. Betsy produced a miscue in the sentence that is semantically acceptable in the whole text when she read, *So the next day the wife went off to the forest,* substituting *day* for *morning,* which is a synonym in the context of this story.

It is possible to examine acceptability for the sentence as it stands alone or within a portion of the text sentence. The overall questions of semantic and syntactic acceptability are always considered within the complete text. However, examining acceptability of portions of sentences or sentences alone and relating acceptability to self-correction is the best way to observe a reader's use of prediction strategies. Because such examination is considered only for Procedure I, partial acceptability will be discussed more fully in the next chapter.

Bilingual Readers

Bilingual students, especially those who are learning English as a second language, may have greater understanding of what they read than is evident in their ability to produce syntactically acceptable sentences. Although with bilingual readers we also consider semantic acceptability to be dependent on syntactic acceptability (that is, semantic acceptability cannot be marked higher than syntactic acceptability), teacher/researchers should carefully take into consideration the linguistic knowledge of their students when responding to syntactic and semantic acceptability questions. This same kind of consideration should apply to the reading of hearing-impaired students who sign; miscue studies by Ewoldt (1977) conclude that these students are bilingual.

Readers who are more proficient in a language other than English (including American Sign Language) may be translating the meanings they are gaining from their reading into their native or dominant language system, even though they are producing English sentences that are syntactically unacceptable. This means that the readers may comprehend more than is revealed by their syntactic and semantic acceptability scores.

Intonation

Intonation patterns of readers can often result in pitch, pause, or stress patterns that differ from the expected response. Such changes may or may not occur in combination with miscues involving words, phrase, or sentence changes. Intonation is a significant clue to a reader's processing of language units. The use of appropriate intonation in oral reading depends on the reader's knowledge of the syntactic structures in the text. Syntactic or semantic miscues involving intonation can be caused either because readers anticipate a different structure or because they are unfamiliar with the author's structures.

When considering intonation, it must be remembered that there is no one-to-one correspondence between written punctuation and oral intonation patterns. Speakers do not stop or pause at the places where periods or commas may occur in written language. *Punctuation* in English occurs at the end of a phrase, clause, or sentence. However, appropriate *intonation* must be predicted *before* the beginning of the linguistic unit. For example, in a declarative sentence the heaviest stress usually falls on the subject of the sentence, while in an interrogative sentence the heaviest stress may be on the initial question marker. In line l04 of A *Man Who Kept House,* Betsy has to deal with just such an intonation problem. In predicting a declarative sentence, Betsy places heavy stress on the pronoun *I.* Had she predicted a question, her stress pattern would have been different. She finally self-corrects and adjusts her intonation appropriately.

Because of the lack of direct relationship between intonation and punctuation, it is often appropriate for readers *not* to pause at commas or periods. By listening to the whole sentence contour, especially the intonation at the beginning of clauses and sentences, teacher/researchers can become better judges of the appropriateness of intonation. Contrary to popular belief, neither pausing at punctuation nor dropping the voice at the end of all sentences is necessarily appropriate. Rather it is the intonation contour of the whole sentence, the degree of stress and pitch that flows from the beginning to the end of the sentence and from one phrase to another that is significant.

In order to mark the miscues on lines 312 and 313 in Betsy's reading of *The Man Who Kept House,* we listened to the recording a number of times. It became obvious that Betsy ended her sentence after *hard work,* and that she intoned *then I thought* as the beginning of the dialogue carrier that went with the next sentence. The major difference between *then* and *than* is not in the sound of the vowel, which most speakers of English pronounce the same, but in the intonation that signals whether the word is the beginning of a clause as a connective or as a comparative. The former gets a good deal more stress than the latter.

Intonation variations are not marked as miscues simply on the basis of pauses or lack of pauses. Intonation shifts due to pitch, stress, and pauses are considered miscues when they change or disrupt the meaning or the syntax of a sentence. It is important to become proficient at hearing syntactically or semantically related intonation shifts in order to verify that readers have actually produced a change in the syntax or meaning of the text and that they have not simply produced an acceptable alternate or optional intonational pattern. By learning to listen carefully to intonation it becomes possible to know whether a reader means *to, two,* or *too,* or whether *can* is a question marker as in *Can you do this?*, a noun as in *Put this in the trash can*, or a verb as in *We will can tomatoes today*.

In early miscue procedures, intonation was marked as a separate category. For the purposes of the procedures in this book, it was decided to consider the appropriateness of intonation as part of the questions concerned with syntactic and semantic acceptability. Anyone who wishes to examine intonation as a separate category can add the question and coding procedures to the Coding Form (see original RMI questions in Appendix D).

The two questions related to semantic and syntactic acceptability are the most important questions in miscue analysis because they center on the major purpose of the reading process—to produce a meaningful and understandable text that sounds like language. These two questions also provide the greatest insight into a reader's proficiency.

Syntactic Acceptability Does the miscue occur in a structure that is syntactically acceptable?

Semantic Acceptability Does the miscue occur in a structure that is semantically acceptable?

For most of the miscue analysis procedures the term *structure* used in the two questions will refer to a sentence. However, depending on the teacher/researcher's purposes, other definitions for structure can be used. For instance, in miscue analysis research using the Goodman Taxonomy, the main clause and all its dependent clauses, or a minimal terminable unit, according to Hunt (1965), was used to define the linguistic unit or structure analyzed for acceptability. In order to use the minimal terminable unit, or T-unit, it is necessary to understand the linguistic concept of the clause. Because the concept of the sentence is more generally understood than the concept of the clause, the primary linguistic unit used for the four procedures will be the sentence.

Meaning Change

The question concerning meaning change provides the opportunity to examine the degree to which miscues retain the author's intended meaning. In many ways, the question related to meaning change is the most difficult to consider because it is used to evaluate the degree to which the reader changes the author's text. It is important to stress that no one is privy to the author's meaning unless the author is there to provide such information. The issue, therefore, becomes *whose* text is being changed. When responding to the question about the degree of change to the text, does the person doing the analysis consider what the degree of change is to the reader or what it is according to the teacher/researcher? In order to consider the degree of change according to the reader, the reader needs to be consulted for each miscue. Since teacher/researchers seldom code miscues with the reader present, it is necessary to keep in mind the concept of expected response; that is, the degree of meaning change is related to what the teacher/researcher expects the meaning to be. In responding to this question, the reader's culture, dialect, and knowledge must be taken into consideration.

Issues about how miscues affect meaning change emerge from and are based on our view of the reading process. All readers have their own interpretation of text and are always constructing text on the basis of their interpretations. The degree to which any teacher/researcher believes a particular miscue has changed a text will depend on many factors. It will depend on the individual's own interpretation of the text as well as on what each teacher/researcher believes was the author's intention. Because of such personal interpretations, the greatest amount of variation from one coder to another occurs on this question. This is especially true for those just beginning to do miscue analysis. However, when people learn to do miscue analysis together they develop similar criteria for marking the degree of meaning change as they build shared understandings about the meanings of texts.

The substitution miscue Betsy made of *basket* for *bucket* on line 313 is a good example to help clarify this issue. Many might think that a basket cannot hold water and therefore decide that it is a major change to the meaning of the story. However, people who are aware of basket-weaving and know that baskets can be watertight would argue that since you can get water from a well with a basket, this miscue causes only a minimal change to the story. However, if Betsy had substituted *pail* for *bucket* in the same context, there would be no change to the meaning since in most cases *bucket* and *pail* are synonyms and refer to the same object. The more miscue analysis is used and discussed with others, the more consistent the answers become for the individual coder, and a high level of agreement among coders results.

The question of degree of meaning change is often difficult to answer for structures that readers render unacceptable. The Goodman Taxonomy codes this question only for structures that are fully acceptable semantically and syntactically. During the development of the RMI, an effort to simplify its use, the question of meaning change was asked for every miscue. Years of research and use support the wisdom of the Taxonomy coding procedures and the conclusion that change will be judged and coded for sentences deemed to be fully acceptable both semantically and syntactically.

meaning change Does the miscue result in a change of meaning?

The question related to meaning change is easier to answer if the significance of the section of the text to the whole meaning of the story or article is kept in mind. For example, as the teacher/researcher is coding each miscue the following criteria should be considered:

Is there any change at all to the text? If the answer is *not at all*, then a *no* answer is acceptable. However, if the answer is *yes*, then the coder has two alternatives:

Is there a change, inconsistency, or loss to *minor* facts, concepts, incidents, characters, or sequences in the text? In this case, the result is a minor, minimal or partial change of meaning;

Is there a change, inconsistency, or loss to *major* facts, concepts, incidents, characters, or sequences in the text? In this case, the result is a major change of meaning.

Dialect

All readers react to the acceptability of language according to their own expectations. Language is judged by what *sounds right* to the language user. When the language a reader or speaker hears *sounds right*, it usually falls within the range of the individual speaker's language use and the use of the language that is part of the commummity. Such community or individual variation in language is known as dialect. There is a great deal of discussion among educators concerning the effects of dialect on learning to read (K. Goodman, 1965; K. Goodman and Buck, 1973). By examining the dialect question in relation to other questions concerning meaning change and acceptability, teachers and researchers can investigate the issue for themselves. If the dialect of the reader or the dialect of the author cause problems in the student's attempt to gain meaning, this will become evident through miscue analysis.

All questions are evaluated with a knowledge of the reader's language and taking the reader's dialect into consideration. In other words, the acceptability questions are answered in terms of whether the miscue would be syntactically or semantically acceptable *within the reader's dialect*—not the dialect approved by the school, teacher, or text. The issue, as it relates to reading, is the gaining of information and meaning—not the use of an approved dialect.

Dialect is generally considered when there is a difference between the dialect the author used in the text and the reader's dialect, what the reader usually says. However, what teacher/researchers decide to code as dialect will obviously depend on their own dialect and its variations from that of the reader's. Therefore, teacher/researchers should know the language of their students well enough to recognize the forms that they use in their oral language. Being knowledgeable about issues related to dialect and the features of dialect used by the readers in the school community is important (Christian, 1979; Christian and Wolfram, 1979; Wolfram, Potter, Yanofsky, and Shuy, 1979).

Dialect miscues can occur as variations of language with respect to sounds, syntax, vocabulary, and meaning, as shown by the examples in the box. Some of the dialect variations listed in the *reader* column may be the preferred forms of those who are reading this manual. If so, they highlight the importance of the concern with dialect in miscue analysis. Too often, judgments about oral reading are based on what a teacher/researcher believes to be correct according to the standards of society and not according to the language that readers usually use

Examples of Dialect Variations

Reader	*Text*
	Sound Variations:
pitchur	picture
idear	idea
lot bub	light bulb
wif	with
amond	almond
cot	caught
	Vocabulary Variations:
goed	went
headlights	headlamps
bag	sack
greens	salad
pop	soda
	Syntactic Varations:
he don't	he doesn't
John be going	John was going
Stand on line	Stand in line
Everybody pet	Everybody's pet
Everyone get in their seat.	Everyone get in his seat.
two boy	two boys
That ain't no cup	That isn't a cup
None of us never	None of us ever
Do it quickly!	Do it quick!

to communicate and understand their world. The purpose here is not to resolve the issues surrounding a standard dialect of English. Miscue analysis is concerned with the degree to which readers understand what they are reading. Evidence about reader's comprehension is provided when dialect is examined. When reading results in sentences that are syntactically and semantically acceptable in the reader's preferred dialect, it becomes obvious that readers are actually translating the written language form of the author into their own oral language variation. Appropriate translation in language is only possible if the meaning of the statements is fully understood.

Miscue analysis has looked at many aspects of dialect features in reading (K. Goodman, 1965; K. Goodman and Buck, 1973; K. Goodman and Y. Goodman, 1978). The analysis of dialect in reading provides documentation for the conclusion that proficiency in reading is not constrained by the speaking dialect of the reader. Speakers of all variations of English dialects are proficient readers of English. Nevertheless, teachers sometimes make readers feel self-conscious about their oral language dialect, a situation that may actually cause problems in the reader's developing proficiency.

Dialect-related miscues are marked with a small *d* in a circle on the typescript but may not always be selected for coding. In most cases, we recommend that syntactic and vocabulary dialect variations be coded, but not phonological dialect differences. For example, coding language that sounds something like *dat* for *that* or *walkin'* for *walking* can become quite time-consuming. Sophisticated listening devices are often needed to help the teacher/researcher hear sound variations. Since speakers produce phonological variations for most sounds depending on the surrounding phonological context, a great deal of effort, as well as knowledge about phonology and dialects, would be required to evaluate all the variations appropriately. Only when the teacher/researcher has specific reasons for analyzing the relationship between certain oral and written features of the language should phonological features be coded. Phonological feature differences may be marked on the reader's typescript even if they are not coded.

In all of the procedures of miscue analysis, dialect is always evaluated as part of the questions about syntactic and semantic acceptability: In the dialect of the reader is the miscue syntactically and semantically acceptable? However, if a teacher/researcher has a special purpose for coding dialect separately, the question used in the original *RMI: Is a dialect variation involved in the miscue?* may be considered.

To repeat, the dialect of the reader is taken into consideration whenever issues of semantic and syntactic acceptability, meaning change, and sound similarity are considered. If the reader being analyzed is a speaker or signer of languages other than English, the dialect question can be expanded to include second language influences.

Correction

Corrections or lack of them in relation to miscues provide insight into the reader's confirming strategies. When readers become aware that they have made a miscue, they may attempt to self-correct either silently or orally, or they may choose to continue reading without correction. Examining correction in conjunction with syntactic and semantic acceptability gives an indication of readers' success in self-correcting and in their judgments concerning which miscues should be corrected.

Readers are considered efficient when they produce miscues that result in sentences that are semantically and syntactically acceptable and then do not correct such miscues. Such activity shows that readers have predicted appropriately and, while confirming, decide there is no reason to self-correct because the language and meaning are acceptable and meaningful. In fact, readers are often unaware of making these types of high-quality miscues.

When miscues result in sentences that are syntactically unacceptable and readers correct such miscues, this shows that readers are concerned with the linguistic structure of their reading and that they are concerned that their reading sound like language. When miscues result in sentences that are both syntactically and semantically unacceptable and readers correct, this indicates that readers are concerned that their reading makes sense.

Less proficient readers, however, show that they are not always concerned that their reading make sense. They do not appear to be monitoring their reading to the same degree as proficient readers since they often do not correct miscues that are unacceptable.

However, when patterns of self-correction indicate that the readers tend not to correct miscues that result in unacceptable sentences, then there are a number of possibilities to consider. It is important to keep in mind that readers do *not* correct all of their miscues. *Correction must be understood in relation to the quality of the miscues produced.* In general, proficient readers correct a higher percentage of low-quality miscues (miscues that result in unacceptable sentences) than less proficient readers, but they don't have as many such miscues to correct because they don't produce as many miscues that result in unacceptable sentences.

However, even proficient readers do not *always* correct unacceptable miscues because they may not consider the miscue significant to their development of meaning. Proficient readers correct their miscues selectively, indicating that they know what aspects of the text are important.

Many readers, even proficient readers, will tend not to correct if there are too many low-quality miscues clustered in the same phrase. In such a situation, it seems as if the reader produces a structure that he or she does not know how to unravel or does not choose to take the time to do so. In such cases, many readers rethink the problem as they continue reading, gathering new information and constructing new meanings in the process.

The retelling often provides evidence that the reader has reconsidered throughout the reading and by the end has constructed a meaning that fits into the structure of the story even though a few highly disruptive miscues are left uncorrected. To make appropriate judgments about a reader's proficiency, therefore, it is important to examine the correction patterns of all the miscues coded and include the information from the retelling.

Betsy has problems with the structure *stay home and keep house* throughout her reading of *The Man Who Kept House.* Although she has a tendency to correct often, she leaves the miscues in *I'll start house and keeping house* on line 113 with no attempt to correct at all. However, examination of all her strategies each time she interacts with this structure (lines 106, 107, 113, 114, 312, 611, 616) indicates she is aware of the problem and that she continues to work on it. Her retelling adds to the evidence that she built an understanding of the phrase *keeping house* through her reading of the story.

Some readers correct high-quality miscues—miscues that are semantically or syntactically acceptable and make little or no change to the meaning of the text. Such cases provide evidence that the reader is paying too close attention to the graphic information in the text. For example, such readers may anticipate a contraction as they come to the phrase *could not* (as Betsy did in line 210), will read aloud *couldn't,* then regress, and finally self-correct. Most proficient readers simply continue reading without self-correction at this point.

Readers' corrections range from approximately 10 to 40 percent of all miscues. Some readers correct few miscues, while others correct many more. The percentage of correction by itself provides no insight into the proficiency of any reader (K. Goodman and Burke, 1973). Sometimes very good readers who are confident of their reading and gain meaning even from some very disruptive miscues correct little. Some poor readers also correct very little because they are not paying attention to meaning, and keep reading regardless of whether something makes sense.

Examination of partial miscue attempts adds to information about self-correction and reading proficiency. Partials occur when a reader produces an initial syllable or two but does not produce enough of an observed response to provide adequate information about grammatical function or word meaning. Whenever partials are not corrected (the vast majority are corrected), they are treated as omissions in miscue coding. Corrected partials are not coded because the reader does not provide enough information to answer the miscue analysis questions. However, all partials are marked on the typescript in order to add to the reader's profile. In one miscue study (K. Goodman and Burke, 1973), corrected partials were counted to evaluate their influence on miscue frequency. Proficient readers produce more partials that are immediately corrected than less proficient readers. Although proficient readers produce fewer miscues than less proficient readers do, when corrected partials are added to the number of other miscues, the number of miscues per 100 words seems to be about the same for all readers. This finding suggests that proficient readers may begin to produce as many miscues as less proficient readers, but their effective use of confirmation strategies allows more efficient self-correction.

As teacher/researchers observe and analyze readers' use of confirmation strategies through self-correction, they develop insight into its signficance.

Correction Is the miscue corrected?

The amount of text that is reread in making a correction is shown on the typescript by the length of the regression line underlining the structure reread. Although the length of regression is not collected on the Coding Form or Reader Profile, it should be examined because it provides cues into the size of the language units being processed by the readers and possible reasons readers choose to correct. These reasons are identified by the letter or letters placed in the circle at the beginning of the regression line (see earlier discussion of marking procedures). Sometimes the reader regresses to correct and produces another miscue. Sometimes the reader actually produces the expected response and then abandons that response in favor of a miscue. These possibilities are considered in responding to the question dealing with correction.

Graphic Similarity and Sound Similarity

Questions concerning graphic and sound similarity provide evidence about the degree to which readers make use of the graphophonic system as they read. The graphophonic system includes the graphic (the orthography or print) cues, the sound (the phonology or oral language) cues, and the relationship between the two (the phonic system). In addition to using the semantic and syntactic systems to predict words and phrases, readers can anticipate a word either by relating its physical characteristics to known items that look similar or have similar patterns or by assigning possible sounds to its various letters and letter combinations. The two related systems, graphic and sound, are evaluated separately in the procedures of miscue analysis.

Only word-for-word susbstitutions are examined for graphic and sound similarity. If it is not possible to determine which word is substituted for which because the miscue is complex, is an insertion or omission, or involves *only* punctuation or intonation variations, then the characteristics of graphic and sound similarity cannot be evaluated and these questions are not asked.

The graphic and sound systems of English and their relationship to each other are very complex. Contrary to the belief suggested by the way many instructional programs are organized, there is no one-to-one correspondence between letters and sounds. Readers' miscues often show that they are aware of the complexities of these systems.

Readers do not use all the graphophonic information available when they read. They sample enough information to be able to predict the language and the meaning of the text. Betsy's miscues of *when* for *while* and *always* for *away* in line 105 are good examples of this. She was beginning to understand that the husband was complaining about his wife, so all Betsy needed was a bit of graphic information to be able to predict that a time-related clause marker *(when)* would probably occur, to introduce a clause in which another time-related adverb *(always)* would be acceptable. She also chose terms that may be more common in her own language and conceptually easier to understand.

Readers also refer to the graphophonic system when they use confirming strategies. On line 318, Betsy provides a good example. She has predicted using both grammatical and semantic knowledge that the second clause in the sentence should begin with *I'll.* Since the first clause begins with *I'll,* it is to be expected that the clause following the *and* will begin in the same way. But *I'll* does not work with the subsequent information in the sentence, so Betsy picks up additional graphophonic information in order to self-correct. A similar phenomenon occurs at the end of the sentence when she predicts *in a flash* for *in a few minutes.*

Even proficient readers do not use the graphic and sound systems to a high degree all the time. In fact, studies of these readers show that about half of their substitution miscues will have only some degree of similarity to the text item (K. Goodman and Burke, 1973). On the other hand, the readers who are evaluated as needing help in reading often overuse their knowledge of the relationship between sounds and letters and often have higher scores on the degree to which they use sound and graphic similarity than more proficient readers. Results of miscue analysis research indicate that graphic similarity scores are usually higher than sound similarity scores for all readers. This suggests that the way a word looks and the patterns related to the visual organization of a word provide important cues to the reader.

When judging graphic similarity, the sequence and shape of the written miscue and the text word must be examined with no concern for pronunciation. The coder should simply look at the two items to *see* the degree to which they are alike. When marking graphic similarity, especially for dialect miscues, it must be remembered that there are often varieties of pronunciation for the same graphic item. Regardless of whether a speaker says *offen* or *often,* the word is always spelled *often.* All speakers use varying pronunciations for certain words depending on the phonological features of the words in the surrounding context. In the next sequence of sentences, the variations of *and* provide a good example to illustrate this issue.

Richard an' Doug will be the ones picked.

Ham 'n' cheese sandwiches are delicious.

And, let me tell you one more thing.

No matter how speakers may say or read these variations of *and,* when they write the word, they spell it *and.* Therefore all the sound variations must be considered graphically identical to the written word *and.*

When judging for sound similarity, on the other hand, the graphic shape or sequence of letters is *not* considered. Instead, coders close their eyes and say the two items, keeping in mind the way the reader pronounces them.

Evaluating the sound and graphic systems separately will provide teacher/researchers with a great deal of information about how the graphophonic system works in English. This procedure also reveals the sophistication the reader has in using the graphophonic system.

Graphic similarity How much do the two words look alike?

Word-level substitutions are evaluated for their graphic similarity by dividing both the observed response (OR) and the expected response (ER) into three parts: the beginning, middle, and end syllables or letters. If two of the three parts of the OR (beginnings and middles; beginnings and ends; or middles and ends) look like two of the three parts of the ER (beginnings and middles; beginnings and ends; or middles and ends) and occur in the same location within both words, then a *high* degree of graphic similarity exists between the OR and the ER.

If the OR and the ER have only one or more graphemes in common (only at the beginning or the middle or at the end) or if there is general configuration in common, such as for the words *am* and *in,* then *some* degree of similarity exists between the OR and the ER.

If there are no graphemes at all in common, then there is *no* graphic similarity between the two items. It is sometimes difficult to code words that cannot be conveniently divided into three parts or to compare long words when substituted for or by short words. Such problems are treated in greater depth in the discussion of Procedure I in Chapter 5.

Sound similarity How much do the two words sound alike?

To consider sound similarity, the two substituted items should be evaluated by dividing each into three parts: the beginning, the medial, and the ending sounds or syllables. If two of the three parts sound alike, (beginnings and middles; beginnings and ends; or middles and ends), and if the two similar parts are heard in the same location (beginnings, middles, ends) within both words, then a *high* degree of sound similarity exists between the OR and the ER.

If only one of the three parts is similar (beginnings, middles, or ends) then *some* sound similarity exists between the substituted word and the expected response.

If there are no sounds in common between the two substitutions, then the OR and ER have *no* sound similarity. Special problems arise when the OR and ER cannot conveniently be divided into three sound segments and when long and short words are compared (see Chapter 5).

Other Possible Questions

Some researchers may be interested in knowing the degree to which miscues can change the syntax of a passage, the kinds of grammatical transformations that can occur to the text or the types of pragmatic changes particular kinds of miscues can cause. Teachers, on the other hand, may want to look at the semantic relationship between substituted words in the text in order to gain some insights into a student's concepts and vocabulary.

Miscue analysis can be expanded and adapted to the particular concerns and questions of teacher/researchers by adding questions of specific interest. Those who want to make additions need to develop a rationale for such uses and tie the questions to their beliefs about the reading process. A discussion of questions concerning grammatical function similarity and peripheral field used in earlier miscue analysis procedures will show how a rationale is developed and how to state the questions. Although these categories will not be used in the procedures developed in this book, many users of miscue analysis have found them useful in adding to their own understandings of the reading process and in gaining insights into a reader's knowledge about language.

Grammatical Function

Words in context can almost always be assigned a grammatical function. The variety of grammatical functions that will fit into any one position within a sentence is limited. Readers make intuitive use of the grammatical constraints of their language to help them predict grammatical function on the basis of preceding structures. The degree to which miscues retain the same grammatical function as the text word it is substituted for indicates the reader's knowledge of English sentence structure. Although readers do not always substitute words of the same grammatical function, often at least 75 percent of the time nouns are substituted for nouns, verbs for verbs, adjectives for adjectives, and function words for function words. In many cases in which the miscue substitution is not the same grammatical function as the text word, the reader produces an alternative grammatical structure in order to produce a syntactically acceptable sentence. Therefore, it should not be expected that all miscues will be replaced by words that serve the same grammatical function; acceptability depends on the ways in which a particular sentence can be transformed.

When the miscue involves the substitution of a single word or nonword for a text word, it is interesting to note the grammatical difference between the reader's substitution and the text word. The reader's intonation and the use of inflectional endings usually make it possible to assign a grammatical function even for nonwords.

Grammatical Function Similarity Is the grammatical function of the miscue the same as the grammatical function in the text?

Possible answers include *yes,* the substitution is identical, or *no,* the substitution is not identical. In a few cases in which the miscue disrupts the text a great deal and the reader does not provide appropriate intonation to help clarify the ambiguity of the syntax, it is necessary to indicate that the grammatical function of the substitution cannot be determined. Such miscues are coded as *indeterminate.*

The coding of grammatical function similarity will depend on the knowledge of the coder. For most purposes, it is sufficient to use the common notions of noun for noun, verb for verb, adjective for adjective, adverb for adverb, or function word for function word. However, some may want their coding to reflect greater sophistication and indicate the degree of grammatical function similarity and will code grammatical similarity depending on additional features such as common noun for common noun, proper noun for proper noun, transitive verb for transitive verb, intransitive verb for intransitive verb, etc. The Goodman Taxonomy provides such a system for comparing similarity (see Appendix D). Anyone developing a grammatical function category must carefully define the features of grammatical function that are to be compared.

Peripheral Vision

To what degree do readers pick up graphic information in the periphery of the text being processed? Teacher/researchers may want to gain insight into the issue of perception in reading. They may be interested to discover how much peripheral information readers use or the degree to which readers stick closely to the written text. Depending on their particular concerns or interests, questions may vary. We suggest the following:

Is the miscue word or phrase within the near periphery?

Is the miscue word or phrase within the far periphery?

The Goodman Taxonomy of Miscues, which includes this category, defines the near periphery as the line immediately above or below the point of the miscue; the far periphery is defined as the second or third line above or below the line in which the miscue occurs. In the Taxonomy, only a complete word or phrase is considered in coding peripheral field. If parts of words or whole words that are parts of other words are involved, these are not coded as being in the peripheral field. If a researcher wants to look at parts of words in the peripheral field, clearly stated questions and definitions need to be established. For example, if the reader reads *her* for *the* in a line and the word *other* appeared in the line directly above the word, this would not be considered in the periphery if the linguistic unit to be considered is defined as being a complete word unit. If on the other hand, any string of letters in the same order is defined as the linguistic unit under consideration, then words such as *other, thermometer,* and even *periphery* need to be considered. Conclusions about peripheral field resulting from miscue research include: (a) Miscues that are most often in the periphery are function words such as articles, prepositions, and verb particles; (b) In most cases, proficient readers produce more peripheral miscues than less proficient readers; and (c) Insertion miscues can often be found in the near periphery (K. Goodman and Burke, 1973; Goodman and Goodman, 1978).

In this chapter, we have presented the questions that are asked about reader's miscues and the theoretical rationale that drives those involved with miscue analysis to seek answers to these questions. Miscue analysis is a heuristic tool that allows teacher/researchers using a similar framework to expand on the work presented here and answer their own questions about the nature of reading, the reading process, and reading instruction.

5

Alternative Procedures for Miscue Analysis

One of our purposes is to help teacher/researchers make independent decisions about ways to use miscue analysis that will accommodate their particular concerns and questions. Teacher/researchers will decide which of the four procedures presented in this and the next chapter they will select depending on their particular purposes and functions. The specific procedures are concerned with which miscues to select for coding, which questions to use for analysis, how to read the text for purposes of analysis, and how to score and record the evaluation of the miscues and the retelling.

Procedure I

Procedure I examines separately each miscue the reader makes, while simultaneously evaluating the influence of the reader's knowledge of the world and language in relation to the context of the miscue. It also examines the reader's use and control of the language systems and reading strategies while reading orally. Except for the omission of a few categories, Procedure I is most similar to the original Reading Miscue Inventory (Goodman and Burke, 1972). Because of its potential for in-depth investigation, this procedure is recommended for researchers, reading specialists, and special education teachers concerned with developing in-depth knowledge about their students' reading.

Selecting Miscues for Coding

When the tape recording of the student's reading and retelling are completed and the miscues are marked on the typescript following the general procedures in Chapter 3, the typescript is ready for miscues to be selected for numbering and coding.

Miscues selected for transfer to the coding sheets include: substitutions (including reversals), omissions (including uncorrected partials), insertions, and intonation shifts that cause changes to the syntax or meaning of the text. These miscues are coded even if they are subsequently corrected. The first complete observed response is selected for coding.

Miscues that are not selected for coding (unless there are specified reasons to do otherwise) include: corrected partials, substitution of alternative sound variations involving phonological dialect, misarticulations and split syllables, some repeated miscues, and new miscues made during a correction attempt.

Repetitions or regressions and pauses are strategies readers use for a variety of reasons and are not considered miscues. Regressions that are attempts at correction are taken into consideration as part of miscue analysis, but other regressions and pauses are not noted on the coding sheet. All of these phenomena provide interesting information about the reader. Information that is not coded but is of interest to teacher/researchers can be examined directly from the typescript and listed under the *comments* section on the Reader Profile. Examples of miscues and regressions not selected for coding follow:

B0302 all the cells and . . .

(Corrected partial is not coded. Caution: uncorrected partials are coded as omissions—see marking of omissions Chapter 3.)

Get in the game with the kids!

(Phonological dialect is not coded.)

They slid on the linoleum floor.

(Misarticulation is not coded.)

What a pretty sight!

(Split syllable is not coded.)

B0212–213 . . . the heartbeat of a friend

(Repetition is not coded.)

. . . she hung between the room.

(Pause is not coded.)

Repeated Miscues

The analysis of repeated miscues examines what readers do when the same linguistic unit (usually a word or phrase) occurs across the text and the reader miscues on the unit at least twice. Some repeated miscues are not coded depending on the nature of the text item. When readers *substitute* or *omit* the identical observed response for the identical text item of nouns, pronouns, verbs, adjectives, and adverbs two or more times in the same text, such miscues are numbered and coded only for the first occurrence. Subsequent occurrences are marked RM on the typescript and are not coded to avoid inflating the statistical data. Repeated identical miscues are marked RM only if the OR and ER have the same meaning and serve the identical grammatical function.

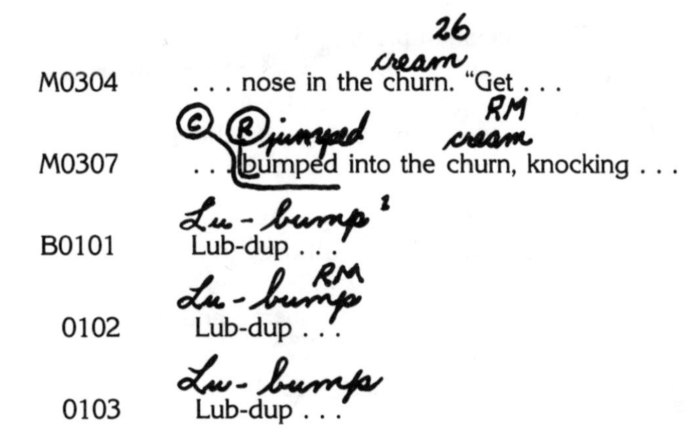
M0304 . . . nose in the churn. "Get . . .

M0307 . . . bumped into the churn, knocking . . .

B0101 Lub-dup . . .

0102 Lub-dup . . .

0103 Lub-dup . . .

Only the first substitution of *cream* (miscue #26) for *churn* and *Lu-bump* (miscue #1) for *Lub-dup* are numbered and, therefore, selected for coding. The subsequent identical repeated miscues are marked RM on the typescript. These are not listed on the Coding Form. However, since repeated miscues provide important insights into a reader's transaction with the text, there are opportunities to examine this process by collecting all repeated miscue data on the Reader Profile even though they are not coded (see the Reader Profile later in this chapter).

Sometimes readers use different strategies in response to the same text item. They may substitute a variety of expected responses or they may omit. Each new observed response for the same text item across the text is coded.

M0205 the cream into the churn, he said, . . .

Betsy substituted a nonword *$shurn* (miscue #13) for the first occurrence of *churn*. On the second occurrence of *churn* (line 304, shown earlier), she substituted *cream* (miscue #26), which was a new observed response. This miscue is numbered and coded. The third occurrence of *churn* (line 307) is marked RM because it is an identical substitution for the same text item.

Whenever the grammatical function of the expected response changes, however, any miscues that occur on that item will be coded. For example, if *pat* is substituted for *pet* (a noun), and later *pat* is substituted for *pet* (a verb), these are not identical miscues; both, therefore, are numbered and coded.

Substitutions for and omissions of function words (determiners, verb markers, conjunctions, prepositions, etc.) are always coded each time they occur because they often mark different kinds of relationships in each text occurrence.

Multiple Miscues

Readers occasionally produce two or more observed responses on the same text item. When such multiple miscues occur, the first complete observed response (OR) (word or nonword, but *not* a partial) is coded. The first miscue is selected in order to evaluate the reader's initial predicting and subsequent confirming strategies. The reader's final attempt at a single text item is taken into consideration when other miscues in the sentence are coded. In the other three procedures, all the miscues are related and coded at the same time within the entire sentence, which allows the final miscue attempts to be considered. These differences will be explained as appropriate for each procedure.

Because all miscue attempts on a single text item are interesting to examine, they are all carefully marked on the typescript in order to provide information about what cues and strategies the reader is using. Multiple attempts are listed sequentially above the text item starting with the first attempt closest to the item.

M0308 . . .The cream splashed all over the room.

(*shout* for *splashed,* miscue #31, is numbered and coded.)

Poor Freddie was in trouble again.

(*$trub,* miscue #2, is numbered and coded.)

Complex Miscues

Sometimes miscues involve words or phrases in such a way that it is not possible to determine word-for-word relationships. When this occurs, the entire sequence is marked, numbered, and coded as one complex miscue.

To determine whether a miscue is complex, the teacher/researcher should attempt to relate the observed response (OR) to the expected response (ER) on a word-for-word level. If it is easy to see that the first OR is substituted for the first text item and the second OR is substituted for the second text item, then each miscue is numbered and coded separately. These are not complex miscues.

M0211 . . . her. She was not . . .

He is going to

Complex miscues are marked, numbered, and coded as one single miscue when it is obvious that the ER and the OR relate in complex ways and that there are no one-to-one relationships between individual words in the ER and the OR. These often involve syntactic shifts or transformations.

M0104 . . . he said to his wife, "What do you

105 do all day . . .

Betsy substitutes the entire clause *I want you* for the entire text clause *What do you.* She has predicted a declarative sentence instead of an interrogative one. It is not possible to say *I* is substituted for *What,* or that *want* is substituted for either *do* or *what.* In fact, Betsy's *you* is the object of the clause she predicted instead of the subject as occurs in the published text. Because it is not possible to separate the miscues, the substitution of one clause for another is treated as a single complex miscue. Because this miscue is in the first few paragraphs of Betsy's reading, it is not part of the coded portion of miscues assigned a miscue number. If it were to be coded it would be marked as a single miscue.

M0204 . . . make some butter. As he put

205 the cream into the churn, he said, "This is

By substituting *and* for the *period* and *As,* Betsy produces a conjoined sentence with two independent clauses rather than starting the second sentence with a dependent clause. This substitution of one word for a period and a word is treated as a complex miscue. This miscue causes her to produce another miscue, the substitution of the period for the comma after the word *churn.* Her intonation indicates that she not only ended the sentence but that she began a new sentence with *He said.*

Often insertions or omissions with related substitution miscues are considered complex.

He could stay at home.

The insertion of *have* and the substitution of *stayed* for *stay* is inseparable and coded as one complex miscue because the reader's prediction of a shift of tense required the substitution.

. . . never been a rule against pets in

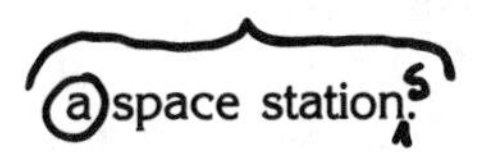

In places where omissions and insertions occur within a noun or verb phrase, the miscue is often complex. In this example, the omission of the determiner *a* and insertion of *s* on *station* indicates the reader has substituted a plural noun phrase for a singular one.

The reversal of sequential words and the omission of two or three sequential words or lines in the text are also treated as complex:

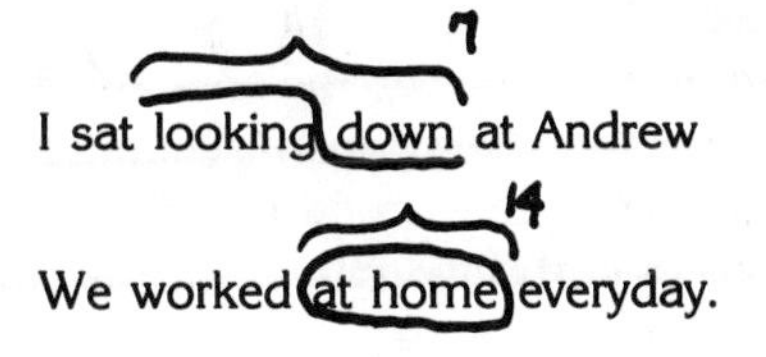

I sat looking down at Andrew
We worked at home everyday.

Teacher/researchers should try to avoid line omissions during the data collection session by asking readers to read the omitted line at the time the omission occurs. However, if they are not noticed and occur, they are treated as a single complex miscue.

Laura wanted to eat

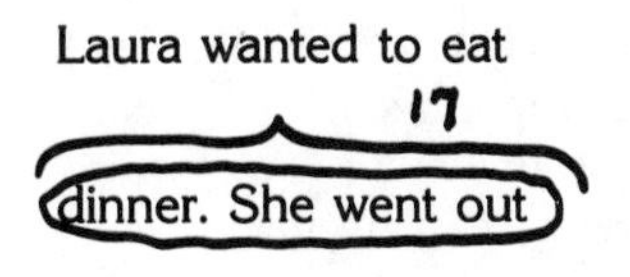

with her good friends.

The reader omitted a line. The omitted line is numbered as a single complex miscue and read and coded using the reader's intonation to decide whether the resulting transformation is semantically and syntactically acceptable. In this case, the reader's intonation indicated that she moved from one line to the next without interrupting the pattern of the sentence. She read: *Laura wanted to eat with her good friends.*

Occasionally, even though it is possible to find a word-for-word relationship, the OR words are related in complex ways to the ER words, graphophonically, syntactically, or semantically, and it is impossible to code each one separately without losing information about the whole complex miscue. In these cases the miscues are also treated as complex!

17 seven 18 pets 19 were

In no time at all, Sven's pet was everybody's pet.

The omission of the comma noted from the reader's intonation is considered a separate miscue since it could have occurred whether the following cluster of miscues occurred or not. However, the cluster of miscues following the comma *(seven pets were)* needs more consideration to determine the number of miscues involved. *Seven pets* for *Sven's pet* is considered one complex miscue not simply because of the relationship of the syntactic cues of plurality but also because of the possessive graphophonic cue involved with the insertion of *s* on *pets*. The need to decide whether the substitution of *was* for *were* is part of the complex miscue is a borderline situation. We suggest it be coded separately because it involves a point at which the reader could have corrected rather than making the form of *be* be consistent with the subject. Many miscues result from readers accommodating following text to prior miscues. If these were all coded as complex miscues, we would lose important insights into the reader's strategies.

the 21 passes

The rest of us passed around the oxygen bottle.

The complex syntactic and semantic meaning changes caused by the substitution of a noun phrase *(the passes)* for an object of the preposition plus a verb makes this miscue too interrelated to code separately.

There is a continuum between the obvious sequence of simple word-for-word substitution miscues and the obvious inseparable complex miscue. In borderline cases, there may be evidence to code in either manner. Experience with miscue analysis provides the opportunity to build consistent rationales and aids in decision making.

Complex relationships between a cluster of miscues and text items are not always discovered until the miscues are being coded. This often results in renumbering all miscues. Because of this, novices to miscue analysis should number and code miscues sentence by sentence until they become adept at discovering complex miscues. It also helps to place a bracket on the coding form in the Text column to highlight all the miscues in one sentence whether they are complex or not, and to keep in mind their relationship (see Betsy's Coding Form later in this chapter and Gordon's in Appendix B).

Numbering Miscues

As the miscues are selected for coding, they are also numbered (see Betsy's typescript in Chapter 1 and Gordon's in Appendix B). It is expedient for those who are using miscue analysis for the first time to number and code only a few miscues at a time (always use pencil). This procedure will eliminate the need to renumber an entire typescript if an additional miscue is discovered or if two or more miscues are considered to be a single complex miscue.

For those using this text in order to learn to do miscue analysis, now is the time to begin numbering and coding miscues and to follow the instructions for each procedure as they are presented. It is advisable to complete each task as it is described and then check the completed forms for confirmation. Often rereading the appropriate sections related to the tasks clarifies problems and misconceptions.

A blank form of *The Man Who Kept House* is provided if you wish to use this story with another reader (see Appendix C). Marked copies of Betsy's and Gordon's typescripts, blank Coding Forms, and Reader Profiles are also provided. We suggest that one copy of each blank form in Appendix C be photocopied and kept as a master form. Additional forms may be photocopied as needed. (This permission covers only the blank forms in this book and does *not* cover *any* other parts of the text.)

In the coding of *The Man Who Kept House*, it makes sense to number the first four miscues, starting with the miscue in the paragraph that is to be coded first. Since we were aware that the text structures of *stay home* and *keep house* were causing Betsy to adapt her reading strategies, we decided to code her miscues starting on line M0112, giving her the first few paragraphs to "settle in" to the text. Teacher/researchers should examine the beginnings of a text carefully in order to decide where to begin coding. The student's familiarity with the context, style, concept density, and predictable structures may all enter into the decision (Menosky, 1971).

After the first four miscues are coded, miscues 5 to 9 found in the next two paragraphs are numbered and coded. For the purpose of evaluating students, at least 25 consecutive miscues need to be coded. In order to provide a wide range of miscue examples for instructional purposes, all of Betsy's miscues have been coded consecutively starting from line M0112. For the same reason, all of Gordon's miscues on *Beat of My Heart* have been coded (see Appendix B). Once the coding of the miscues is started, all subsequent miscues in the text are coded consecutively because overall and continuous patterns are important. Sometimes teacher/researchers decide to code all of a student's miscues if the total miscue number is more that 25 but less than 50. These decisions depend on the development of consistent rationales based on the purposes of the miscue analyses. The line number, miscue number, reader's miscue (OR), and text item (ER) are written on the Coding Form (see Betsy's Coding Form and Gordon's Appendix B).

Beginners to miscue analysis may find it helpful to answer Question 1 for a consecutive group of about 10 miscues, then answer Question 2 for the same miscues, then Question 3, and so forth. As teacher/researchers become proficient with the coding procedures, however, it is preferable to code each miscue right across the coding sheet. In this way teacher/researchers become increasingly aware of how the various language systems and reading strategies interrelate and influence readers' miscues. Practice and patience will result in more proficient coding.

Once miscues are selected and numbered, the questions in the box are used to analyze each miscue. After the questions are listed, there is a discussion to aid in the coding of each question. For purposes of clarification, teacher/researchers may wish to reread the rationale in Chapter 4 for any of these questions.

QUESTIONS

Question 1: *Syntactic acceptability*

Does the miscue occur in a structure that is syntactically acceptable *in the reader's dialect?*

Y (Yes)—The miscue occurs in a structure that is completely syntactically acceptable within the sentence and within the text.

P (Partial)—The miscue occurs in a structure that either is syntactically acceptable with the first part of the sentence or is syntactically acceptable with the last part of the sentence. Or, the miscue is syntactically acceptable within the sentence, but not within the complete text.

N (No)—The miscue occurs in a sentence that is not syntactically acceptable.

Question 2: *Semantic acceptability*

Does the miscue occur in a structure that is semantically acceptable *in the reader's dialect?* Semantic acceptability cannot be coded higher than syntactic acceptability.

Y (Yes)—The miscue occurs in a structure that is completely semantically acceptable within the sentence and within the text.

P (Partial)—The miscue occurs in a structure that is semantically acceptable with either the first part of the sentence or is semantically acceptable with the last part of the sentence. Or, the miscue is semantically acceptable within the sentence, but not within the complete text.

N (No)—The miscue occurs in a sentence that is not semantically acceptable.

Question 3: *Meaning change*

Does the miscue result in a change of meaning? This question is asked only if the miscues are both syntactically and semantically acceptable (Q1 = Y and Q2 = Y).

N (No)—Within the context of the entire passage no change in meaning is involved.

P (Partial)—There is inconsistency, loss, or meaning change of a minor idea, incident, character, fact, sequence, or concept.

Y (Yes)—There is inconsistency, loss, or meaning change of a major idea, incident, character, fact, sequence, or concept (see note below).

Question 4: *Correction*

Is the miscue corrected?

Y (Yes)—The miscue is corrected.

P (Partial)—There is either an unsuccessful attempt to correct, or the expected response is read and then abandoned.

N (No)—There is no attempt to correct.

Question 5: *Graphic similarity*

How much does the miscue look like the text?

H (High)—-A high degree of graphic similarity exists between the miscue and the text.

S (Some)—Some degree of graphic similarity exists between the miscue and the text.

N (None)—No degree of graphic similarity exists between the miscue and the text.

Question 6—*Sound similarity*

How much does the miscue sound like the expected response?

H (High)—A high degree of sound similarity exists between the miscue and the text.

S (Some)—Some degree of sound similarity exists between the miscue and the text.

N (None)—No degree of sound similarity exists between the miscue and the text.

Note: Many have raised questions about the use of Y to equal loss in Question 3, while Y is equal to acceptability in Questions 1 and 2. This is a purposeful shift in order to cause coders not to consider the quality of the miscue in relation to all the cueing systems and strategies automatically.

Analyzing Miscues

In this procedure the influence of each language system on the reading process is analyzed separately through the questions concerning Syntactic Acceptability, Semantic Acceptability, Graphic Similarity, and Sound Similarity (Questions 1, 2, 5 and 6) for each coded miscue. Sociocultural influences, including pragmatics, are considered, along with the semantic system, in the questions concerned with Semantic Acceptability and Meaning Change (Questions 2 and 3).

The relationships of the systems are coded and later analyzed to determine the reader's patterns of strengths and weaknesses. These relationships are marked on the Coding Form under Meaning Construction and Grammatical Relationships.

Syntactic Acceptability and Semantic Acceptability

As discussed earlier, language has both a syntactic organization and a semantic organization. Syntactic Acceptability (Question 1) is concerned with the degree to which the reader produces acceptable grammatical structures. Semantic Acceptability (Question 2) focuses on the success with which the reader produces meaning within an acceptable structure. The dialect of the reader is always taken into consideration when answering these questions.

How to Read for Syntactic Acceptability

Question 1: *Syntactic acceptability*

Does the miscue occur in a structure that is syntactically acceptable *in the reader's dialect?*

In order to answer the question for syntactic acceptability, the entire sentence is read as the reader finally produced it, except for the miscue in question.

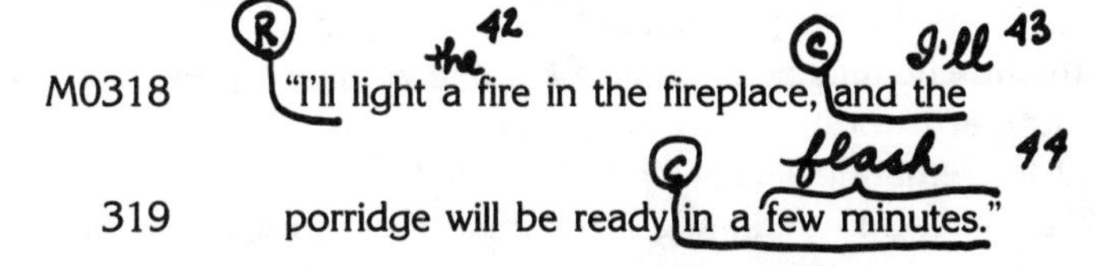

To code the substitution of *the* for *a* the sentence is read: *I'll light the fire in the fireplace and the porridge will be ready in a few minutes.* Since the miscues *I'll* and *flash* were both corrected, they are read as corrected when coding *the.* To code the substitution of *I'll* for *the,* the sentence is read: *I'll light the fire in the fireplace, and I'll porridge will be ready in a few minutes. The* is read as the reader left it because it was not corrected, and *flash* is read as corrected because this is the way the reader left it. To code the substitution of *flash* for *few minutes* the sentence is read: *I'll light the fire in the fireplace, and the porridge will be ready in a flash.* The *the* is read as the reader left it because it was not corrected, and *I'll* is read as corrected because this is the way the reader finally resolved it (see the Coding Form in the following section for coding decisions).

If a miscue is found to be syntactically acceptable within the sentence, the sentence is then read to determine its acceptability within the entire story. Reading the whole story or article up to the sentence often helps to clarify the acceptability of the miscue under question. If the miscue is acceptable within the entire selection, the miscue is coded Y. If the miscue is acceptable only at the sentence level, the miscue is coded P. Syntactic acceptability only at the sentence level rarely occurs. A nonparallel structure caused by a shift in verb tense or a move from singular to plural *may* cause a sentence to be unacceptable within an entire selection.

If the miscue is found to be syntactically *un*acceptable within the total sentence, the next step is to determine whether the miscue is acceptable within the sentence up to and including the miscue or from the point of the miscue to the end of the sentence. Examining acceptability of portions of sentences and relating it to self-correction is the best way to observe a reader's use of predicton strategies. If the beginning portion of the sentence including the miscue is not considered syntactically acceptable, the acceptability of the ending portion of the sentence including the miscue is then judged. If a beginning (including the miscue) or an ending of the sentence (including the miscue) is considered syntactically acceptable, the miscue is coded P. The P category provides a good deal of information about the reader's prediction strategies. If the miscue is an omission, the word beyond the omission or the word before the omission is read when judging for partial acceptability (P) within the sentence. Keep in mind that the sentence is the unit of analysis, therefore, miscues that occur on the first word of a sentence are either acceptable within the total sentence or unacceptable since no portion of the sentence can occur before the miscue. Miscues that occur on the last word of a sentence also can only be totally acceptable or unacceptable.

How to Read for Semantic Acceptability

Question 2: *Semantic acceptability*

Does the miscue occur in a structure that is semantically acceptable *in the reader's dialect?* Semantic Acceptability cannot be coded higher than Syntactic Acceptability.

Semantic acceptability depends on syntactic acceptability. Therefore, if the miscue is syntactically unacceptable (N), the miscue is considered semantically unacceptable and *must* be coded N. If the miscue is syntactically partially acceptable (P), the miscue may be semantically unacceptable (N) or partially acceptable (P). It follows that if the miscue is syntactically acceptable (Y), then the miscue can be coded for semantic acceptability—either Y, P, or N.

To determine semantic acceptability, the miscue is read in exactly the same way it is read to determine syntactic acceptability; that is, the entire sentence, except for the miscue in question, is read as the reader finally produced it.

If the miscue is found to be semantically acceptable within the sentence, the sentence is then read to determine its acceptability within the entire story or article. If the miscue is acceptable within the entire selection, the miscue is coded Y. If the miscue is acceptable at the sentence level only, it is coded P.

If the miscue is found to be semantically unacceptable within the total sentence, the next step is to determine whether the miscue is acceptable with the sentence portion up to and including the miscue or from the point of the miscue to the end of the sentence. If the beginning of the sentence, including the miscue, is not acceptable, an attempt is made to judge the semantic acceptability of the sentence portion from the point of the miscue to the end of the sentence. If the beginning portion (including the miscue) or the end portion of the sentence (including the miscue) is judged acceptable, the miscue is coded P. If the miscue is an omission, the word beyond the omission or the word before the omission is read when judging for partial acceptability (P) within the sentence.

Sometimes miscues that might otherwise be considered acceptable must be coded as unacceptable because prior or subsequent unacceptable miscues in the sentence or the sentence portion result in a structure that is syntactically or semantically unacceptable. Following are examples of responses to Questions 1 and 2 with the reasons for their coding:

Y—The miscue occurs in a sentence that is completely syntactically acceptable within the sentence and within the text.
Y—The miscue occurs in a sentence that is completely semantically acceptable within the sentence and within the text.

It's[4] P heartbeat[5]
B0108 It is the sound of your heart beating

the beat
B0328 Then listen to his heart again.

All of these miscues result in sentences that sound like language and make sense in the total story. They are therefore considered both syntactically and semantically acceptable.

Y—The miscue is completely syntactically acceptable.
N—The miscue occurs in a sentence that is not semantically acceptable.

building
I came down the hill like a boulder.

$mu-si'cle
B0116–18 Your heart is a hollow muscle divided into four parts.

The substitution of *building* for *boulder* is syntactically acceptable because it is a noun for a noun. However, considering English metaphors, the substitution is not semantically acceptable because a person cannot be compared to a building in relation to coming down a hill. The substitution of *$mu-si'cle* for *muscle* is also considered syntactically acceptable. As Gordon read it, his intonation showed that the nonword was a noun and therefore sounds like language. But *$mu-si'cle* is not considered semantically acceptable because there is no such word in English, and therefore the substitution does not make sense.

N—The miscue is not syntactically acceptable.
N—The miscue is not semantically acceptable. The miscue must be marked N; semantic acceptability cannot be coded higher than syntactic acceptability.

$soud P
B0104–107 This strange sound is the sound of a wonderful

m-
m-
machine inside your body.

The omission of the noun *sound,* in this case the subject of the sentence, causes this sentence to be syntactically unacceptable. It is not possible to produce a sentence that begins *This strange is the* . . . Because this miscue is syntactically uancceptable, it will also be coded as semantically unacceptable. The omission also will affect the coding of the next miscue, the nonword $*soud* for sound, which will be discussed later as an example of partial syntactic acceptability.

Here
Her name was Sandy.

The miscue at the beginning of the sentence is considered syntactically and semantically unacceptable. It cannot be acceptable with the prior sentence because the sentence is the unit of analysis in determining acceptability.

Miscues are *partially* syntactically and *partially* semantically acceptable in three ways: (a) partially acceptable with the first part of the sentence including the miscue (and one word beyond when the miscue is an omission), (b) partially acceptable with the last part of the sentence including the miscue (and one word before when the miscue is an omission), or (c) acceptable within the sentence only but not in the entire printed text.

P—The miscue occurs in a structure that is syntactically acceptable with the first part of the sentence.
P—The miscue occurs in a structure that is semantically acceptable with the first part of the sentence.

M0502 . . . He pulled the end of the

503 rope out of the fireplace . . . (© up)

This miscue provides evidence of the reader's ability to predict a possible structure. It is considered acceptable up to and including the miscue although it is not acceptable in the entire sentence. The substitution of *up* for *out* is coded P because it has the potential of resulting in an acceptable sentence if a syntactically acceptable ending is added after the miscue, e.g., *He pulled the end of the rope up (the chimney).* This sentence cannot be coded Y for semantic acceptability because it is not completely semantically acceptable within the sentence or the text, and it cannot be coded higher semantically than it is syntactically. The miscue is coded P for semantic acceptability because it produces a sentence beginning that makes sense up to and including the miscue and has the potential to produce an acceptable sentence as shown in the above example.

The following miscue is also coded P under syntactic acceptability because the sentence portion is acceptable up to and including the miscue.

M0106 "I keep house," replied the wife, "and
107 keeping house is hard work."
and
3. and
2. and keeping house
1. and keeping

This potential is obvious when a syntactically acceptable ending can be added after the miscue e.g., *"I keep house," replied the wife, "and keeping house and (looking after*

you) is hard work". This sentence cannot be coded Y for semantic acceptability because it is not completely semantically acceptable within the text and it cannot be coded higher semantically than it is coded syntactically. The sentence is coded P for semantic acceptability because the sentence portion makes sense up to and including the miscue and it is meaningfully acceptable to read e.g., *"I keep house," replied the wife, and keeping house and (looking after you) is hard work".*

P—The miscue occurs in a structure that is syntacticaly acceptable with the last part of the sentence.

P—The miscue occurs in a structure that is semantically acceptable with the last part of the sentence.

M0112–3 . . . I'll stay home and keep house," said the woodman.

(handwritten above: start, house, keeping)

The substitution of *keeping* for *keep* is coded P because, when included with the last portion of the sentence, the resulting structure is partially syntactically acceptable. This judgment can be facilitated by adding a potential syntactically acceptable beginning e.g., *("I like cooking) and keeping house," said the woodman.* This sentence cannot be coded Y for semantic acceptability because it is not totally semantically acceptable and cannot be coded higher semantically than syntactically. The miscue can be coded P for semantic acceptability.

P—The miscue occurs in a structure that is syntactically acceptable with the last part of the sentence.

N—The miscue is not semantically acceptable.

B0104–107 This strange sound is the sound of a wonderful
machine inside your body.

(handwritten above: $soud; ⓒ m- m-)

Gordon's intonation revealed that his nonword substitution was a noun and that he therefore produced an acceptable structure. However, it cannot be acceptable in the entire sentence because of the omission of the subject. Therefore, *$soud* is syntactically acceptable with the end of the sentence. This nonword substitution then is judged as partially syntactically acceptable with the last part of the sentence and is coded P. The *$soud* for *sound* substitution, however, is not semantically acceptable, and is coded N because it is a nonword and does not carry semantic meaning.

P—The miscue occurs in a structure that is syntactically acceptable with the first part of the sentence.

N—The miscue is not semantically acceptable.

B0110–11 Your heart is a pump which will never
112–13 stop working as long as you live,
114–15 but it can rest even while it is working.

(handwritten above: bump; ⓒ near?; ⓒ 8 E)

To answer Questions 1 and 2 in order to code miscue 8, the insertion of the period, consider how Gordon finally read this sentence: *Your heart is a bump which will never stop working as long as you live, but it can rest. Even while it is working.* The insertion of a period is marked partially syntactically acceptable (P) because of the sentence fragment *even while it is working.* In situations such as this in which readers transform sentences, the unit of analysis for coding acceptability is always considered the sentence as punctuated in the published text. This example is marked semantically unacceptable (N) because of a previous miscue in the sentence, *bump* for *pump* (which is coded Y for syntactic acceptability and N for semantic acceptability). The substitution of *bump* for *pump* is syntactically acceptable because it is a noun substitution; however, it does not make sense in this sentence and is therefore semantically unacceptable.

Y—Syntactically acceptable.

P—The miscue occurs in a sentence that is semantically acceptable with the first part of the sentence (miscue 22) or within the sentence but not within the whole text (miscue 17).

B0301–2 Blood feeds all the cells and organs . . .
(handwritten: R; C feels; C c-; C oranges)

They were coming up the hill toward me, about fifteen ewes and their lambs.
(handwritten: elves)

In each of the above examples, the readers produce syntactically acceptable sentences. In the first, Gordon substitutes the verb *feels* for the verb *feeds* and the noun *oranges* for the noun *organs.* In the other example, the reader replaces the noun *ewes* with the noun *elves.* In each case, therefore, the sentence has retained its grammaticality. However, miscue 22 does not make sense in the complete sentence semantically. The OR *feels* is an example of a miscue that is semantically acceptable with the first part of the sentence and is coded P. The OR *elves* is semantically acceptable within the sentence (it is possible in a fantasy for elves to own lambs), but *elves* is not an acceptable substitution for *ewes* in the context of the entire story and therefore is coded P. The substitution of *oranges* for *organs,* however, would be coded N since it is not semantically acceptable at all.

The following miscue examples will be used to summarize the discussion of the coding of semantic and syntactic acceptability.

B0503–505 Place three fingertips of your right hand on the inside of your left wrist.
(handwritten: 44 C then; 45 fingers; 46 side; 47 UC w- w- $wist worst)

The above miscues are coded as shown on page 89 and on the Coding Form for Gordon's reading of *Beat of My Heart* (Appendix B). Gordon produces a sentence that is complicated to code. In coding *then* for *three* the sentence is read: *Place then fingers of your right hand on the side of your left worst.* Since *worst* is the last attempt for *wrist,* it is read as finally produced in coding the first three miscues in the sentence. In coding *fingers* for *fingertips* and *side* for *inside* the

LINE No./MISCUE No.	READER	TEXT	SYNTACTIC ACCEPTABILITY	SEMANTIC ACCEPTABILITY	MEANING CHANGE	CORRECTION
44	then	three	N	N	—	Y
45	fingers	fingertips	P	P	—	N
46	side	inside	P	P	—	N
47	$wist	wrist	Y	N	—	P

sentence is read in the same way except that *then* is read as corrected. In order to code the last miscue, the sentence is read: *Place three fingers of your right hand on the side of your left $wist.* Therefore, *then* for *three* is both syntactically and semantically unacceptable and coded N because it is not acceptable with either the prior and subsequent portions of the sentence. *Fingers* and *side* would have been fully acceptable both semantically and syntactically except for the other two miscues in the sentence. However, because the miscue on *wrist* is unsuccessfully corrected to a word that does not fit the sentence either syntactically or semantically, *fingers* and *side* must both be coded as acceptable only with the prior portion of the sentence (since the miscue on *three* was corrected), and are therefore coded P under both semantic and syntactic acceptability. Although when the other miscues in the sentence are coded they must be considered with the final attempt on *wrist*, miscue 47 evaluates *$wist* for *wrist* to gain insight into the influence of the initial miscue on the sentence. The substitution of *$wist* is considered syntactically acceptable. As Gordon read it, his intonation showed that the nonword was the object of the preposition and therefore sounds like language. It is not considered semantically acceptable because there is no such word as *$wist* in English and therefore, the substitution does not make sense.

Meaning Change

The focus of this question evaluates the degree to which the reader changes the author's intentions as interpreted by the teacher/researcher.

How to Read for Meaning Change

Question 3: *Meaning change*

Does the miscue result in a change of meaning? This question is asked only if the miscue has been coded completely syntactically and semantically acceptable.

Read the sentence as expected in the published text except for the miscue in question, which is read as the reader produced it. In other words, no matter how many miscues there are in the sentence, change everything back to the expected response except for the miscue under consideration. This causes the teacher/researcher to focus on the potential effect the single miscue has on the entire passage. This focus differs from Questions 1 and 2, in which the influence of all the other miscues in the sentence on the miscue being coded is considered. Following are examples of responses to Question 3:

N—Within the context of the entire passage no change in meaning is involved.

In all of the following examples for Question 3, there is no change of meaning, therefore, each is coded N.

M0201 So the the next morning the wife went off to

202 the forest. The husband stayed home and

203 began to do his wife's work.

B0108–9 It is the sound of your heart beating.

B0121–2 As you grow, it too will grow in size.

B0328 Then listen to his heart again

P—There is inconsistency, loss, or meaning change of a *minor* idea, incident, character, fact, sequence, concept, and so on.

In each of the following miscues, a minor change of meaning is involved, therefore each is coded P:

M0208 Soon the cream will turn into butter.

M0307–308 . . . It bumped into the churn, knocking it over . . .

M0610–612 . . . The wife stayed home to keep house and to look after their child.

Y—There is inconsistency, loss, or meaning change of a *major* idea, incident, character, fact, sequence, concept, and so on.

In the following miscues, a major change of meaning is involved. Because a major incident in each story is changed, each miscue is coded Y:

But the people could not get the fruit from the tree.

. . . so tired from his trip that he got sleepy. Very sleepy.

Mr. Pine could put up the signs.

Correction

Question 4: *Correction*

Is the miscue corrected?

This question examines the overt successful and unsuccessful self-correction attempts that reflect the reader's confirmation strategies.

Y—The miscue is corrected.

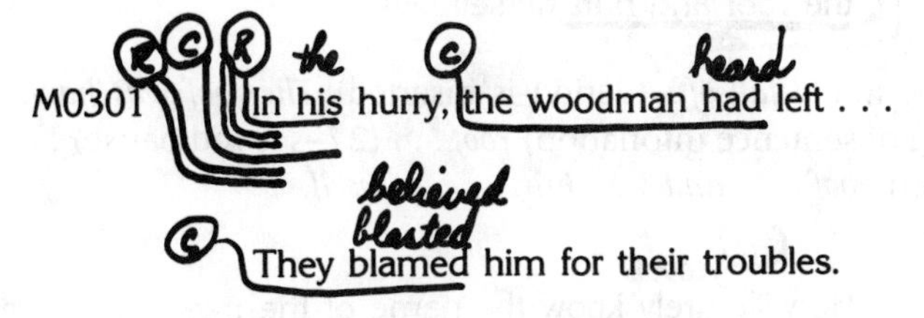

"I know," Ben said. "We could call him up on the telephone.

Read: *"I know," Ben said. "We could call him up on the telephone where everyone. . . "Where?" everyone asked.*

The omission of the period after *telephone* is considered self-corrected even though the reader only corrected by rereading *where* with intonation appropriate to the ER. Since readers almost never regress to a prior sentence when they self-correct beginning sentence intonation, the assumption is made that the correction includes the final punctuation at the end of the previous sentence. If the reader knows how and where the self-corrected sentence begins, this suggests that he or she is aware of the termination of the previous sentence.

P—There is either an unsuccessful attempt to correct (marked **UC**), or the expected response is read then abandoned (marked **AC**).

M0616 . . . stay home and keep house.

Read: . . . *stay home to keep . . . to keep . . . to keep house.*

a kind of backward loop . . .

Read: *a kind of backwa . . . backwards loop.* (Even though backwards is the miscue to be coded, the unsuccessful multiple attempts at correction are marked **UC** .

M0402-403 . . . No one has given her any grass to eat . . .

Read: *No one is . . . No one was . . . (was =* **UC** for *is) . . . giving her any . . . give . . . (give =* **UC** for *giving), No one was . . . (was =* **UC** for *was) . . . giving . . . (giving =* **UC** for *give).*

M0413 Then he was afraid that she would fall off

414 the roof and hurt herself.

Read: . . . *would fall off.* (Period is inserted) *The roof was har-. . . . The . . .* (for beginning of sentence intonation) *roof . . .* (27–second pause) . . . *The . . .* (again for intonation) *roof . . . and . . . hurt . . . himself.*

He will surely know the name of the tree . . .

Read: *He will surely . . . sure know the name of the tree . . .*

His sister Suzanne was hopping around and . . .

Read: *His sister Suzanne was hopping around . . . hoping around and . . .*

N—There is no attempt to correct.

M0600–602 . . . the baby crying, and her husband shouting for help.

B605 and then count once more.

Graphic and Sound Similarity

Question 5:—*Graphic similarity*

How much does the miscue look like the text?

Divide the OR and the ER into three parts in order to judge whether the OR bears high (H), some (S), or no (N) degree of graphic similarity to the ER.

H—A *high* degree of graphic similarity between the OR and the ER. If two parts of the OR look like two parts of the ER and appear in the same location (beginning, middle, or end) of the two words, a *high* degree of graphic similarity exists between the miscue and the text:

always away	house home	heard had	philosophical physical
I'll I'd	first fist	jumped bumped	away any
$soud sound	Well will	Then than	
start stay	$shurn churn	friend's friend	

S—Some degree of graphic similarity between the OR and the ER.

If one part of the OR looks like one part of the ER, and appears in the same location in both words, or if there is the same general configuration of the OR and ER and a letter in common *some* degree of graphic similarity exists between the miscue and the text:

threw / thought — There / She — shout / splashed

when / while — is / was — and / in

bread / butter — forest / far — up / out

job / work — the / his — keep / look

N—*No* degree of graphic similarity exists between the miscue and the text:

to / and — the / your — the / a — And / as

he / did — yet / now — day / morning

Graphic Similarity Problems Sometimes the OR and the ER cannot be conveniently divided into three parts (beginning, middle, and end) for evaluation. When this happens it is important to consider other reasonable visual information; the similar letters and where they appear, the length of the words, the configuration of the words, and whether the letters are both uppercase or both lowercase. Following are guidelines for the coding of miscues that do not easily fall into the stated categories.

High—The entire OR is found in the entire ER:

top / pot — was / saw — no / on — stop / post

High—The entire OR is found in the first 50 percent of the ER or the entire ER is found in the first 50 percent of the OR:

so / some — So / Soon — the / their — as / a — children / child — here / he

High—The entire OR is found in the last 50 percent of the ER or the entire ER is found in the last 50 percent of the OR:

he / she — he / the — she / he — into / to

High—Fifty percent or more of the OR appears in 50 percent or more of the ER or 50 percent of the ER appears in 50 percent or more of the OR.

on / or — the / this — tile / list

Some—The OR and ER have a letter or letters in common, but they do not appear in the same position (beginning, middle, end). Because of common letter(s), similar length and configuration, the miscues can be coded as having some (S) graphic similarity.

the	then	and	up	was	the	you	keep
his	and	in	out	and	his	to	look

When the evaluation of graphic similarity is such that the substitution could be coded in more than one category, the teacher/researcher should develop a rationale for both codings, select the one that seems most in keeping with linguistic knowledge and be consistent with any further coding of that substitution. It is helpful to keep a list of such decisions in order to rethink the rationale and to maintain consistency.

Question 6: *Sound similarity*

How much does the miscue sound like the expected response?

It is important to keep the reader's dialect in mind when sound similarity is being coded. Divide the OR and the ER into three parts in order to code whether the OR bears high (H), some (S), or no (N) similarity to the ER.

H—A high degree of sound similarity exists between the miscue and the text.

If two parts of the OR sound like two parts of the ER and are heard in the same location (beginning, middle, and end), the substituition is considered to have a high degree of sound similarity with the ER:

ways	feels	fat	bump	philosophical
ones	feeds	fit	pump	physical
heard	Well	Then	funny	buttermilk
had	We'll	than	phony	butter
first	light	never	$liver (diver)	
fist	least	over	liver	

S—Some degree of sound similarity exists between the miscue and the text.

If one part of the OR sounds like one part of the ER and is heard in the same location in both words, the substitution is considered to have some degree of sound similarity with the ER:

start	children	when	house	that	
stay	child	while	home	what	
for	the	as	so	is	rate
from	this	and	soon	was	pace

N—No degree of sound similarity exists between the miscue and the text:

job	and	on	away	the	a
work	is	to	any	she	in
There	to	then	cream	on	up
She	she	three	churn	or	out

Sound Similarity Problems Just as words are not always easily divided into three parts for graphic similarity evaluation, they do not always have three distinct sound groupings. In this case, the coder must make use of all sound information: the similarity of the phonemes, where they are heard in the words, and the length of the words.

Following are guidelines for the coding of miscues that do not easily fall into the stated categories.

High—The entire OR is heard in the first 50 percent of the ER, or the entire ER is heard in the first 50 percent of the OR:

some	inside
something	in

High—The entire ER is heard in the last 50 percent of the OR, or the entire OR is heard in the last 50 percent of the ER:

that	into	the	inside
at	to	a	side

High—Fifty percent or more of the OR is heard in 50 percent of the ER or 50 percent of the ER is heard in 50 percent of the OR:

He	I'll	you	he
who	I'd	to	she

The Coding Form

Each miscue is listed on the Coding Form and analyzed for each of the six questions. For ease of reference, the six questions for Procedure I are listed in Appendix A. The Coding Form for Procedure I has been coded for Betsy's miscues and is shown here. A blank Coding Form is available in Appendix C and may be copied and stored for continual use.

Patterns In addition to providing a place where each miscue can be coded, the Coding Form allows for the coding of the patterns of interrelationships for all the answers to Questions 1, 2, 3, and 4. From these patterns, a score is computed to indicate the student's degree of proficiency in using reading strategies. All of this information is subsequently entered on the Reader Profile, which includes data from all aspects of the miscue analysis. Two patterns are coded on the Coding Form to assess the patterns of interrelationships—the Patterns of Meaning Construction and the Patterns of Grammatical Relationships. It is important to keep in mind that these are scores of a reader's ability and do not reflect all aspects of a reader's strengths. Other features of the students' reading include their interests, their language background, and the sociocultural context, which should always be taken into consideration. In addition, these percentages are related to miscue data only and do not reflect all the information about the words, phrases, or sentences that are read as expected.

Patterns for Constructing Meaning These patterns indicate the reader's concern for making sense of the text in relationship to the expected meaning. Note that whenever teacher/researchers compare the reader's meaning with what they believe is the author's intended meaning, they are introducing their own interpretation as the basis for comparison. The patterns indicate the influence the reader's miscues have on Meaning Construction:

MISCUE ANALYSIS PROCEDURE I CODING FORM

READER *Betsy* DATE *Nov. 3*

TEACHER *Mrs Blau* AGE/GRADE *3* SCHOOL *York Elem.*

SELECTION *The Man Who Kept House*

LINE No./MISCUE No.	READER	TEXT	1 SYNTACTIC ACCEPTABILITY	2 SEMANTIC ACCEPTABILITY	3 MEANING CHANGE	4 CORRECTION	MEANING CONSTRUCTION (See 2, 3, 4): No Loss	Partial Loss	Loss	GRAMMATICAL RELATIONSHIPS (See 1, 2, 4): Strength	Partial Strength	Overcorrection	Weakness	5 GRAPHIC SIMILARITY: H	S	N	6 SOUND SIMILARITY: H	S	N
1	so	some	P	P	—	Y	✓			✓				✓				✓	
2	start	stay	P	P	—	N		✓					✓	✓				✓	
3	house	home	P	P	—	N		✓					✓	✓				✓	
4	keeping	keep	P	P	—	N		✓					✓	✓			✓		
5	we'll,	—	Y	P	—	N		✓			✓			—	—	—	—	—	—
6	bread	butter	Y	P	—	N		✓			✓				✓			✓	
7	—	all	Y	Y	N	Y	✓					✓		—	—	—	—	—	—
8	well	we'll	Y	Y	P	N		✓		✓				✓			✓		
9	you	—	Y	Y	P	N		✓		✓				—	—	—	—	—	—
10	day	morning	Y	Y	N	N	✓			✓						✓			✓
11	job	work	Y	Y	N	N	✓			✓					✓				✓
12	©and	. As	Y	P	—	N		✓			✓			—	—	—	—	—	—
13	$shurn	churn	Y	N	—	N			✓		✓			✓			✓		
14	. He	, he	Y	P	—	N		✓			✓			—	—	—	—	—	—
15	the	this	Y	Y	N	Y	✓					✓		✓				✓	
16	So	Soon	Y	Y	N	N	✓			✓				✓				✓	
17	. buttermilk	butter	Y	Y	P	N		✓		✓				✓			✓		
18	couldn't	could not	Y	Y	N	Y	✓					✓		—	—	—	—	—	—
19	There	She	N	N	—	Y	✓			✓					✓				✓
20	is	was	P	P	—	Y	✓			✓					✓			✓	
21	into	to	P	P	—	Y	✓			✓				✓			✓		
22	forest	far	P	P	—	Y	✓			✓					✓			✓	
23	in	to	Y	Y	N	N	✓			✓						✓			✓
24	the	his	Y	Y	N	Y	✓					✓			✓				✓
25	heard	had	P	P	—	Y	✓			✓				✓			✓		
			COLUMN TOTAL																
			PATTERN TOTAL																
			PERCENTAGE																

a. TOTAL MISCUES ____

b. TOTAL WORDS ____

a ÷ b × 100 = MPHW ____

(Goodman, Watson, Burke)

MISCUE ANALYSIS PROCEDURE I CODING FORM

READER *Betsy* DATE *Nov. 3*

TEACHER *Mrs. Blau* AGE/GRADE *3* SCHOOL *York Elem.*

SELECTION *The Man Who Kept House*

LINE No./MISCUE No.	READER	TEXT	1 SYNTACTIC ACCEPTABILITY	2 SEMANTIC ACCEPTABILITY	3 MEANING CHANGE	4 CORRECTION	MEANING CONSTRUCTION (See 2, 3, 4) No Loss	Partial Loss	Loss	GRAMMATICAL RELATIONSHIPS (See 1, 2, 4) Strength	Partial Strength	Overcorrection	Weakness	5 GRAPHIC SIMILARITY H	S	N	6 SOUND SIMILARITY H	S	N
26.	cream	churn	Y	Y	N	N	✓			✓					✓				✓
27.	shout	shouted	P	P	—	Y	✓			✓				✓			✓		
28.	big	pig	P	P	—	Y	✓			✓				✓			✓		
29.	and	the	P	P	—	Y	✓			✓						✓			✓
30.	jumped	bumped	Y	Y	P	Y	✓					✓		✓			✓		
31.	shout	splashed	P	P	—	Y	✓			✓					✓			✓	
32.	I'll	I've	P	P	—	Y	✓			✓				✓			✓		
33.	and	in	Y	P	—	Y	✓			✓					✓			✓	
34.	home	house	P	P	—	P		✓					✓	✓				✓	
35.	and	is	P	P	—	Y	✓			✓						✓			✓
36.	hard	harder	P	P	—	N		✓					✓	✓			✓		
37.	work ‸‸"... thought ⑪	work... thought"	P	P	—	N		✓					✓	—	—	—	—	—	—
38.	Then	then	P	P	—	P		✓					✓	✓			✓		
39.	he	I	P	P	—	Y	✓			✓						✓			✓
40.	the (thə)	a	Y	Y	N	N	✓			✓						✓	✓		
41.	basket	bucket	Y	Y	P	N		✓		✓				✓			✓		
42.	the (thə)	a	Y	Y	N	N	✓			✓						✓	✓		
43.	I'll	the	P	P	—	Y	✓			✓						✓			✓
44.	flash	few minutes	Y	Y	N	Y	✓					✓		—	—	—	—	—	—
45.	is	has	Y	Y	N	P		✓				✓			✓			✓	
46.	giving	given	Y	Y	N	P		✓				✓		✓			✓		
47.	and	.	P	P	—	N	✓						✓	—	—	—	—	—	—
48.	———	he	P	P	—	Y	✓			✓				—	—	—	—	—	—
49.	the (thə)	she	P	P	—	Y	✓			✓				✓					✓
50.	off ‸	off	P	P	—	N		✓					✓	—	—	—	—	—	—
			COLUMN TOTAL																
			PATTERN TOTAL																
			PERCENTAGE																

a. TOTAL MISCUES ____

b. TOTAL WORDS ____

a ÷ b × 100 = MPHW ____

(Goodman, Watson, Burke)

MISCUE ANALYSIS PROCEDURE I CODING FORM

READER *Betsy* DATE *Nov. 3*

TEACHER *Mrs. Blau* AGE/GRADE *3* SCHOOL *York Elem.*

SELECTION *The Man Who Kept House*

LINE No./MISCUE No.	READER	TEXT	1 SYNTACTIC ACCEPTABILITY	2 SEMANTIC ACCEPTABILITY	3 MEANING CHANGE	4 CORRECTION	See 2, 3, 4 MEANING CONSTRUCTION: No Loss	Partial Loss	Loss	See 1, 2, 4 GRAMMATICAL RELATIONSHIPS: Strength	Partial Strength	Overcorrection	Weakness	5 GRAPHIC SIMILARITY: H	S	N	6 SOUND SIMILARITY: H	S	N
51.	was	and	P	P	—	Y	✓			✓					✓				✓
52.	himself	herself	N	N	—	N			✓				✓	✓			✓		
53.	the (thə)	a	Y	Y	N	N	✓			✓						✓	✓		
54.	to	——	Y	Y	P	N		✓		✓				—	—	—	—	—	—
55.	up	out	P	P	—	Y	✓			✓					✓				✓
56.	then	and	Y	Y	N	Y	✓					✓			✓			✓	
57.	he	——	Y	Y	N	N	✓			✓				—	—	—	—	—	—
58.	the	this	Y	Y	N	N	✓			✓				✓				✓	
59.	is	he	P	P	—	Y	✓			✓						✓			✓
60.	hang	hung	P	P	—	N		✓					✓	✓			✓		
61.	never	over	P	P	—	Y	✓			✓				✓			✓		
62.	$ gorun	ground	P	N	—	N			✓				✓	✓			✓		
63.	he	she	P	P	—	N		✓					✓	✓			✓		
64.	cried	crying	P	P	—	N		✓					✓	✓			✓		
65.	shouted	shouting	P	P	—	N		✓					✓	✓			✓		
66.	to	the	P	P	—	Y	✓			✓					✓				✓
67.	And	As	Y	Y	N	Y	✓					✓			✓			✓	
68.	leg	legs	Y	Y	N	N	✓			✓				✓			✓		
69.	her	his	Y	P	—	Y	✓			✓					✓			✓	
70.	keep	look	Y	Y	N	N	✓			✓					✓			✓	
71.	the	their	Y	Y	N	P		✓				✓		✓				✓	
72.	children	child	Y	Y	P	Y	✓					✓		✓			✓		
73.	(9) (11) that he	, "What did you	P	P	—	Y	✓			✓				—	—	—	—	—	—
74.	the (thə)	he	P	P	—	Y	✓			✓				✓					✓
75.	to keep	and keep	Y	Y	N	P		✓				✓		—	—	—	—	—	—
						COLUMN TOTAL	47	25	3	42	5	13	15	33	17	10	26	18	16
						PATTERN TOTAL	75			75				60			60		
						PERCENTAGE	63%	33%	4%	56%	7%	17%	20%	55%	28%	17%	43%	30%	27%

a. TOTAL MISCUES *75*

b. TOTAL WORDS *711*

a ÷ b × 100 = MPHW *10.55*

(Goodman, Watson, Burke)

No loss Miscue patterns include those that are coded as semantically acceptable with no meaning change or, if not acceptable, are corrected.

Partial loss Miscue patterns include those that are coded as fully semantically acceptable with some meaning change or are partially semantically acceptable. Such miscues may have no attempt at correction or an unsuccessful correction attempt.

Loss Miscue patterns include those that are coded as semantically unacceptable with no correction attempt or an unsuccessful correction attempt; or the miscue is partially semantically acceptable with no attempt at correction.

Each number in the following table represents columns from the Coding Form: 2, Semantic Acceptability; 3, Meaning Change; and 4, Correction. Each letter beneath the number represents a possible coding for the column. For example, in the No Loss column, Y N Y under numbers 2 3 4 indicates a miscue that results in a No Loss pattern because it is semantically acceptable with no meaning change and is corrected. The blanks shown for column 3 indicate that the category was not marked because the miscue was not semantically and syntactically fully acceptable.

For the most part, coding the patterns is straightforward. Once a pattern is seen on the Coding Form by looking at the coding of Questions 2, 3, and 4, it is then located on the list of patterns and checked off in the appropriate column under Meaning Construction. However, for one pattern it is necessary for the coder to evaluate the degree of meaning construction. In most cases, a pattern coded as P for Question 2, left blank in Question 3, and not corrected is considered a loss of meaning construction (pattern P–N). However, under two conditions such a pattern results in partial loss: (a) if the miscue had been coded acceptable except for other miscues in the sentence (e.g., Betsy's miscues 5, the insertion of *well* and 6, the substitution of *bread* for *butter*); and (b) if the miscue had been acceptable except for *minor* syntactic shifts, such as connectives, tense, or number (e.g., Betsy's miscues 12, the substitution of *and* for the period and *as*; 14, the substitution of a period for a comma; and 64 and 65, the substitution of *cried* and *shouted* for *crying* and *shouting*).

These should be considered carefully and a consistent rationale developed in making decisions about the Partial Loss Column for such miscues. For example, Betsy's miscue 12, the substitution of *and* for the period and *as*, results in an acceptable clause relationship even though the clause dependencies are changed. This miscue would have been acceptable except for the nonword, $*shurn*. This miscue is, therefore, coded as a partial loss. Miscue 47, the substitution of *and* for a period seems on the surface to be a similar miscue. However, the conjunction *and* in this case is used to connect a declarative sentence within the ongoing narration with a sentence representing dialogue. Therefore, this is not a *minor* syntactic shift and is marked a *loss*.

Patterns for Constructing Meaning

No Loss		*Partial Loss*		*Loss*
2 3 4	2 3 4	2 3 4	2 3 4	2 3 4
Y N Y	Y Y Y	Y P N	Y Y N	N – N
Y N N	P – Y	Y N P	Y P P	N – P
Y P Y	N – Y	Y Y P	P – P	P – N*
			P – N*	

*This pattern will be Loss except in a few cases. The criteria for Partial Loss need to be considered carefully (see discusssion).

Patterns of Grammatical Relationship This pattern indicates the reader's ability to integrate concern for producing sentences that are Syntactically Acceptable (Question 1), Semantically Acceptable (Question 2) and/or Corrected (Question 4). These patterns have been categorized to show a reader's:

Strength of Grammatical Relationships Miscue patterns include those that are syntactically and semantically acceptable and, if not, are corrected

Partial Strength Miscue patterns include those that are syntactically acceptable but not fully semantically acceptable nor successfully corrected

Overcorrection Miscue patterns include those that are fully acceptable both syntactically and semantically and do not need correction but the reader self-corrects

Weakness Miscue patterns include those that are not fully syntactically acceptable nor semantically acceptable nor successfully corrected

Patterns for Grammatical Relationship

Strength	*Partial Strength*	*Overcorrection*	*Weakness*
1 2 4	1 2 4	1 2 4	1 2 4
N N Y	Y N N	Y Y Y	N N N
P N Y	Y P N	Y Y P	P N N
Y N Y	Y N P		P P N
P P Y	Y P P		N N P
Y P Y			P N P
Y Y N			P P P

After finishing the coding of Betsy's, Gordon's, or any other reader's miscues and marking the Meaning Construction and Grammatical Relationship patterns, it is time for a statistical analysis of the data collected. Remember to make a copy of the blank Coding Form (Appendix C) as a master copy for your own continual use.

Statistical Analysis In order to provide statistical data to transfer to the Reader Profile (see below), Questions 5 and 6 and both patterns are tallied as follows:

1. Count the marks made for each vertical column and place the total in the box marked Column Total.
2. Count the marks made for all the columns within each pattern and question and place the total in the boxes on the Coding Form for Procedure I marked Pattern Total. The totals for Questions 5 and 6 may differ from the totals for the two patterns because only word-for-word substitution miscues are coded on the Coding Form for 5 and 6 and every selected miscue is coded for the other questions that result in the two patterns. However, the totals for 5 and 6 should be the same, and the total for the two patterns should be the same.
3. Percentages are computed for each vertical column. Percentages may be computed by using a commercially prepared percentage table, or the teacher/researcher may simply divide the column total by the pattern total coded for the particular question or pattern. The decimal answer is changed into a percentage by multiplying the quotient by 100, or by moving the decimal point two places to the right. To check quickly for accuracy, total the column percentages for each question or pattern. The total should be between 99 and 101 percent.
4. The Procedure I Coding Form also provides a place for the computation of miscues per 100 words. This step is fairly self-explanatory on the coding form.

The number of words read should include only those words read for the miscue portion of the text. Betsy's miscue portion starts on line M0112 and continues through line M0616. There are 711 words in this miscue portion. The total number of miscues coded is divided by the total words read in the miscue portion. The quotient is multiplied by 100, which provides a miscues-per-100-words score.

The statistical data on the Coding Form can be transferred to the Reader Profile in order to have all the statistical as well as qualitative data in one place. For ease of reference, the Patterns of Grammatical Relationships and Patterns of Meaning Construction are available in Appendix A.

Retelling Guide and Scoring

As suggested in Chapter 3, some organization for collecting the retelling should be prepared before the oral reading session. The Retelling Guide that follows is the form most commonly used with Procedure I. However, teacher/researchers may select the Retelling Summary (see Procedure II).

If it is desirable to score a retelling, it is convenient, but not necessary, to set a final total of 100 points, as we have done with *The Man Who Kept House.* The point distribution that the teacher/researcher choses will depend on the passage and the purpose of the retelling score.

Many narrative stories can be divided into 40 points for "character" analysis, and 60 points for "events." Character analysis may be made up of (a) recall of characters, and (b) information concerning each character. The events may include major and minor events or idea units, with appropriate points given for each unit. In *The Man Who Kept House,* 40 points were assigned for character analysis (20 points for naming the three characters, and 20 points for describing them). Six major events were listed with 5–15 points for each, making a total of 60 points for events. In the complete story, 100 points were designated. Theme and plot may or may not be scored, depending on the purposes of the retelling. Although we chose not to score them, Lee and Sadoski (1986) provide research evidence about the advantages of scoring theme and plot.

Typically, but not necessarily, expository text is assigned 40 points for Specifics, 30 points for Generalizations, and 30 points for Major Concepts. Within each category there can be a point range depending on the text emphasis. In *Beat of My Heart* (see Appendix B), 50 points were assigned for Specific Information, and 25 points each for Generalizations and Major concepts. This selection was a bit unusual in that in addition to specific pieces of information, the author provided facts within the context of four experiments that the reader was supposed to do in order to learn about the heart. Although these experiments led to generalizations, their primary intent was to provide specific information.

When assigning points to the retelling, teacher/researchers should take into consideration their goals, the text itself, and the interests, age, and ability of the reader. Standardization of scores is best done on a population similar to the one being used for research purposes. For classroom or school purposes, standardization is best established by keeping students' records over time. Betsy's Retelling Guide of *The Man Who Kept House* follows and has been scored. (The scoring of Gordon's retelling of *Beat of My Heart* is in Appendix B.) It may be helpful to score either or both readers' retellings independently to see the degree to which your scoring matches.

It should be remembered that the language of the Retelling Guide is only to remind teacher/researchers about the published text. If students produce alternate language, plots, themes, generalizations, or events that are appropriate, they should be considered acceptable options and scored accordingly.

Reader: Betsy Date: November 3

Retelling Guide: Procedure I

The Man Who Kept House

Character Analysis: (40 points)

Recall (20 points)
9 – Man (husband) ✓
9 – Woman (wife) ✓
2 – Baby ✓
20

Development (20 points)
Husband
2 – Woodman ✓
3 – Thought he worked very hard ✓
5 – Changed attitude over time 1
Housewife
5 – Worked Hard 4
5 – Accepted challenges 1 11

Events: (60 points)

Woodman thinks he works very hard. He comes home and asks his wife what she does all day. Wife responds that she keeps house and keeping house is hard work. (10 points) 10

The husband challenges the wife to change places. The wife agrees and tells husband what he has to do. The husband says they will change places the next day. (10 points) 8

The wife goes off to the forest and the husband stays home. (5 points) 5

The husband is involved in a number of events that cause problems: (15 points) 13

Butter making 1

Baby cries and woodman goes to find her. He leaves the door open. 2

Pig gets into the house, the woodman chases it and the pig spills the cream. 2

Woodman starts to clean up the mess. 1

The baby cries again and the woodman prepares to feed the baby. 2

The cow's mooing interrupts the woodman who realizes that the cow needs to be fed. He puts the cow on the roof to feed. He is afraid the cow might fall off the roof so he throws the rope from the cow's neck down the chimney. When he gets into the house he ties the rope to his own leg. 4

As he thinks again about the porridge, the cow falls off the roof pulling the woodman up the chimney. Cow and woodman are hanging, one in the house and one outside. 1

As the wife returns home she hears the commotion. She cuts the cow down and then finds her husband upside down with his head in the porridge pot. (10 points) 10

Every day after that the husband goes to his work and the wife to hers. The husband never again asks the wife what she does every day nor says he will do her work. (10 points) 10

Points – character analysis 31

Points – events 56

Total Points 87

Plot:

The old man believes his word is harder than his wife's. When he trades places with her he discovers her work is more complicated and harder than he thought.

I'd say it was about a woodman who thought he had a harder job than his wife and he didn't so he stopped saying it.

Theme:

Things aren't always as easy as they appear to be. Keeping house is demanding work. A woman's job is just as hard as a man's. The grass is always greener on the other side of the fence.

People shouldn't brag about all they have to do. Other people prove that they work just as hard as they do.

The Reader Profile

The Procedure I Reader Profile provides a single form for the most important information from a miscue analysis—information that will be especially helpful for instructional purposes and continuous record keeping. The top of the Reader Profile includes biographical and procedural information that may be changed to accommodate particular interests or concerns of teacher/researchers.

The percentages from the Coding Form that show Patterns for Constructing Meaning, Grammatical Relationships, and Graphic/Sound Relationships are simply taken from the Coding Form and placed in the appropriate spaces on the Reader Profile. The Retelling Score is also carried over from the Retelling Guide.

The time the reading took is optional information that teacher/researchers may find helpful. In addition, miscues per 100 words may be entered from the Coding Form. There is also a general Comments section under which any relevant comments about the reading may be noted.

Repeated Miscues As discussed earlier, the written text provides opportunities for the reader to have multiple encounters with words or phrases. By examining the miscues related to such points in the text, it provides teacher/researchers a window on the reader's selection and use of strategies. Two varieties of repeated miscues get recorded on the repeated miscue section of the Coding Form. One type includes miscues that are repeated identical substitutions or omissions for the same text item. In this case, only the first miscue has been coded on the Coding Form, and the others are collected on the Reader Profile for further examination. The second type of repeated miscue, which also is listed on the Reader Profile, includes instances of varied responses to the same word or phrase. In this case, each varied response has been coded on the Coding Form.

The line number for each repeated miscue is listed because it shows the patterns readers follow to adjust their strategies depending on the density of the repeated words and phrases in the text. It provides clear evidence that readers use the information from the text to change their reading strategies, especially when their miscues do not result in semantically and syntactically acceptable structures.

Information that might be considered significant for further investigation or instructional planning is noted under Comments in the repeated miscue section of the Reader Profile. Examples include:

Contextual circumstances under which readers correct
Contextual influences on changes in the miscues
The particular language system (syntactic, semantic, or graphophonic) that influences readers' use and modification of reading strategies
How particular word sequences influence repeated miscues
Where in the text the same ER does not generate miscues

MISCUE ANALYSIS PROCEDURE I READER PROFILE

	%	%
MEANING CONSTRUCTION		
No Loss	61	96
Partial Loss	35	
Loss	4	
GRAMMATICAL RELATIONS		
Strength	56	80
Partial Strength	7	
Overcorrection	17	
Weakness	20	
GRAPHIC/SOUND RELATIONS		
Graphic		
High	55	83
Some	28	
None	17	
Sound		
High	43	73
Some	30	
None	27	
RETELLING		
Characters	31	
Events	56	
Total	87	
Holistic Score		

MPHW 10.55 TIME 19 minutes

READER Betsy DATE November 3

TEACHER Mrs. Blaw AGE/GRADE 3 SCHOOL York Elem.

SELECTION The Man Who Kept House

REPEATED MISCUES ACROSS TEXT

LINE	READER	TEXT	COMMENTS (place in text, correction, etc.)
113-	start	stay	first occurrence of stay
114	start	stay	start home for stay home 2 times
			gets stayed (202); stay (513) (616)
113	house	home	no miscue on first occurrence (103)
114	house	home	no miscue on home 4 out of 6 times
			miscues home for house (312) but no
			miscue on house 13 times
205	$shurn	churn	never produces ER
304	cream	churn	syn. + sem. acceptable
307	cream	churn	syn. + sem. acceptable
207	the	this	In the majority of cases she gets
505	the	this	the and this appropriately. Her
			substitutions of function words are
			either semantically and
			syntactically acceptable or
			corrected.
510	hang	hung	Only two occurrences of the OR;
512	hang	hung	irregular verb form

COMMENTS For the most part Betsy uses predicting and confirming strategies proficiently. She may be overattending to surface features of text.

(Goodman, Watson, Burke)

Overview of Procedure I

The following provides, in order of recommended use, a list that may be checked off as each of the activities for Procedure I are learned or used to complete a miscue analysis.

- Select student ____
- Select material ____
- Prepare typescript for material ____
- Prepare Retelling Guide for material ____
- Prepare tape recorder and setting ____
- Collect data ____
  - Oral reading and miscue marking ____
  - Retelling ____
- Prepare retelling script ____
  - Score retelling on Retelling Guide ____
- Listen to recording and verify miscue marking ____
- Select and number miscues ____
- Code minimum of 25 miscues for questions 1 through 6 ____
- Code patterns of meaning construction and grammatical relations ____
- Compute statistics for Questions 5 and 6 and for Meaning construction and grammatical relations patterns ____
- Add optional data to Coding Form (MPHW, time) ____
- Complete Reader Profile ____
  - Transfer statistics from Coding Form ____
  - Transfer retelling score ____
  - List repeated miscues and comments ____
  - Add overall comments ____

6

Alternative Procedures II, III, IV

Procedure II

The major focus of attention for analysis in Procedure II is the sentence within the context of the entire text. The taping and miscue marking procedures are the same for Procedure II as those discussed in the General Procedures (Chapter 3). The typescript for Procedure II is identical to the typescript for Procedure I, with one important addition: *each sentence in the text is numbered consecutively.* Sentence numbering is necessary in Procedure II because it examines all the sentences the reader has read whether they include miscues or not (see the typescript for Procedure II later in this chapter for an example of sentence numbering). Procedure II is recommended for classroom teachers or students in teacher education programs. Researchers who do not need the depth of analysis provided by Procedure I may also find this procedure useful.

QUESTIONS

Question 1: *Syntactic Acceptability*

Is the sentence syntactically (grammatically) acceptable in the reader's dialect and within the context of the entire selection?

Y—The sentence, as finally produced by the reader, is syntactically acceptable.

N—The sentence, as finally produced by the reader, is not syntactically acceptable (partial acceptability is not considered in this procedure).

Question 2: *Semantic Acceptability*

Is the sentence semantically acceptable in the reader's dialect and within the context of the entire selection? (Question 2 cannot be coded Y if Question 1 has been coded N).

Y—The sentence, as finally produced by the reader, is semantically acceptable.

N—The sentence, as finally produced by the reader, is not semantically acceptable (partial acceptability is not considered in this procedure).

Question 3: *Meaning Change*

Does the sentence, as finally produced by the reader, change the meaning of the selection? (Question 3 is coded only if Questions 1 and 2 are coded Y).

N—There is no change in the meaning of the selection.

P—There is inconsistency, loss, or change of a *minor* idea, incident, character, fact, sequence, or concept in the selection.

Y—There is inconsistency, loss, or change of a *major* idea, incident, character, fact, sequence, or concept in the selection.

Question 4: *Graphic Similarity*

How much does the miscue look like the text item?

H—A high degree of graphic similarity exists between the miscue and the text.

S—Some degree of graphic similarity exists between the miscue and the text.

N—No degree of graphic similarity exists between the miscue and the text.

Question 5: *Sound Similarity*

How much does the miscue sound like the expected response (ER)?

H—A high degree of sound similarity exists between the miscue and the ER.

S—Some degree of sound similarity exists between the miscue and the ER.

N—No degree of sound similarity exists between the miscue and the ER.

Analyzing Miscues

The Coding Form is divided into two sections, Language Sense and Word Substitution in Context (discussed later in this chapter; also see Appendix C). Each section helps the teacher/researcher view miscues in different ways and at different linguistic levels. The heart of the analysis is the Language Sense section, which evaluates the reader's concern for constructing meaning. All sentences are coded, whether they include miscues or not. In this way, the coder gets a picture of the influence of miscues on the total story and not just on the sentences that include miscues. This part of the analysis may be used alone. The Word Substitution in Context section is *not* useful when used without the information analyzed in the Language Sense section.

Procedure II is easier and less time-consuming than Procedure I because all the reader's strategies in the entire sentence are evaluated at one time. However, teacher/researchers must keep in mind that the strength of readers' prediction and confirming strategies is not as readily perceived in this procedure as it is in Procedure I.

If the material being used for Procedure II has fewer than 40 sentences, each sentence in the story should be numbered. If the material has more than 40 sentences, the teacher/researcher may wish to skip the first paragraph or two, using the same rationale as in Procedure I, and then number the remaining sentences consecutively. If the material is exceptionally long, the user may choose to code only 75 consecutive sentences after skipping the first paragraph or two. We have coded all of the sentences in both of the selections read by Betsy and Gordon (see Betsy's Procedure II Coding Form in this chapter).

Language Sense

This section of the Coding Form is concerned with whether the reader produces sentences that make sense and sound like language. It also evaluates the proficiency with which readers use strategies involving sampling, predicting, confirming, and constructing meaning. Question 1 asks whether the miscues and corrections result in syntactically acceptable sentences (does this sentence sound like language?). Question 2 asks whether the miscues and corrections result in sentences that are semantically acceptable (does this sentence make sense in the context of the entire text?). The information gained from Question 2 is the most useful provided in Procedure II. Question 3 gives information about the degree to which miscues and corrections change the intended meaning of the story according to the teacher/researcher's interpretation.

In preparation for coding, number the text sentences and write the sentence numbers under the column headed Sentence No. In the second column, No. of Miscues, indicate the number of miscues in the sentence. If there are no miscues in the sentence, write 0 in the column. To answer Questions 1 to 3, read each sentence as the reader finally resolves it. In other words, *all corrected miscues or attempts at correction are read as finally uttered by the reader* (see examples later in this chapter). The Patterns of Language Sense are checked off by matching the patterns as coded in columns 1, 2, and 3 with those listed under strength, partial strength, and weakness. Only the latter three columns in this section are computed for statistical information.

Word Substitution in Context

In this section, only substitution word-for-word miscues are evaluated to see the degree to which they are graphically or phonologically related to the text item. The purpose is to help the teacher/researcher determine the graphic and sound cues that influence the reader.

In preparation for coding, write the sentence number and the miscue number in the first two columns of the Coding Form. In the column marked Reader, write the miscue itself. Write the expected response (ER) in the column marked Text. If the reader's dialect has influenced the miscue, mark ⓓ after the miscue. If the miscue is a repeated identical substitution of a noun, verb, adjective, or adverb, do not list the miscue. These repeated miscues are not coded, using the same criteria and rationale stated in Procedure I, but they are listed on the Reader Profile. Following are examples for coding:

M0101 Once upon a time there was a woodman ⓒ .

102 who thought (He threw) that no one worked as hard

103 as he did . . .

Read: *Once upon a time there was a woodman who thought that no one worked as hard as he did.*

This sentence has three miscues, and they are all self-corrected. Therefore it is coded Y, syntactically acceptable, Y, semantically acceptable, and N, no meaning change. *He* for *who* is coded the same under graphic and sound similarity as it is for Procedure I (see the Procedure I Coding Form).

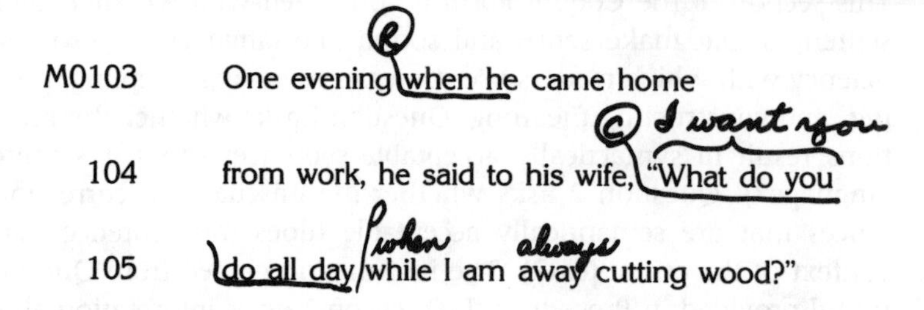

Read: *One evening when he came home from work, he said to his wife, "What do you do all day when I am always cutting wood?"*

This sentence has three miscues. *I want you* is a single complex miscue that is self-corrected. The other two miscues are acceptable in the sentence and the story, and there is no change to the meaning. It is therefore coded Y, syntactically acceptable, Y, semantically acceptable, and N, no meaning change. The first miscue is not a word-for-word substitution and is therefore not coded under sound and graphic similarity. The other two are coded the same as in Procedure I.

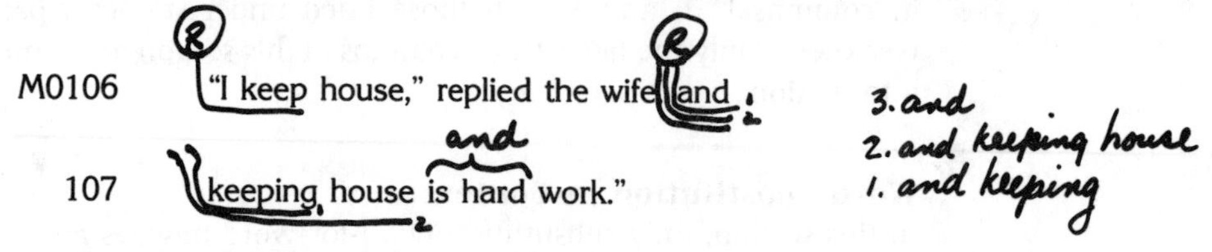

Read: *"I keep house," replied the wife, "and keeping house and work."*

This sentence has one miscue coded N, not syntactically acceptable, and N, not semantically acceptable. Meaning change is not coded because the sentence is syntactically and semantically unacceptable. Graphic and sound similarity are not coded because this is a complex miscue and not a word-for-word substitution.

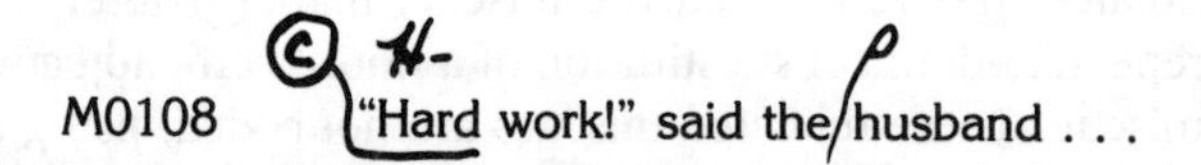

In this sentence, there are no miscues, so the sentence is marked Y, syntactically acceptable, Y, semantically acceptable, and N, no meaning change. There is no reason to code graphic and sound similarity in such sentences.

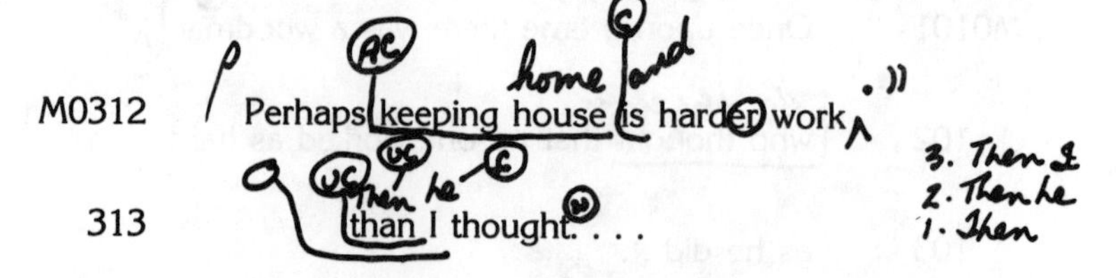

Read: *Perhaps keeping home is hard work." Then I thought.*

This sentence has six miscues and is coded N, syntactically unacceptable, and N, semantically unacceptable. Meaning change is not coded because the sentence is both syntactically and semantically unacceptable. The word-level substitutions are coded for graphic and sound similarity using the same rationale as presented for Procedure I.

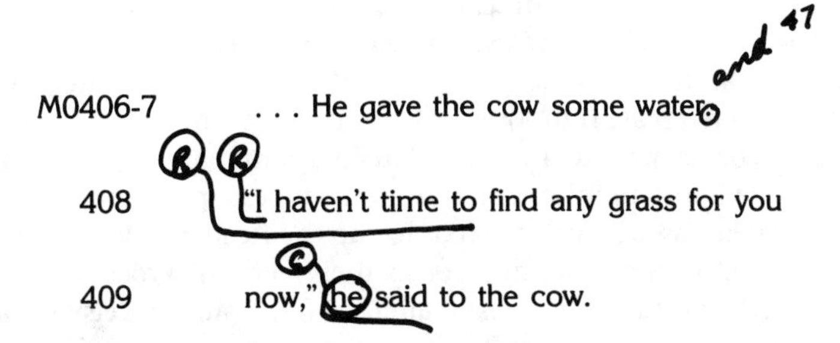

Read: *He gave the cow some water and . . . "I haven't time to find any grass for you now," he said to the cow.*

Sentence 44 has one miscue, the substitution of *and* for the period at the end of the sentence. Betsy's intonation indicates that she expected another clause to follow, but when she starts the beginning of the next sentence (45), she treats it as the beginning of a new sentence, and therefore it is not affected by the miscue. For these reasons, the first sentence in the above example is coded N, syntactically unacceptable, N, semantically unacceptable, and not coded for meaning change. Substitutions of a word for a punctuation mark cannot be coded for sound and graphic similarity. The second sentence in this example (46) is coded Y for syntactic acceptability, Y *for* semantic acceptability, and N for meaning change since the omission of *he* is self-corrected.

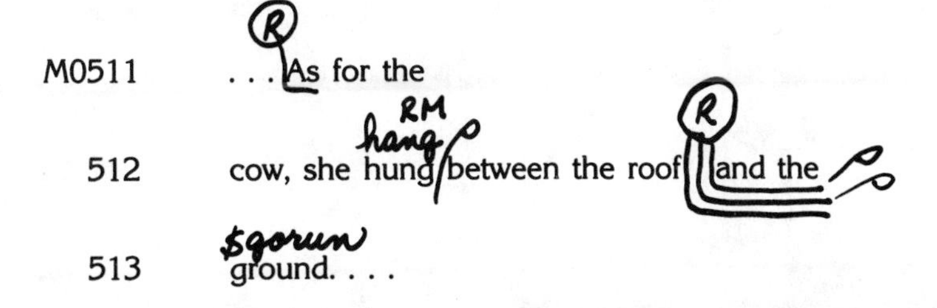

This sentence is coded N for syntactic acceptability and N for semantic acceptability because of the inappropriate form of *hang* and the nonword substitution for *ground.* The substitution of *hang* for *hung* is not coded for sound and graphic similarity in this sentence because it is a repeated identical substitution, but the nonword substitution for *ground* is coded.

The forms for Procedure II follow. Each is filled out in ways similar to those for Procedure I. The computation is either similar to Procedure I or explained directly on the Coding Form and Reader Profile.

The Retelling Summary is anecdotal for this procedure. The reader's plot, theme, inferences, and misconceptions are written exactly as they were said to the teacher/researcher. Keep in mind that misconceptions are not simply errors; rather, they are unexpected responses and reflect inferences students make based on their present knowledge. Comments should reflect the aspects of retelling that the teacher/researcher finds most important and that are not listed under previous sections of the summary.

If a score is considered necessary, teacher/researchers might use a holistic scoring procedure (Irwin and Mitchell, 1983). Holistic scoring provides a view of the retelling by considering its overall gist. The retelling is compared with other students' retellings of the same text, or with previous retellings of other texts by the same reader. The teacher/researcher may use the Retelling Guide as a framework, but *not* as a checklist for evaluation. The holistic score may involve an even-numbered scale (1 to 4) so that there will be no average category, or it may be an odd-numbered scale (1 to 5) in order to provide a midpoint. Space for the optional holistic score is provided on the Retelling Summary.

Any important information from the typescript and the Coding Form, including repeated miscue data are recorded on the Reader Profile. Repeated miscue data are reported in the same manner as they were for Procedure I.

The forms that follow have all been filled out for Betsy's reading of *The Man Who Kept House*. Blank forms for Procedure II are in Appendix C and may be copied for continual use.

MISCUE ANALYSIS PROCEDURE II CODING FORM

READER *Betsy* DATE *November 3*

TEACHER *Mrs. Blau* AGE/GRADE *3* SCHOOL *York Elem.*

SELECTION *The Man Who Kept House*

LANGUAGE SENSE

SENTENCE NO.	No. MISCUES IN SENTENCE	1 SYNTACTIC ACCEPTABILITY	2 SEMANTIC ACCEPTABILITY	3 MEANING CHANGE	PATTERN (See 1,2,3) Strength YYN	Partial Strength YYY YYP	Weakness NN_ YN_
26	0	Y	Y	N	✓		
27	1	Y	Y	N	✓		
28	2	Y	Y	N	✓		
29	1*	Y	Y	N	✓		
30	1	Y	Y	N	✓		
31	0	Y	Y	N	✓		
32	1	Y	Y	N	✓		
33	1	Y	Y	N	✓		
34	6	N	N	—			✓
35	2	Y	Y	P		✓	
36	0	Y	Y	N	✓		
37	0	Y	Y	N	✓		
38	0	Y	Y	N	✓		
39	3	Y	Y	N	✓		
40	0	Y	Y	N	✓		
41	0	Y	Y	N	✓		
42	2	Y	Y	N	✓		
43	0	Y	Y	N	✓		
44	1	N	N	—			✓
45	1	Y	Y	N	✓		
46	0	Y	Y	N	✓		
47	0	Y	Y	N	✓		
48	0	Y	Y	N	✓		
49	4	N	N	—			✓
50	1	Y	Y	N	✓		
		COLUMN TOTAL			21	1	3
		PATTERN TOTAL					
		PERCENTAGE					

WORD SUBSTITUTION IN CONTEXT

SENTENCE No.	MISCUE NO.	READER Dialect ⓓ	TEXT	4 GRAPHIC H	S	N	5 SOUND H	S	N
27		shout	shouted	✓			✓		
28		big	pig	✓			✓		
28		and	the			✓			✓
29		jumped	bumped	✓			✓		
30		shout	splashed		✓			✓	
32		I'll	I've	✓			✓		
33		and	in		✓			✓	
34		home	house	✓				✓	
34		and	is			✓			✓
34		hard	harder	✓			✓		
34		Then	than	✓			✓		
34		he	I			✓			✓
35		the	a			✓	✓		
35		basket	bucket	✓			✓		
39		the	a			✓	✓		
39		I'll	the			✓			✓
42		is	has		✓			✓	
42		giving	given	✓			✓		
49		the	she	✓					✓
49		was	and		✓				✓
49		himself	herself	✓			✓		
50		the	a			✓	✓		
53		up	out		✓				✓
53		then	and		✓			✓	
54		the	this	✓				✓	
			COLUMN TOTAL						
			TOTAL MISCUES						
			PERCENTAGE						

a. TOTAL MISCUES ____ * Not counting RM's.

b. TOTAL WORDS ____

a ÷ b × 100 = MPHW ____

MISCUE ANALYSIS PROCEDURE II   CODING FORM

LANGUAGE SENSE

SENTENCE NO.	No. MISCUES IN SENTENCE	1 SYNTACTIC ACCEPTABILITY	2 SEMANTIC ACCEPTABILITY	3 MEANING CHANGE	PATTERN (See 1,2,3) Strength YYN	Partial Strength YYY YYP	Weakness NN_ YN_
1	3	Y	Y	N	✓		
2	3	Y	Y	N	✓		
3	1	N	N	—			✓
4	0	Y	Y	N	✓		
5	0	Y	Y	N	✓		
6	0	Y	Y	N	✓		
7	1	Y	Y	N	✓		
8	1	Y	Y	N	✓		
9	3	N	N	—			✓
10	2*	Y	N	—			✓
11	1	Y	Y	N	✓		
12	2	Y	Y	P		✓	
13	1	Y	Y	N	✓		
14	1	Y	Y	N	✓		
15	1	Y	N	—			✓
16	2	Y	N	—			✓
17	1	Y	Y	N	✓		
18	2	Y	Y	P		✓	
19	0	Y	Y	N	✓		
20	1	Y	Y	N	✓		
21	2	Y	Y	N	✓		
22	1	Y	Y	N	✓		
23	2	Y	Y	N	✓		
24	2	Y	Y	N	✓		
25	1	Y	Y	N	✓		
		COLUMN TOTAL			18	2	5
		PATTERN TOTAL					
		PERCENTAGE					

READER *Betsy*   DATE *November 3*

TEACHER *Mrs. Blau*   AGE/GRADE *3*   SCHOOL *York Elem.*

SELECTION *The Man Who Kept House*

WORD SUBSTITUTION IN CONTEXT

SENTENCE No.	MISCUE NO.	READER (Dialect ⓓ)	TEXT	4 GRAPHIC H	S	N	5 SOUND H	S	N
1		He	who	✓			✓		
1		threw	thought		✓			✓	
2		when	while		✓			✓	
2		always	away	✓			✓		
7		I'll	I'd	✓			✓		
8		so	some	✓				✓	
9		start	stay	✓				✓	
9		house	home	✓				✓	
9		Keeping	keep	✓			✓		
10		bread	butter		✓			✓	
12		Well	we'll	✓			✓		
13		day	morning			✓			✓
14		job	work		✓				✓
16		$shurn	churn	✓			✓		
17		the	this	✓				✓	
18		so	soon	✓				✓	
18		buttermilk	butter	✓			✓		
21		There	She		✓				✓
21		is	was		✓			✓	
22		into	to	✓			✓		
23		forest	far		✓			✓	
23		in	to			✓			✓
24		the	his		✓				✓
24		heard	had	✓			✓		
25		cream	churn		✓				✓
			COLUMN TOTAL						
			TOTAL MISCUES						
			PERCENTAGE						

a. TOTAL MISCUES ____   *Not counting RM's
b. TOTAL WORDS ____
a ÷ b × 100 = MPHW ____

(Goodman, Watson, Burke)

MISCUE ANALYSIS PROCEDURE II CODING FORM

READER Betsy DATE November 3

TEACHER Mrs. Blau AGE/GRADE 3 SCHOOL York Elem.

SELECTION The Man Who Kept House

LANGUAGE SENSE

SENTENCE NO.	No. MISCUES IN SENTENCE	1 SYNTACTIC ACCEPTABILITY	2 SEMANTIC ACCEPTABILITY	3 MEANING CHANGE	PATTERN (See 1,2,3) Strength YYN	Partial Strength YYY YYP	Weakness NN_ YN_
51	1	Y	Y	P		✓	
52	0	Y	Y	N	✓		
53	3	Y	Y	N	✓		
54	1	Y	Y	N	✓		
55	0	Y	Y	N	✓		
56	0	Y	Y	N	✓		
57	3	N	N	—			✓
58	2*	N	N	—			✓
59	0	Y	Y	N	✓		
60	2	N	N	—			✓
61	1	Y	Y	N	✓		
62	0	Y	Y	N	✓		
63	1	Y	Y	N	✓		
64	2	Y	Y	N	✓		
65	0	Y	Y	N	✓		
66	3	Y	Y	N	✓		
67	1	Y	Y	N	✓		
68	2	Y	Y	N	✓		
Totals	for	Sentences		51-68	14	1	3
"	"	"		26-50	21	1	3
"	"	"		1-25	18	2	5
		COLUMN TOTAL			53	4	11
		PATTERN TOTAL			68		
		PERCENTAGE			78%	6%	16%

WORD SUBSTITUTION IN CONTEXT

SENTENCE No.	MISCUE NO.	READER Dialect ⓓ	TEXT	4 GRAPHIC H	S	N	5 SOUND H	S	N
57		is	he			✓			✓
57		hang	hung	✓			✓		
57		never	over	✓			✓		
58		$gorun	ground	✓			✓		
58		he	she	✓			✓		
60		cried	crying	✓			✓		
60		shouted	shouting	✓			✓		
61		to	the		✓				✓
63		And	As		✓			✓	
64		leg	legs	✓			✓		
64		her	his		✓			✓	
66		keep	look		✓			✓	
66		the	their	✓				✓	
66		children	child	✓				✓	
68		the	he	✓					✓
			COLUMN TOTAL	36	19	10	28	21	16
			TOTAL MISCUES	65			65		
			PERCENTAGE	55%	29%	15%	43%	32%	25%

a. TOTAL MISCUES ____ * Not counting RM's

b. TOTAL WORDS ____

a ÷ b × 100 = MPHW ____

(Goodman, Watson, Burke)

MISCUE ANALYSIS PROCEDURE II READER PROFILE

READER Betsy — DATE November 3

TEACHER Mrs. Blau — AGE/GRADE 3 — SCHOOL York Elem.

SELECTION The Man Who Kept House

	%	%
LANGUAGE SENSE		
Strength	78	84
Partial Strength	6	
Weakness	16	
GRAPHIC/SOUND RELATIONS		
Graphic		
High	55	84
Some	29	
None	15	
Sound		
High	43	75
Some	32	
None	25	
RETELLING		
Holistic Score		

or Comments Very complete unaided retelling. Doesn't always seem to understand concept of cow on roof of sod house. Uses pictures to aid retelling. Tone toward story always serious

MPHW ____ TIME 19 minutes

REPEATED MISCUES ACROSS TEXT

LINE	READER	TEXT	COMMENTS (place in text, correction, etc.)
113-	start	stay	first occurrence of stay
114	start	stay	start home for stay home 2 times
			gets stayed (202); stay (513) (616)
113	house	home	no miscue on first occurrence (103)
114	house	home	no miscue on home 4 out of 6 times
			miscues home for house (312) but no
			miscue on house 13 times
205	$shurn	churn	never produces ER
304	cream	churn	syn. + sem. acceptable
307	cream	churn	syn. + sem. acceptable
207	the	this	In the majority of cases she gets
508	the	this	the and this appropriately. Her
			substitutions of function words are
			either semantically acceptable or
			corrected.
510	hang	hung	Only two occurrences of the OR;
512	hang	hung	irregular verb form.

COMMENTS For the most part Betsy uses predicting and confirming strategies proficiently. She may be overattending to surface features of text.

MISCUE ANALYSIS PROCEDURE II RETELLING SUMMARY

READER *Betsy*
DATE *November 3*
SELECTION *The Man Who Kept House*

Holistic Retelling Score (optional): *N/A*

Plot Statements *It was about a woodman who thought he had a harder job than his wife had and he didn't so he stopped saying it.*

Theme Statements *Maybe about how people shouldn't brag about all they have to do. They get in trouble and other people prove they work as hard as they do.*

Inferences
- *wife got blister*
- *wife left home with ax (in picture)*
- *discusses personality traits of major characters*

Misconceptions
- *poured buttermilk in the jar*
- *cow fell over the house*
- *calls cow "he"*
- *cow drinks milk*

Comments *Very complete unaided retelling. Doesn't always seem to understand concept of cow on roof (sod house). Uses pictures to aid retelling. Tone toward story always serious.*

(Goodman, Watson, Burke)

Overview of Procedure II

The following provides a list that may be checked off as each of the activities for Procedure II is learned or used to complete a miscue analysis on a reader.

Select student ____
Select material ____
Prepare typescript for material ____
Prepare Retelling Guide ____
Prepare tape recorder and setting ____
Collect data ____
  Oral reading and miscue marking ____
  Retelling ____
Complete Retelling Summary ____
Listen to recording and verify miscue marking ____
Number sentences ____
Code miscues on Procedure II Coding Form ____
  Code Questions 1 to 3 ____
  Code patterns ____
  Code Questions 4 and 5 ____
Compute statistics for Coding Form ____
  Transfer statistics from Coding Form ____
  List repeated miscues and comments ____
  Add overall comments ____

Procedure III

Procedure III provides the same kind of information about a reader as does Procedure II. It too is constructed so that its major focus is on the sentence within the story or article. The major difference between Procedures II and III is that in Procedure III, *the typescript is used for marking the miscues as well as for coding them.* It is therefore less time-consuming because the marking, coding, and analysis are all on the typescript. *Neither a Coding Form nor a Reader Profile is necessary.* The data collection and miscue markings are the same as those discussed under General Procedures (Chapter 3). In this procedure, the miscues need not be numbered, but the sentences must be numbered.

This procedure will be most helpful for classroom teachers and may be helpful in preservice and inservice teacher education programs.

QUESTIONS

Question 1: *Syntactic Acceptability*

Is the sentence syntactically acceptable in the reader's dialect and within the context of the entire selection?

Y—The sentence, as finally produced by the reader, is syntactically acceptable.

N—The sentence, as finally produced by the reader, is not syntactically acceptable (partial acceptability is not considered in this procedure).

Question 2: *Semantic Acceptability*

Is the sentence semantically acceptable in the reader's dialect and within the context of the entire selection? (Question 2 cannot be coded Y if Question 1 has been coded N.)

Y—The sentence, as finally produced by the reader, is semantically acceptable.

N—The sentence, as finally produced by the reader, is not semantically acceptable (partial acceptability is not considered in this procedure).

Question 3: *Meaning Change*

Does the sentence, as finally produced by the reader, change the meaning of the selection? (Question 3 is coded only if Questions 1 and 2 are coded Y.)

N—There is no change in the meaning of the selection.

P—There is inconsistency, loss, or change of a *minor* idea, incident, character, fact, sequence, or concept in the selection.

Y—There is inconsistency, loss, or change of a *major* idea, incident, character, fact, sequence, or concept in the selection.

Question 4: *Graphic Similarity*

How much does the miscue look like the text item?

H—A high degree of graphic similarity exists between the miscue and the text.

S—Some degree of graphic similarity exists between the miscue and the text.

N—No degree of graphic similarity exists between the miscue and the text.

Analyzing Miscues

The right margin of the typescript serves as a coding form for the first three questions. It is preferable to number each sentence first, then with a ruler move down the typescript and place a line next to every line with a period in it that ends a sentence. The coding for the first three questions is placed on this line (see Betsy's Procedure III typescript). Each sentence is read and then coded as the reader left it. Sentences in which no miscues occur are coded YYN.

To code for graphic similarity, the marking H (high), S (some), or N (none), is placed in a circle directly above the word-level substitution on the typescript. As in the other procedures, omissions, insertions, repeated miscues, intonation, complex miscues, and punctuation are not coded for graphic similarity. The miscues are coded using the same criteria as in the earlier procedures.

bump

B0224–5 When it goes dup, it is pushing blood out

RM
your

226 to all parts of the body. YYN

Read: *When it goes bump, it is pushing blood out to all parts of your body.*

The substitutions of *bump* for *dup* and *your* for *the* produce a syntactically and semantically acceptable sentence with no meaning change. Only *bump* for *dup* is coded for graphic similarity because *your* for *the* is a repeated miscue.

Ⓟ

B0226–7 Your heart has this most important job to do—

Ⓒ pum-

228–29 pumping blood to all parts of your body. YYN

Since there is only one partial miscue corrected in this sentence, it is read as: *Your heart has this most important job to do—pumping blood to all parts of your body.* It is coded YYN. There is nothing to code for graphic similarity.

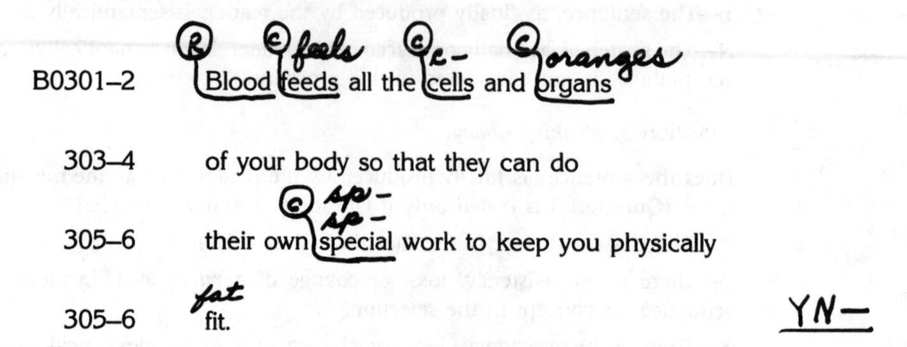

B0301–2 Blood feeds all the cells and organs

303–4 of your body so that they can do

305–6 their own special work to keep you physically

305–6 fit. YN–

Read: *Blood feeds all the cells and organs of your body so that they can do their own special work to keep you fat.*

The observed responses of *feel* and *oranges* are corrected; *fat* for *fit* is not corrected. The sentence is coded syntactically acceptable (Y) because the substitution miscues all retain the same grammatical functions. However, although *fat* for *fit* produces a sentence that sounds like language, it doesn't make sense within the total context. Therefore, the sentence is coded unacceptable semantically (N). Since it is not fully acceptable both semantically and syntactically, it is not coded for meaning change. The word-for-word substitutions are all coded for graphic similarity using the same criteria as in the earlier procedures.

Betsy's Procedure III Typescript

The Man Who Kept House

0101 Once upon a time there was a woodman

0102 who thought that no one worked as hard as

0103 he did. One evening when he came home ① YYN

0104 from work, he said to his wife, "What do you

0105 do all day while I am away cutting wood?" ② YYN

0106 "I keep house," replied the wife, "and

0107 keeping house is hard work." ③ NN–

0108 "Hard work!" said the husband. "You don't ④ YYN

0109 know what hard work is! You should try

0110 cutting wood!"

0111 "I'd be glad to," said the wife.

0112 "Why don't you do my work some day? I'll

0113 stay home and keep house," said the woodman.

0114 "If you stay home to do my work, you'll

0115 have to make butter, carry water from the

0116 well, wash the clothes, clean the house, and

0117 look after the baby," said the wife.

0118 "I can do all that," replied the husband.

0119 "We'll do it tomorrow!"

0201 So the next morning the wife went off to

0202 the forest. The husband stayed home and

0203 began to do his wife's work.

0204 He began to make some butter. As he put

0205 the cream into the churn, he said, "This is

0206 not going to be hard work. All I have to do

0207 is sit here and move this stick up and down.

0208 Soon the cream will turn into butter."

0209 Just then the woodman heard the baby

0210 crying. He looked around, but he could not

0211 see her. She was not in the house. Quickly,

0212 he ran outside to look for her. He found the

0213 baby at the far end of the garden and

0214 brought her back to the house.

0301 In his hurry, the woodman had left the

0302 door open behind him. When he got back to

0303 the house, he saw a big pig inside, with its

0304 nose in the churn. "Get out! Get out!"

0305 shouted the woodman at the top of his voice.

0306 The big pig ran around and around the

0307 room. It bumped into the churn, knocking it

0308 over. The cream splashed all over the room.

0309 Out the door went the pig.

0310 "Now I've got more work to do," said the

0311 man. "I'll have to wash everything in this

0312 room. Perhaps keeping house is harder work

0313 than I thought." He took a bucket and went

0314 to the well for some water. When he came

0315 back, the baby was crying.

0316 "Poor baby, you must be hungry," said the

0317 woodman. "I'll make some porridge for you.

0318 I'll light a fire in the fireplace, and the

0319 porridge will be ready in a few minutes."

0320 Just as the husband was putting the

0321 water into the big pot, he heard the cow

0401 mooing outside the door. "I guess the cow is

0402 hungry, too," he thought. "No one has given

0403 her any grass to eat or any water to drink

0404 today."

0405 The man left the porridge to cook on the

0406 fire and hurried outside. He gave the cow

0407 some water.

0408 "I haven't time to find any grass for you

0409 now," he said to the cow. "I'll put you up

0410 on the roof. You'll find something to eat

0411 up there."

0412 The man put the cow on top of the house.

0413 Then he was afraid that she would fall off

0414 the roof and hurt herself. So he put one

0415 end of a rope around the cow's neck. He

0416 dropped the other end down the chimney.

0501 Then he climbed down from the roof and

0502 went into the house. He pulled the end of the

0503 rope out of the fireplace and put it around

0504 his left leg.

0505 "Now I can finish making this porridge,"

0506 said the woodman, "and the cow will

0507 be safe."

0508 But the woodman spoke too soon, for just then

0509 the cow fell off the roof. She pulled him up

0510 the chimney by the rope. There he hung,

0511 upside down over the porridge pot. As for the

0512 cow, she hung between the roof and the

0513 ground, and there she had to stay.

0514 It was not very long before the woodman's

0515 wife came home. As she came near the

0516 house, she could hear the cow mooing, the

0601 baby crying, and her husband shouting for

0602 help. She hurried up the path. She cut the

0603	rope from the cow's neck. As she did so,	62 YYN
0604	the cow fell down to the ground, and the	
0605	husband dropped head first down the chimney.	63 YYN
0606	When the wife went into the house, she	
0607	saw her husband with his legs up the	
0608	chimney and his head in the porridge pot.	64 YYN
0609	From that day on, the husband went into	
0610	the forest every day to cut wood. The wife	65 YYN
0611	stayed home to keep house and to look	
0612	after their child.	66 YYN
0613	Never again did the woodman say to his	
0614	wife, "What did you do all day?" Never	67 YYN
0615	again did he tell his wife that he would	
0616	stay home and keep house.	68 YYN

no. of Sentences 68

Question 1: no. of Y 60 88% ; no. of N 8 12%

Question 2: no. of Y 57 84% ; no. of N 11 17%

Question 3: no. of Y 0 0% ; no. of P 4 7% ; no. of N 53 93%

Question 4: no. of H 36 55% ; no. of S 19 29% ; no. of N 10 15%

Statistical Analysis

The summary is placed at the bottom or on the back of the last page of the typescript, or it may be placed on a separate page.

Syn. Accept. Y____% N____% No. Sentences Coded____
Sem. Accept. Y____% N____% No. Sentences Coded____
Mean. Chng. N____% P____% Y____% No. Sentences Coded____
Graphic Sim. H____% S____% N____% No. Miscues Coded____

Comments:

Optional:

Total No. Miscues____ No. Words Read____
MPHW (miscues per hundred words)____ Time____

To compute MPHW, count the total number of miscues, divide by the number of words read, and multiply by 100. Time may be included if the teacher is concerned with the amount of time it takes a particular student to read a selection.

To compute syntactic acceptability, count the number of sentences marked Y in the Syntactic Acceptability column and the number of sentences marked N (syntactically unacceptable) in the same column. Place the number on the appropriate line. Divide each number by the total number of *coded* sentences in the text and write the result on the appropriate percentage line.

To compute semantic acceptability, count the number of sentences marked Y in the Semantic Acceptability column and the number of sentences marked N (semantically unacceptable) in the same column and place the number on the appropriate line. Divide each number by the total number of *coded* sentences in the text and write the result on the appropriate percentage line.

To compute meaning change, count the number of Ns (no meaning change), Ps (partial meaning change), and Ys (meaning change) in the appropriate column. Determine the percentages of each by dividing each number by the number of sentences *coded for meaning change.* Sentences not coded for meaning change (marked with a dash) are not counted.

To compute graphic similarity, count the number of Hs (high graphic similarity), Ss (some graphic similarity), and the number of Ns (no graphic similarity). Determine percentages by dividing each H, S, and N by the number of *coded word-level substitutions.*

If desired, the Reader Profile for Procedure II may also be used for Procedure III. The Retelling Summary for Procedure II may be used to evaluate the Retelling. Anecedotal information about the retelling may be written under Comments.

Overview of Procedure III

The following list includes each of the activities for Procedure III, which may be checked off as each is learned or used to complete a miscue analysis.

Select Student	____
Select Material	____
Prepare typescript for material	____
Prepare retelling guide for material	____
Prepare tape recorder and setting	____
Collect data	____
Oral reading and miscue marking	____
Retelling	____
Write comments or holistic score of retelling on typescript	____
Listen to recording and verify miscue marking	____
Prepare typescript for coding	____
Number sentences and mark lines	____
Code sentences for questions 1 to 3	____
Code substitutions for graphic similarity	____
Compute statistics	____
Add comments	____

Procedure IV: The Reading Conference Form

Procedure IV provides a vehicle for those very familiar with miscue analysis to do a quick evaluation of a student's reading. It is especially helpful for the classroom teacher during an individual reading conference or for an initial evaluation by a reading specialist or special education teacher. Procedure IV focuses on the most important questions used in miscue analysis: semantic acceptability and correction. As discussed concerning earlier procedures, the significance of the interrelationship between these two phenomena has been highlighted by a great deal of miscue analysis research. This interrelationship of these two questions results in a *comprehending score.*

Procedure IV does not require tape-recording readers, and a typescript is unnecessary. Instead, the teacher listens to students read and keeps a tally of the coded sentences by responding to the question: Does the sentence as the reader left it, make sense within the context of the selection? Those that are fully semantically acceptable (assuming total syntactic acceptability) with the context of the total story or article and those that are partially acceptable or unacceptable but corrected are coded *yes.* Those that are partially acceptable or unacceptable within the context and not corrected are coded *no.*

Procedure IV is for teachers who know miscue analysis *well* enough to make use of miscue concepts whenever they listen to readers. When the teacher and the reader have an individual conference, the material can, in most cases, be what the reader has chosen for recreational reading, or informational material the reader is using for a project or report. The student is asked to read from the point in the text at which he or she stopped reading before the conference. This assures the reading of new material at the same time that the reader has the background of the material read previously. As the student reads, the teacher simply tallies each sentence.

The Conference Form provides directions for computing the comprehending score, which is found by dividing the total number of sentences (listed on the form) into the total number of sentences coded *yes.* The quality of the presentation, which should follow each reading, is noted by the teacher under Retelling Information. As part of the conference, the teacher engages the reader in a discussion about what he or she has been reading and about any problems that have arisen in relation to reading or information seeking. This discussion often covers more than the material read during the conference. Comments and anecdotes collected during the conference are also listed on the form, especially information that can help with planning continuous reading instruction. Such information might include: what and how much the student is reading; the student's current interests; projects the student is working on; resources being used; reading strategies the reader is trying to use with greater facility; or any other information related to the reader's strengths or weaknesses.

MISCUE ANALYSIS PROCEDURE IV INDIVIDUAL CONFERENCE FORM

READER Betsy DATE November 3

TEACHER Mrs. Blaw AGE/GRADE Grade Three

SELECTION Man Who Kept House

Does the sentence, as the reader left it, make sense within the context of the story?

Yes ~~||||~~ ~~||||~~ ~~||||~~ ~~||||~~ ~~||||~~ ~~||||~~ ~~||||~~ ~~||||~~ ~~||||~~ ~~||||~~ ~~||||~~ || Total 57

No ~~||||~~ ~~||||~~ | Total 11

Number of Sentences 68 Comprehending Score 84%

Divide total Yes by Total number of sentences for Comprehending Score 57÷68 = .84

Retelling Information Very complete retelling. Doesn't always seem to understand concept of cow on roof (sod house). Uses pictures to aid retelling. Tone towards story always serious.

Comments For the most part Betsy uses predicting and confirming strategies proficiently. She may be over attending to surface features of text.

Involve Betsy in reading a variety of material. Help her choose her own reading. Perhaps suggest some humorous reading such as Robert Munsch. Concepts about churns and sod roofs may be extended as appropriate.

(Goodman, Watson, Burke)

Overview of Procedure IV

The following activities may be checked off to complete Procedure IV:

Select Student	____
Select Material	____
Prepare setting	____
Listen to oral reading	____
Tally sentences onto Procedure IV Form	____
Request retelling	____
Enter comments about retelling on Procedure IV Form	____
Confer about other concerns	____
Enter comments about other concerns	____
Compute appropriate statistics	____

Part III

Miscue Analysis and Curriculum Development

Miscue analysis leads both researchers and teachers to a revaluing of the reading process, the reader, and reading instruction. While researchers use miscue analysis to answer specific questions about reading, teachers use miscue analysis to develop important insights about their students' reading, insights that empower teachers to make critical decisions about curriculum development and instructional procedures. The suggestions presented in the final section of this book grow out of information about language, the reading process, and a specific reader, Betsy—presented earlier.

In Chapter 7, three models of reading instruction are discussed with examples of three students who hold these views. The essentials of a reading program consistent with a holistic model of reading instruction are presented, along with a sketch of the teacher who might coordinate such a program. Chapter 8 considers the information gained through miscue analysis as the basis for a reading program for Betsy and other students.

7 Whole Language Reading Curriculum

We've said that after completing just one Reading Miscue Inventory (RMI), teachers never again listen to students read in the same way. We also believe that after studying several readers, teachers begin to rethink their beliefs about reading and consequently reexamine their own reading curricula. During such evaluation, teachers often consider whether their beliefs and their programs are consistent with what they have learned about the reading process through miscue analysis.

Because what students and teachers believe about reading powerfully affects teaching and learning, we first discuss three models of reading instruction. Knowledge of these views will help teachers understand their own beliefs, as well as their students' ideas about reading.

Three Models of Reading Instruction

Miscue analysis has been instrumental in the development of holistic views of reading. However, other views of reading are held by most members of society and are reflected in published reading schemes or programs. All members of a literate society develop views, ideas, and attitudes about reading. One purpose of miscue analysis is to help teacher/researchers examine beliefs about reading held by students or research subjects that need to be considered in understanding readers' attitudes toward reading and in planning reading instruction.

Understanding how readers view what happens as they read and how reading instruction relates to how they read can help explain the strategies readers use. When students or teachers are involved in miscue analysis and instructional activities that help them raise questions about their own personal views of reading, the ways in which they think about the reading process often change. The Reading Interview discussed later provides an additional way to gain access to the ways in which people view reading and how their views change. It may be helpful, however, to first explore the views of reading that are most commonly held.

Beliefs about reading may be categorized into three major models of reading instruction: a subskills or phonics view, a skills or eclectic view, and a whole language view (P. Anders, in press; Reed, 1982).

Subskills Model

The subskills model of reading instruction is based on behaviorist learning theory. The underlying assumptions include that reading must be taught in an explicit way, that reading is learned from parts to wholes through a carefully worked-out sequential hierarchy of skills; and that each skill must be taught, positively reinforced, mastered, and tested before the next appropriate skill in the hierarchy is presented. The simplest units of language are assumed to be letters and sounds. These smallest units of language are carefully introduced one at a time before the teaching of word-recognition skills. Instruction directed toward the mastery of subskills usually precedes a focus on understanding the meaning of what is being read. Generally, consonants are introduced first, followed by long vowels and short vowels. The reader is taught larger units of language after tests show that beginning subskills have been mastered.

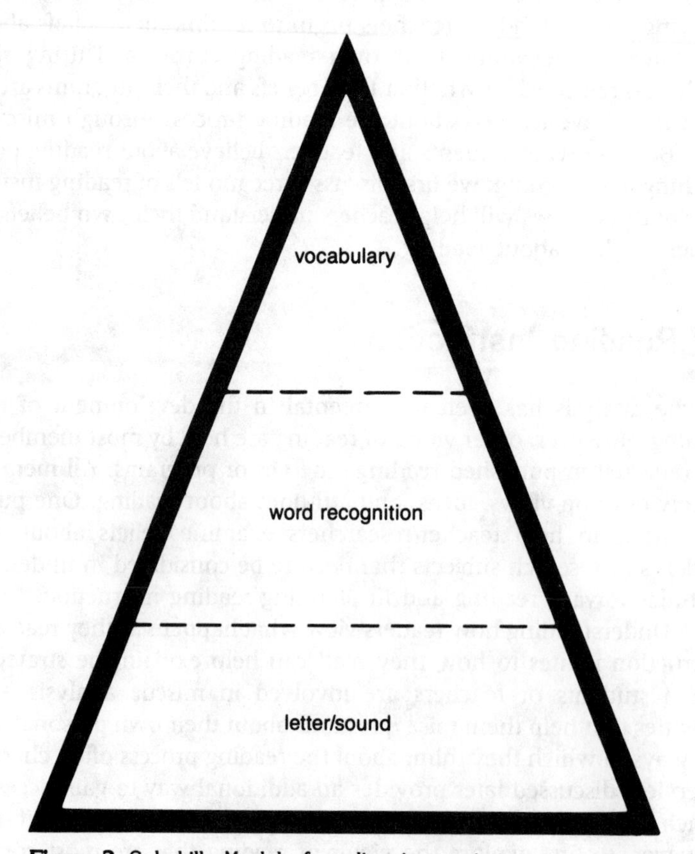

Figure 3 Subskills Model of reading instruction.

Practice leads to mastery of the hierarchically arranged skills. Errors are unacceptable because they become learned responses. To discourage errors, reading instruction is carefully organized and directed to ensure exact responses. The teacher monitors the reader's progress and uses a test-teach-test curriculum model. This model of reading instruction can be depicted as a triangle (Figure 3) with a strong base of letter-sound relationships, which supports the next hierarchical level of word recognition, which in turn supports the top tier: word meanings or vocabulary. The tiers are separate and hierarchical.

Skills Model

The skills model of reading instruction represents the most common view held and is reflected in most basal readers—the most prevalent reading-instructional tool. The proponents of this view often claim that they are eclectic, using what they believe represents the best insights from all views of reading. Beginning reading instruction includes the teaching of relationships between letters and sounds. In many programs, irregular words are taught as whole units through flash cards or games focusing on words in isolation. In addition to the teaching of phonics, word recognition, and vocabulary, instruction may include the reading of children's literature and the integration of the other language arts (writing, speaking, and listening) with reading instruction. All three language cueing systems (graphophonics, syntax, and semantics) are taught, although each is usually presented in separate lessons using prescriptive language rules.

Basal readers are written to reflect control of letter-sound relations, word frequency, spelling patterns, and grammatical structures. In recent years, basals include excerpts from professionally authored literature and genre other than narrative. Meaning is important to this view but is often organized as a hierarchical set of comprehension skills. Those who support this view think of reading as a set of hierarchical skills and believe that the teaching of language must be simplified in order for children to learn to read. This model can be shown as a circle with equal divisions provided for comprehension, phonics, and vocabulary skills (Figure 4).

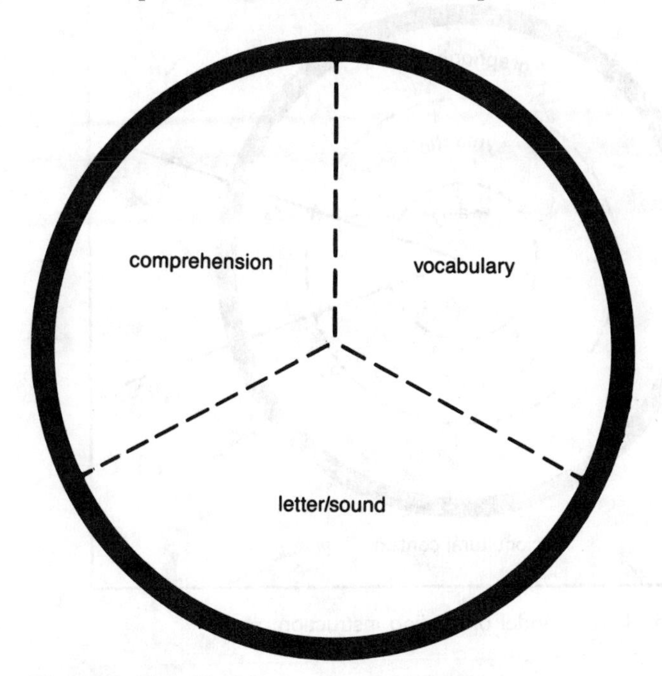

Figure 4 Skills Model of reading instruction.

Holistic Model

The holistic model of reading instruction reflects a transactional, psycholinguistic, and sociolinguistic view of the reading process (see Chapter 2), which has been discussed at length throughout this book. This view can be pictured as a multi-layered circle that represents meaning (Figure 5). At the heart of the sphere is the semantic system. Surrounding and supporting the semantic system is the syntactic system of language, and on the surface is the graphophonic system of language. All the systems are used simultaneously within a sociocultural context. In order to construct meaning, the reader must use all the language systems within a social-cultural context.

We have summarized the three models of reading instruction for the purpose of providing a background to explore how different readers view reading and how their views may affect their reading proficiency. We reject both the subskills and the skills view of reading instruction since they are not based on what research in miscue analysis has revealed about the integration of the language cueing systems and the reading strategies.

The Reading Interview

In order to plan reading instruction for students, it is important to be aware of their beliefs about reading and to speculate on the ways in which their reading proficiency has been influenced by reading instruction. We believe that what students believe about reading and reading instruction affects decisions they make about strategies to use during reading. Responses to the Reading Interview provide information about the reader's metalinguistic knowledge about reading—the language people use to talk about reading as an object of study. Readers' responses (Burke, 1980) often correspond to the models of reading instruction and provide a way of understanding the reader's views.

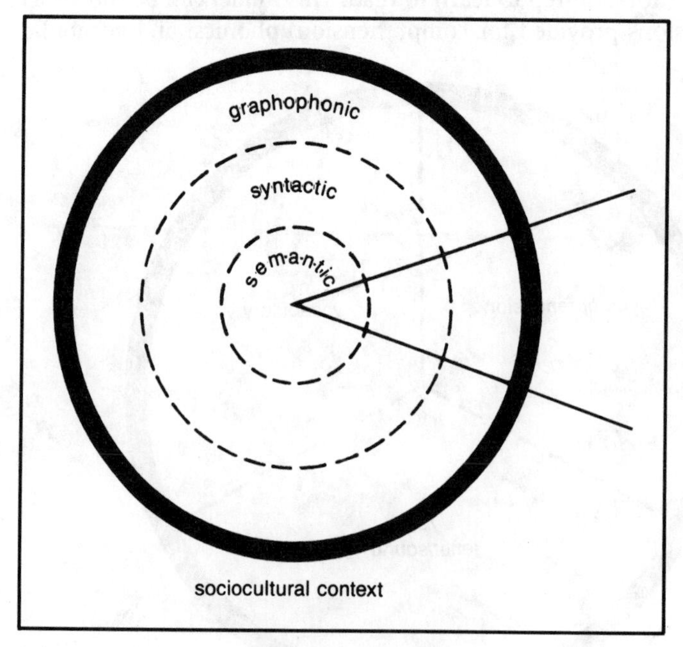

Figure 5 Holistic Model of reading instruction.

By examining readers' responses to the Reading Interview, it is possible to categorize their views of reading according to the three different views described in the previous section. When readers' responses are compared at different times, the influences of reading instruction on readers' metalinguistic awareness can be compared. No single question on the interview provides a profile of a student's personal view of reading. In fact, some readers respond differentially to the questions if the procedure is done in different settings or with different types of materials (Coles, 1981). However, since a good deal of reading is done in school, examining how readers respond in school settings is most illuminating. Given the nature of the reader and the purpose of the teacher/researcher, it may be important to conduct more than one Reading Interview with students in different sociocultural contexts.

Because the Reading Interview provides access to people's views about reading, it is helpful for teacher/researchers to respond to the interview in writing and then compare and discuss the responses with other adult readers (see Appendix C for a blank form). These responses may then be compared with students' responses, including the responses that follow.

After we list each question from the Reading Interview, we discuss its significance and then present the responses of three different readers.

Question 1: *When You Are Reading and Come to Something You Don't Know, What Do You Do?*

One issue addressed by this question is what the student believes the word *something* refers to. The response to this question shows what linguistic unit (words, letters, phrases, sentences, or sections of text) the reader is concerned with. A second issue concerns strategies readers believe they use when they come to the unit of language that they don't know. Their answers indicate whether they believe it is best to sound out, skip, substitute, or keep reading, as well as who or what the reader depends on for help while reading.

The major purpose of the follow-up question—*Do you ever do anything else?*—is to gain additional information about the characteristics of what the *something* refers to. In addition, this question provides insight into whether readers have a single strategy in mind or if they believe that they need to change strategies depending on purpose or setting.

Question 2: *Who Is a Good Reader You Know?*

This question provides insight into what readers believe about the characteristics of a good reader. Students' views of a good reader are useful for comparison with answers to subsequent questions. It is revealing when students indicate they do not know any good readers or nominate themselves as good readers.

Question 3: *What Makes ________ a Good Reader?*

This question adds to the reader's list of characteristics of a good reader. The blank is filled with the name or pronoun of the person mentioned in answer to Question 2.

Question 4: *Do You Think ________ Ever Comes to Something He/She Doesn't Know?*

This question relates to Question 1. If students, in response to Question 4, say that good readers never come to something they don't know, this suggests that the student's view of reading equates good reading with errorless performance on the part of totally knowledgeable human beings. Such students would believe they are not smart enough to learn to read. Different questions are asked next depending on whether the response to Question 4 is *yes* or *no.*

Question 5: *(Yes) When ________ Does Come to Something He/She Doesn't Know, What Do You Think He/She Does?*

(No) Suppose ________ Comes to Something He/She Doesn't Know?

With this question, the reader is encouraged to take a stand on what aspect of language is most important in reading and what strategy is most productive.

Question 6: *If You Knew Someone Was Having Trouble Reading, How Would You Help That Person?*

The response to this question reveals whether the reader believes troubled readers are or should be treated differently from other readers.

Question 7: *What Would a/your Teacher Do to Help That Person?*

This is similar to Question 5, in which the reader is again asked to focus on what is important in teaching, especially for the less able reader. Questions 6 and 7 together suggest the extent to which instruction may have influenced the reader's beliefs.

Question 8: *How Did You Learn to Read?*

People who have pleasant memories about learning to read often think they learned to read before school or don't even remember learning to read. Such readers often credit family members—parents, grandparents, or siblings—with having taught them to read, or they remember being told that they were self-taught readers who were reading before they came to school. Readers who believe that they are problem readers often remember vivid and sometimes negative experiences while learning to read in school settings.

Question 9: *What Would You Like to Do Better as a Reader?*

This question provides additional information about readers' beliefs about the reading process. Even good readers think that they would like to be able to read faster or remember everything that they read. This question provides an opening to discuss reading in terms of the limitations of the reading process and the need for prior knowledge.

For very young children, this question may need to be rephrased: *Would you like to read better? How could you do that?*

Question 10: *Do You Think You Are a Good Reader? Why?*

By the time this question is asked, teacher/researchers can often predict the answer.

The following responses to the Reading Interview questions are from readers who represent different views of reading. Since the Reading Interview was not available when we taped Betsy's reading, we do not have her responses to the questions. However, we believe that her responses would be similar to Sara's. Sara's and Julia's interviews were done by their teachers (T). Brian's interview was done by a researcher (R).

Reading Interview

Students Being Interviewed

Name	*Age*	*Education Level*	*Sex*
Sara (S)	9	3	F
Brian (B)	8	3	M
Julia (J)	8	3	F

When you are reading and come to something you don't know, what do you do? [Question 1]

S: I ask you.
B: Figure it out—like break it into two parts.
J: Do you mean when I don't understand something?
T: Yes, anytime you come to something . . .
J: I usually can work it out. I keep reading.
Do you ever do anything else?
S: I look close at the word. I sound it out and I try to figure it out.
T: What do you mean? How do you figure it out?
S: I sound it out. Sometimes I try to see if I know the beginning and the end.
B: My mom helps me. She tells me it's something else but what it really is. Say the word is *not* and she will say: You were (blank) there. And that will help me.
J: Well if I'm really interested when I'm finished I might look back at it and work it out.

Who is a good reader you know? [Question 2]
S: You're a really good reader. *(talking to teacher)*
B: My mom.
J: My dad is a good reader.

What makes (me, your mom, your dad) *a good reader?* [Question 3]
S: You know all the words. When you read to us it's really good.
B: She just reads a lot.
J: He reads a lot and he knows a lot.

Do you think (I, your mom, your dad) *ever come/s to something I/she/he don't/ doesn't know when reading?* [Question 4]
S: No!
B: Yes.
J: Well, maybe.

Yes. When (your mom, your dad) *does come to something she/he doesn't know, what do you think she/he does?* [Question 5]
B: She might say a wrong word, and then she'll try to say it again.
R: What does she do to figure it out?

B: There's a hard word or something, she says like . . . she might say a wrong word or something. She will say it a couple more times and it will come out all right.
R: What do you think she's doing when she says it a couple of more times so that it comes out right?
B: Thinking about it.
J: He thinks about it, I guess. Sometimes he talks about what he is reading to us . . . to mom and me.

No. Suppose (I) *came to something* (I) *didn't know. What do you think* (I'd) *do?* [Question 5]
S: You always know it.
T: Just suppose—pretend.
S: You would ask your husband.
T: Who else is a good reader?
S: Janis. (another student is class)
T: Why?
S: Because she can pronounce all the words.
T: What does Janis do when she doesn't know?
S: Asks the teacher.
T: Anything else?
S: She sounds it out.

If you knew someone was having trouble reading, how would you help that person? [Question 6]
S: Tell them to ask the teacher.
T: Anything else?
S: Give them a worksheet.
B: I don't know . . . do shared reading.
R: What's shared reading?
B: One person reads a page and then the other one does. Or you read three pages and they read three pages.
R: How does that help?
B: I don't know. You just . . . it's just like . . . they just get to read and like if they make mistakes it doesn't matter. Or something like that.
J: I'd take them to the library.

What would a/your teacher do to help that person? [Question 7]
S: Tell them to sit down and work on the word 'til they get it.
B: Just have them read and then stop them.
R: What would they do after they stopped them?
B: I don't know.
R: That's okay. I'll give you a couple of minutes to think about it.
B: They would read with them and do written conversation and read stories like picture books and stuff.
J: She'd give them some good stories to read and try to get them to understand it.

How did you learn to read? [Question 8]
S: I don't know. I learned at school. My teacher helped me. I learned from her. I needed help.
B: By my mom helping me and teachers helping me.
R: Tell me the kinds of help your mom and your teachers gave you.
B: They just gave me some encouragement to read it and stuff. That's about all.
R: They never told you to do anything?

B: Well, they told me not to give up and stuff . . . just to keep on trying.
R: Can you remember when you were in first grade?
B: Yeh.
R: When you went to reading circle tell me what happened?
B: I was in the low reading group.
R: Well, what did you do in the low reading group?
B: We read like easy books. But my mom said . . . like some of the kids that were higher, they were making fun of us kids that were low, because we weren't that good of readers . . . And my mom said ignore it. Then in the second grade my teacher tutored me.
R: And what kinds of things did she do?
B: We just read books. I read books to her and that helped me.
R: When you came to something you didn't know what did your teacher do?
B: She told me to sound it out.
R: Did she ever tell you to do anything else?
B: No.
J: My dad. He taught me to read and then I read and then my teacher taught me too.

What would you like to do better as a reader? [Question 9]
S: I'd like to know all the words.
B: Just read quicker.
R: What do you think it is you might do to be able to read quicker?
B: Practice a lot.
R: What would you practice?
B: Books, just reading books and stuff. And words, just like saying them.
R: What do you think will help you say the words better?
B: Just saying them over and over, I guess.
J: Understand everything in the book.

Do you think you are a good reader? [Question 10]
S: No. Maybe, sometimes . . . a little bit.
B: So-so.
J: Yes, because people tell me I am.

Sara's responses show a focus on atomistic language units. She "looks close at the word"; tries to see whether she knows the beginning and end; believes good readers know everything and never have problems with reading. Sara also believes when readers have problems they usually rely on other people for help and that she herself is "maybe, sometimes . . . a little bit" a good reader. Sara's answers reflect a subskills view of reading.

Brian is more eclectic in his views. He thinks reading is focusing on words "like break it into two parts" or "just saying them (words) over and over." But he also thinks that "reading books and stuff" is part of reading practice and he has some idea that making a mistake "doesn't matter." Unlike Sara, Brian does not lack confidence in himself as a good reader, even though he does not seem strong in his convictions.

Julia's responses always focus on reading for meaning as she places the reader in a position of power: "I usually can work it out. I keep reading." ". . . if I'm really interested . . . I might look back."

Together with the information resulting from miscue analysis, the responses from the Reading Interview help teachers understand students' views about reading. What the teacher believes about the reading process and what students believe have powerful influences on how reading is taught and learned. When both the Reading Interview and the student's miscue analysis reflects a subskills or skills view of reading, then reading instruction has to take into consideration ways of helping readers view reading in a more holistic and personal way. Readers develop control over reading when they are aware that reading is for their own personal use and that the major focus while they are reading is to construct meaning.

The Reading Interview adds information to a reader's profile. It is a good tool to use at the beginning and end of an instructional program because it shows a student's shift in attitudes about reading and the reading process. It has been used in research to show readers' metalinguistic knowledge about reading and the impact each model of reading instruction has on readers' beliefs about reading and on how they read (Harste and Burke, 1977). Similar research has been used in the examination of teachers' views about reading and reading instruction (DeFord, 1981).

Essentials of A Whole Language Curriculum

As teachers develop "miscue ears" and focus on the process of students constructing meaning through reading, they realize that all readers, whether proficient or not, in regular or special classes, improve their reading when they are in an instructional setting with a teacher who: (a) places students at the center of the program; (b) begins the program with a focus on students' strengths; and (c) selects materials and instructional procedures that integrate all the cues of language.

Research in reading using miscue analysis as an investigative tool shows that the more personally involved students become in their reading, the more proficiently they read (Allen and Watson, 1976; K. Goodman, 1973). This understanding makes it clear that we must develop reading programs that center on students' needs and interests. When students are at the heart of the curriculum and are continually observed by informed teachers (through miscue analysis, for example), the curriculum is inevitably in process, changing to suit emerging needs and situations, and constantly supports the strengths of learners. Such a curriculum—a whole language reading program—facilitates learning to read by inviting students to participate in meaning-centered language events that are linguistically and pragmatically holistic.

Although whole language progams may mean different things to different people, one essential attribute provides the foundation for all such programs—students must be involved in a literacy curriculum that *keeps the systems of language unified in a mutually supportive way*. When language systems are kept whole, as they are naturally integrated in real reading and writing, students are *never* given instructional materials that fragment the systems into small, abstract, and isolated units. Rather, students are invited to participate in a program that is meaningful—a program in which they learn their language by *using it*. Instructional experiences are based on the belief that in using all the available linguistic cues, readers have the opportunity through their active involvement to select the information they need in order to construct personal meaning.

Experiences that are essential to a whole language curriculum should be *part of every student's reading program:* listening to literature; reading; writing; integrating past experiences, knowledge and language with life and learning in the classroom; and becoming consciously aware of reading and the reading process.

Listening to Literature

Telling stories and reading to students (of all ages) every day is an essential part of a whole language program. In addition to providing sheer enjoyment, hearing a good story told or read well presents students with an invitational model for the students' own future *reading and writing*. That is, teachers not only demonstrate the reading act, but in effect help students *value reading*, inviting them to find time to read to themselves and to others. The content and form of a variety of stories that students listen to expand their linguistic experiences and provide a model for writing. Literature heard is then extended as students are invited to add another chapter, verse, or incident to the story read or told by the teacher or to write their own stories.

When stories and poems are shared in the classroom, the literature becomes similar to loved family stories; shared literature helps create a bond between students and teacher. Sharing and experiencing the culture of other groups and societies presented through their literature is an equally important reason for the daily presentation of stories.

When teachers read or tell stories, there is no academic pressure. Students comfortably draw on and create personal meanings. They see that stories are supposed to make them laugh and cry. Students easily become aware of the parallel between listening and reading. When teachers encourage listeners to predict what will happen next in a story or to guess how a character might solve a problem, they are inviting students to take linguistic risks—a way of becoming actively involved in gathering information and constructing meaning.

Newspapers, magazines, and nonfiction literature are other sources for shared reading experiences. When readings relate to interesting current events and controversies, or when they are a part of thematic units and content areas, the experience has the potential of providing students with concepts and labels (vocabulary) that are significant to the particular subject matter. By listening to their teachers read, students become familiar with the structures of news features, scientific reportings, political essays, and other forms while they share their concerns about the significant events of the day. In addition to sharing professionally authored texts, students' compositions are read aloud—an exciting way to value and celebrate authorship.

Personal Reading of Literature

Personal reading—daily, silent reading from a variety of materials—is a distinguishing characteristic of a whole language program. Students are encouraged to choose their own fare, while at the same time teachers organize the curriculum and the environment as an invitation to readers to try different materials with a variety of messages and with diverse literary forms. To bring students and good reading material together, teachers obviously need to know not only their students' interests and abilities, but also the literature that is available and suitable for them. Excellent annotated resources are available for keeping informed and up to date on books and magazines for children and youth (see the bibliography).

Writing

In a whole language program, students (all ages, including those in kindergarten, and all groups, including those in special education) are invited and expected to write daily. Students write notes and letters; keep logs, records, journals, and diaries; make lists, labels, captions, and learning plans; order materials and supplies; organize books, materials, and portfolios; author stories, poems, plays, and research reports; and publish magazines and books. Their writing is responded to by the audiences for whom it is intended.

When reading and writing are a continuous part of the curriculum, students "learn to read like writers" (F. Smith, 1983). They begin to ask, "Why and how did the author do that?" and then they use the information, including conventions of writing, in their own compositions. The rich background that reading provides and the need to write for a variety of personal and social reasons influences and motivates the writer.

Students who control their own writing do not compose anything that does not have semantic intent; therefore, as readers they expect to encounter meaning and demand it from authors as they demand it from themselves. Such expectations, combined with meaning construction through writing, support all the reading strategies.

Through reading, students explore the many uses of written language, and through writing they use the written language in order to convey innumerable meanings to innumerable audiences.

Experience and Language

In a whole language program, students are encouraged to bring their experiences and their language into the classroom. A great deal of talk takes place about ideas, events, and people that are already of interest to students or have *the potential* of stimulating their interests and imaginations. Students talk (question, discuss, argue, debate) with each other and with the teacher; they sing; they dramatize; they read and they write; and they do this all day—in science, math, social studies, art, and physical education. Content areas especially give students an opportunity to express concerns about the world in which they must grow up—about exploration in space, nuclear potential, democratic or rigged elections, starvation, poverty, health, and love. These topics are not contrived, but are just as real for students as they are for teachers and parents. The world with all its wonders and all its worries is brought into a whole language classroom, and students attempt in various ways to solve its problems and answer their own questions.

When first-graders teach a jump rope rhyme to their teacher, who writes it on the board (under their watchful eyes), the children are using their own resources and familiar language. When they write (whether it be scribble, mock letters, "pretend," or conventional print), or when they dictate to their teacher, they are using their memory of past experiences as well as the language itself to help them write and then to read what they have composed.

When older students share the language unique to teenagers and write a dictionary of their vocabulary, they learn about the variations of language, and how and why it changes. Students' familiar language not only includes their natural conversations but also songs, school chants and cheers, jokes, finger plays, advertisements, and commercials. Students make books of family sayings and stories (see the Foxfire Series), nursery rhymes, song lyrics, favorite recipes—anything that brings their world and the language that thay know and use comfortably into the classroom. Students share familiar written language by way of menus, posters, signs, newspapers, magazines, leaflets, maps, record album and videotape jackets, package labels, baseball cards, bumper stickers, and T-shirts.

Conscious Awareness of the Reading Process

In a whole language program, all students, regardless of proficiency, talk about their reading. These metalinguistic and metacognitive discussions take place in large- or small-group sessions in teacher-student or student-student interactions. Students talk about what people read, why they read, and what is important about reading. They make lists of everything they have read recently, exploring why each was read and how the reading influenced them. Students evaluate their own and their teacher's miscues and discover that miscues often help them in their attempt to construct meaning. They notice that miscues are related to editing the author's text and to translating the author's language to the reader's. Students explore how they discover meaning, decide what happens next, and know what certain words or phrases mean.

The Reading Interview, discussed in the previous section, reveals that many students have a subskills model of reading even though they use the reading process with moderate proficiency. This gap between what students think they should do and what they actually do when they are reading often causes problems, especially when students come to difficult or unpredictable text. Through discussions about how people read and the support of strategy lessons (Chapter 8), students focus on their own use of the reading process. This powerful experience allows students, often for the first time, to realize that what they thought was wrong to do is exactly what they *should* do in order to construct meaning. For proficient readers, discussions that highlight the reasons for initiating, selecting, predicting, and correcting confirm their view of reading.

Daily experiences of students in a whole language classroom include:

Hearing a story told or read
Reading real literature
Writing real compositions
Sharing their life and language
Talking about reading and the reading process

Sketch of a Whole Language Teacher

Whole language teachers have individual and unique personalities, interests, strengths, and styles, but there are some important attributes that appear to be universally characteristic.

Whole language teachers learn about and from students by kid-watching (Y. Goodman, 1976). By becoming enlightened observers of students, and by using learners as informants (Harste, Woodward, and Burke, 1984), teachers find out what kids are trying to do and then they help them do it. They value and respect the language and experiences of students. As they observe students' expansion of language use, they participate in the joy of success and are supportive when problems occur. As evidence of respect, whole language teachers: (a) maximize readers' literacy strengths (students are not underestimated); (b) involve students as the touchstone for curriculum development (students are not underrepresented); and (c) encourage students' independent and personal use of language (students are not undervalued).

Whole language teachers know what they are talking about and what they are doing. That is, they are able to support, with theory based directly on research, their decisions about curriculum and instruction in their classrooms. They not only know about human development, but understand language development as well. Because of what they know, what they believe, and what has been proven by experience with learners, they encourage students to engage in certain strategies such as hypothesizing about language, being linguistic and cognitive risk takers, and focusing on the construction of meaning.

Whole language teachers do not ignore problems, but at the same time are not preoccupied with the elimination of mistakes, errors, and deficiencies. Rather, miscues are used to show evidence of the students' growth, logic, interpretations, and intellectual functioning. Students' strengths, rather than their difficulties, become the basis for lesson development.

Whole language teachers are risk takers. One recently wrote about her experiences:

> Do you realize how much courage it took me to read aloud to high school students. (I was terrified they'd say, "That's kid stuff." and some did); to share my own writing with students; to stand up to district-wide mandates incompatible with whole language; to tear up a book to make "skinny books"; to say to students, "You have a choice"; to demonstrate extensions of books such as creating dramatic readings, art work and pantomimes (Aren't you embarrassed doing that? asked one student); to bite my tongue; dig in my toes, but keep quiet so that a student could figure out meaning for himself?
>
> I tell you I have taken *risks* this year and it's becoming easier!
>
> Marné Isakson

Whole language teachers do not tolerate artificial reading activities that fragment language, destroy the reading process, and defeat students. Rather, they make available a world of materials with all kinds of real messages in them, and see that ample time is available for readers and authors to come together in order to benefit from these messages. They fervently encourage students to become involved in creating meaning, not only by reading but by writing as well.

Whole language teachers create an environment in which students perceive themselves, their peers, and their teachers as readers and writers; *everyone* in the whole language classroom is a participating member of an active literacy community. *All* come to value themselves as language users. Whole language teachers:

Use information gained from their students to develop curriculum
Involve students in curriculum planning, and self-evaluation
Use information from research, theory, and experience to develop curriculum
Focus on students' strengths
Take risks
Integrate language and the language arts with content areas
Create a community of language users

8

The Reader and the Program

When a reading miscue analysis is completed, a great deal of information is available in several forms and in several places: the marked typescript, the Coding Sheets, the list of repeated miscues, the reader's retelling, the teacher's written comments, and the Reading Interview. The Reader Profile summarizes much of this information and provides a good starting point for investigating the reader's strengths and weaknesses.

The RMI is not a prescriptive instrument. We cannot compute the scores, categorically label students as good or poor readers, and then present a programmed set of skills for students to master. The Reading Miscue Inventory is an analytical and descriptive instrument. It is a tool for teachers to use in concert with their own knowledge about kids, language, and learning. This chapter is designed to help teachers use all the descriptive information gathered during the miscue analysis sessions to develop an appropriate reading program. The RMI information must always be combined with what the teacher already knows about students and with what is understood from reading research and practice that is based on language in use. After a discussion of Reader Profiles and other RMI data, recommendations are given for developing a reading program for Betsy and other students.

Reader Profile Information

The Reader Profile indicates the proficiency with which students use the systems of language and the reading strategies. It is not our intention to place students in absolute categories or to attach restrictive labels on them; it does however, facilitate discussion to categorize to some degree the reader's proficiency. Terms that will be used to describe readers are: proficient, moderately proficient, and nonproficient.

K. Goodman (1978) describes proficient readers as those who make both effective and efficient use of the language cueing systems and the reading strategies. Such readers produce syntactically and semantically acceptable structures most of the time, either by predicting appropriate structures or by correcting unacceptable ones using graphophonic information selectively. Proficient readers' graphic and sound similarity scores may be in a moderate range, and may be lower than those of less proficient readers who depend heavily on graphophonic information.

One proficient reader showed the following percentages on his Procedure I Reader Profiles.

Proficient Reader Profile

Meaning Construction		
No Loss	70%	89% (No Loss + Partial)
Partial	19%	
Loss	11%	
Grammatical Relations		
Strength	61%	90% (Strength + Partial Strength + Overcorrection)
Partial Strength	20%	
Overcorrection	9%	
Weakness	10%	
Graphic Similarity		
High	62%	79% (High + Some)
Some	17%	
None	21%	
Sound Similarity		
High	62%	78% (High + Some)
Some	16%	
None	22%	

This proficient reader uses all the cues of language to produce syntactically and semantically acceptable miscues (shown by 89% Meaning Construction and 90% Grammatical Relations). He selects graphophonic cues but does not overuse them, as 21 percent and 22 percent of his graphic and sound similarity scores reveal miscues with no similarity at all. This suggests that he makes high-level substitutions that have little or no letter-sound relationship, but that does not change the meaning of the passsage.

Readers can be moderately proficient. Most moderately proficient readers make effective use of reading strategies but are not very efficient. These readers produce syntactically and semantically acceptable structures most of the time, but tend to rely a great deal on graphophonic information. They have a tendency to correct miscues that are semantically and syntactically acceptable. Their reading may be slow and they may regress often. When this is the case, they are constructing meaning but they are not efficient in their selection of cues. Such readers may be able to retell a great deal of the story, although they may not understand subtlety. Betsy is a moderately proficient reader who is effective in her use of predicting and confirming reading strategies, but she is not efficient since she overuses graphic and sound information, overcorrects, and makes a large number of repetitions. Her scores, a profile, and a discussion of reading strengths and weaknesses are included in the next section.

Occasionally, moderately proficient readers may be efficient but not effective in their use of reading strategies. These readers are usually proficient with predictable and familiar texts. However, when these students read unfamiliar texts with complex sentence structures or with multiple concepts, especially the sort that occur in content-area materials, they may be able to produce a fairly high percentage of syntactically and semantically acceptable sentences while they may not construct a great deal of meaning of the text as a whole. Their miscues often result in sentences with partial or extensive meaning changes. Efficient readers may have few repetitions and few overcorrections. Although they may read quickly with appropriate intonation, they are unable to organize their retellings and often retell facts or events rather than relationships between characters and among concepts.

Nonproficient readers produce unacceptable and uncorrected structures. These readers often rely too heavily on graphophonic information and fail to relate the text to their lives and their background knowledge. They are easily distracted and often resist reading.

The following is a Procedure I profile of a nonproficient reader.

Nonproficient Reader Profile

Meaning Construction		
No Loss	35%	55% (No Loss + Partial)
Partial	20%	
Loss	45%	
Grammatical Relations		
Strength	48%	57% (Strength + Partial Strength + Overcorrection)
Partial Strength	3%	
Overcorrection	6%	
Weakness	43%	
Graphic Similarity		
High	68%	93% (High + Some)
Some	25%	
None	7%	
Sound Similarity		
High	62%	92% (High + Some)
Some	30%	
None	8%	

This nonproficient reader's primary reading strategy is sounding out letters, syllables, and words. Her percentages for graphic and sound similarity are very high. Less than half of her miscues result in sentences that are semantically and syntactically acceptable or that are corrected with little or no meaning change, as shown by the 45 percent *loss* of Meaning Construction and 48 percent *strength* of Grammatical Relations.

The Reader Profiles are offered with a note of caution. No single measure, including one RMI, can be used exclusively to evaluate readers. The *text* the student is asked to read constitutes a major influence. If the text is not well written or has not been selected with the interest, age, and background of the reader taken into consideration, scores are likely to be depressed. Proficiency is influenced not only by how well readers control the process, but also by how interested they are in the material, their purpose for reading, and the background of information they bring to the reading. One student may be a highly proficient reader of novels, but only moderately proficient in the reading of knitting instructions. Another student may construct a great deal of meaning while reading historical fiction, but respond to a history textbook with nonproficient strategies. Reader Profiles may be kept over a period of time and used for comparison purposes.

Betsy's Reader Profile

One way to consider the information summarized on the Reader Profile is to focus on categories and patterns that deal specifically with the reading strategies: initiating and sampling, predicting, confirming, and correcting (see Chapter 2). Betsy's scores from the Reader Profile of each procedure are summarized below as a means to examine and discuss how the scores reflect her use of the reading strategies.

Procedure I Reader Profile: Betsy

Meaning Construction		
No Loss	63%	96% (No Loss + Partial Loss)
Partial Loss	33%	
Loss	4%	
Grammatical Relations		
Strength	56%	80% (Strength + Partial Strength + Overcorrection)
Partial Strength	7%	
Overcorrection	17%	
Weakness	20%	
Graphic Similarity		
High	55%	83% (High + Some)
Some	28%	
None	17%	
Sound Similarity		
High	43%	73% (High + Some)
Some	30%	
None	27%	

Repeated miscues: See List on Profile
Retelling total: 87 pts.
Reading time: 19 min. MPHW: 10.55

Procedure II Reader Profile: Betsy

*Language Sense**		
Strength	78%	84% (Strength + Partial Strength)
Partial Strength	6%	
Weakness	16%	

*See Procedure I above for other scores.

Procedure III Reader Profile: Betsy

Syntactic Acceptability	
Yes	88%
No	12%

Semantic Acceptability	
Yes	84%
No	17%

Meaning Change	
Yes	0%
Partial	7%
No	93%

Graphic Similarity		
High	55%	84% (High + Some)
Some	29%	
None	15%	

Procedure IV: Betsy

There is no profile form, but the teacher can check scores, and *Comments* on the Conference Form for references to the reader's use of strategies.

Note: Scores from the procedures will vary somewhat because unequal numbers of miscues and sentences are coded in each procedure and the questions in each procedure focus on different linguistic units and patterns.

Initiating and Sampling

Betsy's initiating and sampling strategies are reflected in her use of graphic and sound information (see Chapter 5). The combined totals of *high* and *some* graphic and sound similarity (83 and 73 percent respectively) on her Procedure I Reader Profile show that she is knowledgeable about the graphophonic cueing system but is not very selective in her sampling strategies. Her slow reading rate and her overcorrection score of 17 percent add evidence that she is not efficient in her use of surface text features.

Predicting and Correcting

Betsy's *strength* of Grammatical Relations in Procedure I shows that 80 percent of the time she produces sentences that have at least some degree of acceptability in the text. Overcorrections are included in the total with other acceptable structures because, although they indicate that Betsy is overusing the surface text features, they are structures that make sense and sound like language in the story. Her *strength* of Grammatical Relations shows that she makes appropriate use of predictions as she moves through the text or that she self-corrects when her predictions do not result in acceptable structures. Her graphic and sound similarity scores suggest that she uses a great deal of letter-sound information as she predicts.

Her Meaning Construction scores show that 96 percent of the time she is making sense within the context of the story and producing structures that do not change the author's meaning (as interpreted by the coder) to any major degree.

Other RMI Information

Coding Form

Although the Reader Profile summarizes much of the data provided by the Coding Form, it does not reflect it all. For this reason, teachers may want to review the Coding Form to consider information that does not appear on the Reader Profile.

On the Procedure I Coding Form, important questions about readers' strengths and weaknesses are answered including the following:

1. Do readers construct meaning as they read? (Meaning Construction)
2. Do readers' miscues result in appropriate structures on which they can construct meaning? (Grammatical Relations)
3. To what degree do readers use graphic and sound information as they read? (Graphic and Sound Similarity)

The results of asking these questions are shown on the Reader Profile.

Other information found on the Procedure I Coding Form has to do with the kinds of miscues (substitutions, insertions, etc.) the reader is making. By scanning the Coding Form, the observed response (OR) listed under *reader* can be quickly compared with the expected response (ER) listed under *text.* Knowledge concerning the kinds of miscues a reader makes can help teachers select appropriate strategy lessons and instructional procedures. For example, many omissions of nouns and verbs would suggest a reader is not willing to risk making predictions, while acceptable insertions and substitutions indicate a reader who is using cues selectively and constructing meaning confidently.

On the Procedure I Coding Form, the teacher may look at the coding for correction, syntactic acceptability, semantic acceptability, and meaning change separately, not as part of the Reader Profile patterns (Grammatical Relations and Meaning Construction). Examination of a reader's partially acceptable (P) miscues, under the syntactic and semantic acceptability headings in relation to correction, provides insight into the reader's prediction and confirmation strategies. Examination of the kinds of partially acceptable miscues that are corrected can reveal the degree to which a reader is understanding certain concepts or plot development.

The Procedure II Coding Form shows the number of miscues in each sentence in the second column of the first section *language sense.* For Betsy, sentences such as those numbered 34 and 49 (see Procedure III typescript) reflect large numbers of miscues that may be investigated to determine whether the syntactic structure and concept load of the text may be responsible for the miscues produced. The second section, word substitution in context, provides a comparative look at the OR (listed under *reader*), and the ER (listed under *text*), of all word-level substitution miscues.

The Procedure I and Procedure II Coding Forms indicate the miscues that involve influence of the reader's dialect with a *d* inside a circle beside the OR under the *reader* column. (Dialect is discussed in Chapters 2 and 3.)

Typescript

Teachers may consult the typescript directly for confirmation and clarification of Coding Form and Reader Profile information, or for data that do not appear on other forms:

1. Repeated Identical Miscues **RM** *on a Single Item Across Text* Studying a reader's response to the same linguistic unit throughout the entire text can help the teacher identify the many strategies a student uses. For example, if a student reads a text in which the word *canary* occurs eight times substitutes *cannery* for *canary* three times (each marked as a repeated miscue), then substitutes *carry,* then *cardinal,* then again *cannery,* and finally reads the last two occurrences correctly as *canary,* it is interesting to look at the text for factors influencing the OR changes. Because repeated miscues provide a powerful way to view students' changing strategies through transaction with the text, a place is provided to summarize repeated miscue information on the Reader Profiles for Procedures I and II. Betsy's repeated miscues are examined in this way later.

2. Multiple Miscues on a Single Text Item If a reader substitutes two or more words for a single text item, the first complete word or nonword is coded. The additional attempts on the same item may provide information about the reader's use of strategies. In the following example, the reader activates more and more information on each effort, in the attempt to produce the final observed response. His first strategy makes most use of graphophonic cues. By the time he substitutes *songs* for *signs,* he is using both syntactic and graphophonic cues with little focus on meaning.

(UC)
songs
song
sing
Mr. Pine put up all the signs in Little Town.

3. Partials Investigating partial attempts on words can help confirm what the Reader Profile and Coding Forms indicate in terms of the reader's sampling and predicting strategies. Frequency of partials gives information about reading efficiency. Proficient readers tend to produce more partials than less proficient readers, but these partials are almost always immediately corrected. Partials provide information on the reader's use of initial consonant and vowel cues. Betsy's miscue number 22 indicates she uses graphophonic, grammatical, and semantic information to produce *f-, forest* before she self-corrects to the ER, *far.*

4. Repetitions The position, extent, and frequency of repetitions reflect the reader's lack of efficiency and confidence. Examining points in the text where the reader's repetitions diminish or increase may indicate the predictability and complexity of the passage. After Betsy turns the second page of the story, she meets an unusual use of an idom on line M0301. The common idiom *in a hurry* is written as *in his hurry.* Betsy possibly predicts that the author is providing information about what is *in the house,* but *hurry* doesn't fit. Her grammatical and semantic sense cause her to correct, but she has to assure herself by repeating several more times. Is it possible that the author originally wrote *in his haste,* and an editor, thinking this was too complicated for a young reader, produced a more complex structure by substituting a higher frequency word?

5. Peripheral Field The possibility and extent to which something in the ER periphery can influence readers, possibly causing them to miscue, can be investigated only by looking at the typescript. Although there are syntactic and semantic considerations in Gordon's reading, his substitution of *your* for *the* may have been influenced by *your* appearing in the preceding line:

B0211 pointing to your heart.

212 Listen to the heartbeat

6. *Corrections* Both unsuccessful attempts to correct and instances in which a correct reading is abandoned are marked P on the Procedure I Coding Form. The markings on the typescript will clarify this coding. See Betsy's miscue on line 312 for an example of an *abandons correct* form rather than the more usual unsuccessful attempt at correction.

7. *Pauses* Pauses made during reading may indicate that the reader is sorting out information, hesitating before taking a risk, anticipating syntactic or semantic problems, working with unpredictable text, and so on. Betsy's three pauses in line 512 indicate that she is reflecting—possibly on the improbability of a cow hanging anywhere, especially between the roof of a house and the ground.

8. *Additional Miscues* Miscues other than those in the coded portion, as well as dialect and misarticulations, are available for analysis.

9. *Types of Miscues* The kinds and complexity of miscues (omissions, insertions, substitutions, etc.) can be identified and evaluated in the context of the total text. A reader who constantly omits words is less of a risk taker than one who is willing to predict and produce a substitution miscue on the basis of syntactic or semantic cues. Such information helps the teacher select and develop appropriate strategy lessons.

10. *Miscue Clusters* Examination of text units (words, phrases, clauses, sentences, etc.) in which there are large numbers of miscues can help identify points in the text that are complex and affect the reader's performance. Analysis of the text at these points may reveal unpredictable beginnings, extraneous or irrelevant information, or abrupt shifts in the expected linguistic or conceptual sequence. Betsy's miscue numbers 50 and 51 illustrate how a text may not be supportive of a reader's expectations.

11. *Location of Miscues* Examination of the typescript may shed light on where certain readers tend to miscue. For example, more miscues may occur during sections of narrative or dialogue, at the beginning or ending of a sentence, at the beginning, middle, or ending of a passage, in headings, or in the body of the text.

12. *Comments Written in the Margin of the Typescript* The reader's extraneous remarks (*that's a hard word, I'm going to skip that,* or deep sighing), as well as the teacher's comments about the reader's behavior during the session *(working hard with text, pointing, laughed out loud, enjoying story)* can be of help when describing the reader.

Some of these features have been researched in depth (Gollasch, 1982; Goodman and Goodman, 1978). Teacher/researchers may want to build on the available research or collect samples of one or more of the features to use as a focus for their own study.

Retelling

Teachers are often surprised when students who are considered to be poor readers present extensive and in-depth retellings. By the same token, when students who appear to read well orally fail to give substantial retellings, teachers are often bewildered.

Despite what may be considered by many as a halting and slow (19-minute) oral reading, during which Betsy produces many miscues per 100 words, her retelling indicates that she understood a great deal of the story. She especially had a good grasp of setting, characterization, and inferential information, such as theme and plot. Both Betsy's miscues and her story retelling indicate that she has a sense of the author's grammar; her retelling includes phrases and clauses that closely follow the author's sentence construction. Betsy has a sense of story grammar in that she uses her knowledge of the structure of stories to provide an orderly retelling with little change between her retelling presentation and the author's presentation of the text. Betsy's grasp of sentence and story grammar are strengths that should become part of the foundation of her reading program.

As Betsy retold the story, there was no indication that she saw any humor in it or that she related it in any way to her own life or to literature she may have heard or read previously. One reader was reminded as he read *The Man Who Kept House* of something that happened to him and his family; he gave this personal response:

> I was thinking about when we first moved into our new house. There was a garage outside that was full of junk and stuff people left. We had to do so much. It seemed like every time we got one thing done there was lots more things to do. It took us forever to get everything right. The harder the woodman worked the bigger mess he made. That was kind of like us.

Reading Interview

The views students have about reading and reading instruction may cause problems, especially for those who think of themselves as poor readers (see the discussion of the Reading Interview in the previous chapter). Students such as Betsy and Sara believe they are not good readers, and are willing to rely on their teachers or parents to help when they have a problem rather than to capitalize on their own resources. When readers have no faith in themselves, they often find themselves in instructional programs that confirm their views; the negativism is circular. At school, Betsy is considered to be a remedial reader, a label given to her when she first started reading instruction. This identification and the program developed for her may have contributed to Betsy viewing herself as a nonproficient reader.

Betsy's self-esteem as a reader must be heightened. She must concentrate on reading strategies that are productive and that help her to construct meaning. Strategies that inhibit and interfere with her reading progress will diminish as Betsy becomes more proficient at what she is already doing well and as her successful reading strategies are brought to conscious awareness through strategy lessons and discussions about her reading.

Betsy as a Reader: All RMI Data

When planning a reading program it is necessary to look at the readers' strengths first and then to consider areas in which they might improve. In this way it becomes possible to develop a whole language program in which strategy lessons can be used to support and capitalize on assets while minimizing weaknesses.

The Reader Profile indicates, and the other RMI data confirm, that Betsy is a moderately proficient reader. Obviously this young reader is doing many things right, and these are the things we must consider first.

Betsy's Use of Language Systems

Betsy's ability to predict on the basis of all the language systems, but especially through the use of grammatical structure, is evident (Grammatical Relations on Procedure I and Language Sense on Procedure II indicate this strength). Her ability to make predictions not only moves her along in the text, but allows her to disconfirm and then correct a response that does not sound right to her. She tries to make her reading syntactically acceptable; that is, she is concerned that her reading sounds like language.

To get a better understanding of Betsy's ability to use the grammatical system of language, it is a good idea to consult the Coding Forms and the Typescript, as well as the Reader Profile. Only twice in the coded section of *The Man Who Kept House* did Betsy produce a *totally* syntactically unacceptable sentence. In the first case, she corrected the miscues, and the second time she did not:

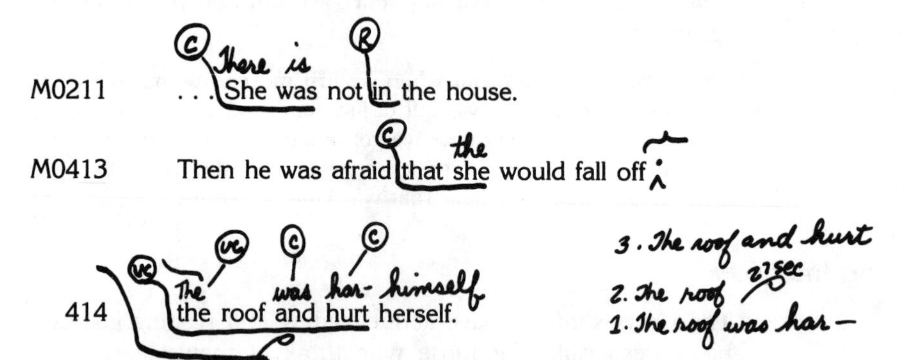

In M0211, Betsy had not yet firmly established the gender of the baby, and therefore she may have predicted a more generalized structure, such as *there is (no one to help the woodman in the house).* The structure itself supports her correcting strategy; that is, it does not sound like English to read: *there is not in the house.* However, in M0413, once Betsy predicted that *fall off* was the end of a sentence, she tried to make the first part of the next line into a sentence beginning. These miscues are obvious by her intonation patterns. She attempted to correct, not realizing that the problem was with an earlier segment of the sentence rather than at the beginning of the line (M0414). Betsy eventually continues reading, leaving a syntactically unacceptable segment of the original sentence (line M0414).

When readers make a number of miscues in a short amount of text (as with lines M0413 to 14), they are often overwhelmed with the complexity of the situation and, consequently, may leave the unacceptable segment without being able to correct it to an acceptable form. When this happens, it is important to check the retelling to determine whether the reader corrected silently and subsequently understood all or part of the section of the text.

When Betsy's miscues were syntactically acceptable, they almost always were semantically acceptable as well; or she corrected to achieve total acceptability. When the miscues were partially syntactically acceptable, they were also partially semantically acceptable, or Betsy corrected them to acceptability. Such strategies indicate proficient use of syntactic information and meaning construction.

Betsy's score of 17 percent on *overcorrection* in Procedure I Grammatical Relations does not interfere with her story comprehension because all the miscues in the *overcorrection* category are both syntactically and semantically acceptable. The miscues are marked *overcorrection* because in the total context of the story, correction is unnecessary. Betsy's *overcorrection* score confirms what was indicated by her intonation when reading and by her numerous repetitions—she overuses graphophonic features and is hesitant to allow even a completely acceptable miscue without correcting it. The three following examples illustrate that this overuse does not diminish Betsy's effectiveness as a reader, but does diminish her efficiency.

M0118 "I can do all that," replied the husband.

M0207 is sit here and move this stick . . .

M0615–6 . . . he should stay home and keep house.

The Reader Profile indicates that 20 percent of Betsy's miscues resulted in a *weakness* in Grammatical Relations. Almost all of these miscues were a result of partial syntactic acceptability and partial semantic acceptability; that is, Betsy was able to use the beginning of the sentence to help her make reasonable predictions. Unfortunately, she did not always confirm that these reasonable predictions were actually acceptable.

For the most part, however, Betsy produced language that was acceptable English structure. In the following instances, apparently the language was acceptable to Betsy's ear, she did not attempt to correct, and there was not enough semantic disruption to cause a reconsideration of her reading:

M0516 . . . she could hear the cow mooing, the

M0517–18 baby crying, and her husband shouting for help.

We have seen how Betsy's use of Grammatical Relationships give her a base for all the reading strategies. We will now look at the pattern of Meaning Construction (Procedure I) that focuses on Betsy's intent to build meaning as she reads. The role of Meaning Construction is especially apparent when we consider the correction strategy. Let's first investigate what Betsy did to cause 61 percent of her miscues to result in *no loss* of meaning. By referring to the Procedure I Coding Sheet, columns 2, 3, and 4, which comprise the patterns for Meaning Construction, we find that Betsy produced only three miscues that were semantically unacceptable after correction; about half of the remaining miscues were semantically acceptable. This consistent production of totally or partially acceptable miscues leads us to believe that Betsy was monitoring her reading to make sure it was making sense; that is, she was concerned with comprehension and therefore seldom accepted nonsense.

When her miscues resulted in partial semantic acceptability, Betsy corrected them well over half the time. These miscues show that she predicted potentially meaningful sentences. Following are typical corrections:

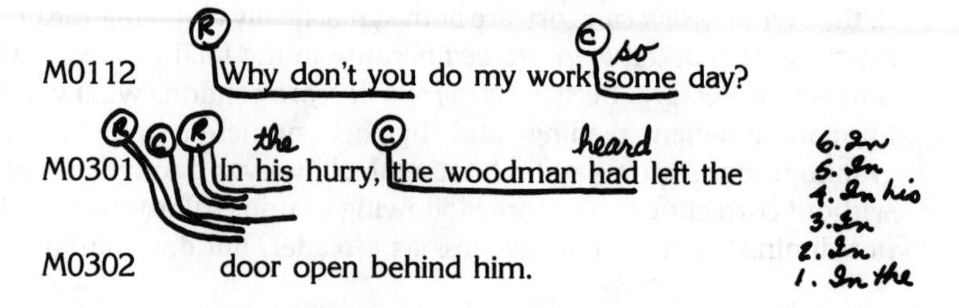

For the most part Betsy did not bother to correct miscues that were semantically acceptable and caused no change in meaning:

M0111 "I'd be glad to," said the wife. (I'll)

M0201 So the next morning the wife went off to (day)

202 the forest. The husband stayed home and

203 began to do his wife's work. (job)

When Betsy produced a semantically acceptable miscue that caused a minor meaning change in the text, the Partial Loss column reflects the fact that she usually did not correct:

M0208 Soon the cream will turn into butter." (So; buttermilk)

M0415–16 . . . He dropped the other end down the chimney. (to; 18 sec.)

Betsy's Use of Reading Strategies

At this point it is appropriate to look further at Betsy's correction strategies. From the preceding information it appears that Betsy used the correction strategy proficiently; that is, she corrected when the miscues were not completely semantically acceptable, and she often went right on reading when the miscue did not cause a significant change in the meaning of the total text. However, to understand Betsy's use of correction strategies more fully, we need to look at the patterns that emerge in the Loss column of Procedure I. On only three occasions did Betsy allow a completely semantically unacceptable miscue to go without correction. Twice she substituted a nonword for a text item (on M0205, $*shurn* for *churn*, and on M0513, $*gorun* for *ground*), and once she substituted a masculine pronoun for a feminine pronoun (on M0414, *himself* for *herself*). The long pause before $*shurn* and the regressions before $*gorun* indicate that Betsy thoughtfully made her best attempts.

In the case of the pronoun substitution, we will see that Betsy may have predicted a masculine pronoun related to the male woodman rather than a feminine pronoun related to the female cow. It also may be possible that 9-year-old Betsy did not attribute a gender to cows, or that she considered all cows to be male. Also, because it may have been incomprehensible for a cow to be on a roof, Betsy could not confirm the meaning at this point.

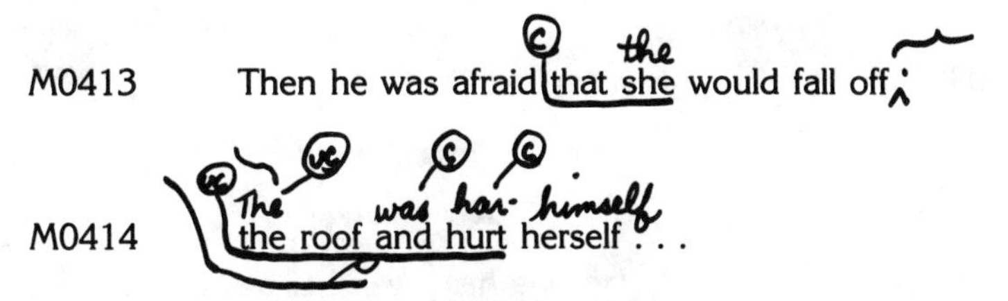

M0413 Then he was afraid that she would fall off
the
M0414 the roof and hurt herself . . .
The was har- himself

The remainder of the miscues that constitute Loss of Meaning Construction were partially semantically acceptable and were not corrected. Betsy makes many regressions and unsuccessful attempts at correction, suggesting that she was *aware* of her problems, but not proficient enough to make them acceptable. The complexity of *keeping house* was discussed earlier, in Chapter 5. The following represent typical partially semantically acceptable but uncorrected miscues.

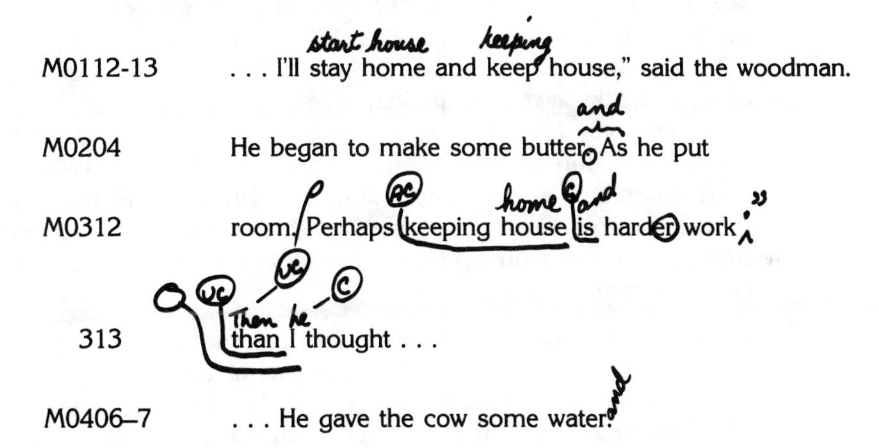

M0112-13 . . . I'll stay home and keep house," said the woodman.
start house keeping
M0204 He began to make some butter. As he put
and
M0312 room. Perhaps keeping house is harder work.
home and
313 than I thought . . .
Then he
M0406–7 . . . He gave the cow some water.
and

Betsy's Procedure I Reader Profile indicates that her use of graphic similarity is 55 percent *High*, 28 percent *Some*, and 17 percent *None*, and her use of sound similarity is 43 percent *High*, 30 percent *Some*, and 27 percent *None*. When the combined scores of *High* and *Some* are considered, we see that in 83 percent of Betsy's miscues, she produces a response that involves her use of graphic cues, and that in 73 percent she uses sound cues. Such high scores indicate a heavy reliance on the surface features of the text. On the other hand, Betsy is able to sample graphic and sound information when the meaning of the text is clear to her. This is evident from the Procedure I and Procedure II Coding Forms. In every instance of either no graphic or no sound similarity, Meaning Construction is marked *No Loss*, and Grammatical Relations is marked *Strength*. A look at such substitutions in context illustrates this pattern:

M0201 So the next ~~morning~~ *day* the wife went off to

M0214 brought her back ~~to~~ *in* the house.

Betsy's numerous repetitions on a single text item indicate that she is overly concerned with surface-level (graphophonic) accuracy; because she works hard at her problem, the difficulty becomes greater. Betsy is attending so closely to the letters and words (*has given* in M0402, following) that she doesn't sample on a broad enough base; she continues to work without the information more text could give her.

M0301 In his hurry . . .

M0402–3 . . . "No one has given her any grass to eat . . .

Betsy's repeated miscues show her strengths as well as some obstacles as she transacts with the text. Such miscues also indicate that a well-written story provides many opportunities for students to learn more about reading at the same time they are learning about the content of the selection. For example, *house* and *home* occur frequently throughout the text. While *house* occurs 14 times (in lines 106, 107, 113, 116, 211, 214, 303, 312, 412, 502, 516, 606, 611, and 616), *home* occurs six times (in lines 103, 113, 114, 202, 611, and 616). It is important to determine not only *when* Betsy miscued on these two words, but also when she predicted either *house* or *home* appropriately.

Betsy read *home* as expected once, before she miscued on it; she read *house* seven times before she miscued on it. She miscued on *home* twice out of the six text possibilities, and on *house* once out of the 14 text possibilities. If we collected and counted miscues without studying the text, it would be easy to conclude that Betsy confused the two words. When the context is examined, however, the following pattern emerges:

1. *home* is miscued on only when *stay* precedes it.
2. *house* is miscued on only when *keeping* precedes it.
3. There are regressions before *keep* and *keeping house* in lines 106 and 107.
4. Betsy never uses the term *keeping house* in the retelling.
5. Betsy eventually, by transacting with the story, solves the problem of *staying house* and *keeping house.*

We can conclude that Betsy has a problem with the concept of *keeping house,* which she ultimately resolves in her reading. Her retelling reveals that she understands the concept when she tells about the chores the woodman became involved in as he attemped to keep house.

Her substitutions of *$shurn* (M0205) and *cream* (M0304 and M0307) for *churn* also show Betsy's concern for making sense. She first substitutes a nonword (*$shurn*), then predicts a meaningful real word *(cream)* the next two times the word *churn* occurs. By doing this, she produces semantically and syntactically acceptable sentences. Betsy shows through her repeated miscues that she can develop her reading by transacting with a story that is meaningful to her and is long enough to allow her to learn from the text.

Betsy's Strengths and Weaknesses

Although we have pointed out Betsy's strengths, it is helpful to summarize her abilities, for it is on these abilities that her reading program will be built.

1. Within a moderately proficient range, Betsy uses all the reading strategies to comprehend and move forward in the text. Betsy uses *initiating and sampling strategies* by readily attempting assigned stories, reading the title and beginning the story in the conventional upper left-hand corner. Many of her miscues indicate that she samples on the basis of all available language cues. However, on occasion she labors over discrete surface-text features to the point of disrupting her reading. Betsy's *predicting strategies* are evidenced by her use of all the systems of language, especially the grammatical system, to take linguistic risks. Her *correcting strategies* are revealed in her concern with constructing meaning by making her reading sound like language and make sense; she often corrects her miscues to achieve these aims.
2. Betsy *learns from text.* Her repeated miscues indicate that she uses text to develop familiar concepts and language structures.
3. Betsy uses her *knowledge of story grammar.* Her miscues, especially those made during the last two-thirds of the text, along with her retelling, indicate her knowledge of how a story is organized. Such knowledge helps her move through the text and aids in her retelling of the passage.
4. Betsy's insight into *characterization* and her ability to gain information even when it is not explicitly stated in the text is revealed in her retelling.
5. Betsy uses *background experiences and information.* She brings to the reading of *The Man Who Kept House* some knowledge about folk tales and the chores males and females are usually assigned in such stories. She understands things about porridge and fireplaces.
6. Betsy has *control of language.* Her retelling indicates that she can take turns during a conversation. She is able to articulate her ideas and thus communicate by using language.

Areas of concern have become evident through the analysis of Betsy's miscues, retelling, and by looking at her current reading program:

1. Betsy lacks concepts relating to a sod house, to cows eating on roofs of houses, and to making butter in churns.
2. Betsy lacks linguistic experiences related to certain idioms and structures, i.e., *in his hurry, keeping house,* and the past perfect tense, *has given.*
3. Despite her understanding of the plot, Betsy is unaware of mood (humor) in the story.
4. Occasionally, Betsy overuses the surface-level cueing systems involving graphics and sounds.
5. Betsy lacks confidence in herself. This is shown through her hesitancy in selecting her own reading material as well as her failure to understand that past experiences are of value and should be brought to the reading task.
6. Betsy holds a view of reading and of herself as a reader that does not always support her risk-taking abilities.

An Instructional Program for Betsy

With the information gathered from the analysis of Betsy's reading and with knowledge about the reading process and reading instruction, we are now ready to develop a whole language program including personalized strategy lessons for Betsy (Y. Goodman and Burke, 1980).

Whole Language Experiences for Betsy

Betsy must be invited daily to listen to literature, read or told, to read and write on her own, and to enter into discussions with her peers and teachers about literature and about the reading and writing processes.

Betsy's teacher, Ms. Blau, reads to the students on a fairly regular basis. This practice not only should be continued but should be thought of as a necessary and integral part of the reading curriculum. By hearing stories, Betsy can use the strategies of sampling, predicting, and correcting in a stress-free listening setting. Ms. Blau might enlist the librarian's help in selecting folktales and other genres that will broaden and deepen Betsy's and her classmates' knowledge of literature.

Betsy is willing to read, for short periods of time, materials selected for her by Ms. Blau. An important step in becoming an independent reader is learning that reading involves self-selection of reading material. Betsy must take some initiative in finding her own material, or at least in making selections from a collection of materials made with her interests and abilities in mind. Teachers can help Betsy make selections by introducing her to stories that reflect her background, experiences, and interests, and by not withholding the kind of written material she sees the more proficient students reading.

By self-selecting stories, poems, and books from a variety of genres (folk stories, fiction, fantasy, realism, history, etc.), Betsy can become immediately involved in personal reading. She should be encouraged to have at least three kinds of reading material in her desk at all times. Many teachers encourage students to have a book of their own choosing *(mine),* a book suggested by the teacher or librarian *(yours),* and a book mutually chosen with the teacher, a friend, a penpal, or a parent *(ours).* By having a combination of materials, such as a magazine, a novel, and a poetry book immediately available, Betsy can again make choices about her own reading—the beginning of a sense of control and accomplishment.

Throughout the reading and retelling of *The Man Who Kept House,* Betsy showed no signs of enjoying or being amused by the story. In the stories read to the class, the teacher may select several that move both children and teacher to laughter or tears. The teacher may also invite Betsy to read books that will help her realize that authors stir emotions, so it is acceptable and expected that readers will laugh or shed a tear when they read or hear such literature. Betsy might be moved by *A Taste of Blackberries* by Doris Buchanan Smith and amused by *You Can't Catch Me!* by Michael Rosen, a British poet, *Putrid Poems,* a collection of Australian poems compiled by Jane Covernton, or *Jacob Two-Two and the Hooded Fang* by Canadian author Mordecai Richler. Laura Inglis Wilder's books not only reach out to children emotionally, but provide background knowledge (for example, information about sod houses) that help children when they read stories such as *The Man Who Kept House.*

Betsy's reading program should include individual and small-group reading conferences in which she is invited to discuss with the teacher and with other students the relationship between her life and the literature she is reading. To ensure that she has ample opportunity to talk about her reading, *Literature Groups* may be organized. In this activity, four or five books are carefully chosen with the student's interests and abilities in mind. The students are invited to indicate their first and second preferences of books. On the basis of their selections, the readers are placed into groups of five or six. The most proficient and the least proficient readers may be in the same group. Each student in a group has a copy of the book. The group decides on a minimum number of pages to be read in the time between group meetings. Those who want to read beyond the minimum number may do so.

Because students move right along in the text, it usually takes no more than two weeks to read and discuss a book.

The students often keep a log in which they note their reactions and responses to the literature, as well as any questions they may have. Twice each week the children and teacher come together to discuss the book, other literature, and their own reading. They share the impact and the influence the literature has on them. For their own reasons (*it grabbed me, I didn't understand this; this is a good description; this part reminds me of* The Great Gilly Hopkins; *I wish I could write like this*), they may want to read short sections from their book to other members of the small group.

During such shared reading, students begin to use and appreciate their own background of experience and come to realize how what they already know helps them understand what the author is expressing. Students in their *Literature Groups* compare themes and plots of stories, talk about similarities and differences in characters and in relationships, and use their reading to learn. They learn that people do not always respond in the same way and that it is possible to learn different things from the same reading experience. Students broaden their own views about the many ways to respond to literature. The teacher, as a member of the *Literature Group,* is expected to read, write, and respond along with the students.

Students benefit greatly from the continuity of their group meetings during the reading of the selected book: If it is not possible to meet regularly, there are other ways to participate in shared reading. One means of organization is to ask students to write on the board their names and the titles of the books they have finished and are ready to discuss. When enough class members have read the same book, they come together to share their responses to the literature. Initially the teacher meets with the groups to discuss and demonstrate ways of sharing literature; some students are soon able to handle literature-sharing groups on their own.

Betsy needs to read silently most of the time to develop more effective reading. If she is going to read aloud it should be a genuine literacy event: reading stories and making tape recordings for younger children, reading her own writing to interested classmates, reading recipes and directions to others, and participating in plays, reader's theater, and choral reading. Betsy's text repetitions and multiple attempts on single words will diminish when she has a real audience for which to prepare her reading. Such an activity will help her become a more efficient reader.

Work in the content areas of social studies, science, math, art, and others can provide evidence that build concepts for reading literature. For example, a visit to a farm, discussions of shelters including sod houses, and investigation of an old-fashioned churn at a local history museum (actually seeing and handling one, as well as gathering information from reference books), can help Betsy build a background of knowledge that will help her understand the confusing parts of *The Man Who Kept House.*

When content-area textbooks are unsuitable for Betsy because of difficult syntax, format, or concepts, a group of conceptually related materials may be selected to provide support. These materials (often called "skinny books") include professionally authored single-concept texts, materials written by teachers or students, and short chapters or articles taken from other books, magazines, or newspapers that add appropriate and related background information. Topical collections of books, stories, poems, games, newspaper articles, and so on, help many students gather and organize information by presenting related concepts in a variety of formats and genres. Betsy's use of syntactic and semantic cues indicate that she can handle difficult concepts if they are presented in cohesive and predictable structures.

Students must have time to read. Betsy's reading strategies will become stronger when she has the opportunity to practice her reading undisturbed over reasonable amounts of time and on a daily basis. We suggest that 70 to 80 percent of the time allotted to reading instruction be devoted to real reading and writing, with 20 to 30 percent of the time spent working on instructional strategy lessons that include thinking and talking about reading and writing.

Betsy not only needs to talk and read about experiences that connect with her life and interests; she needs to write about them as well. With constant invitations and support, Betsy can generate her own topics for writing stories, poems, articles, and plays. She may be invited to write in journals or learning logs. For example; "This is what I learned in science today, and here are my questions" or "*The Summer of the Swans* made me think about people with handicaps." Betsy may also want to respond to literature by extending it (e.g., writing another chapter or changing the ending of *The Man Who Kept House*).

Reading Strategy Instruction

The activities presented here are intended to build on Betsy's strengths in using all the systems of language. They will help her gain more proficiency in sampling, predicting, and confirming. These lessons are suitable not only for Betsy, described as a moderately proficient reader, but for many other readers as well. Teachers will need to modify the strategies to make them suitable for their own students.

Reading strategy instruction is a major component of a whole language program. Proficient readers know tacitly that sampling from print, predicting, and confirming or disconfirming their predictions through correction procedures are necessary reading strategies. Proficient readers are constantly asking and answering the questions: "Does this make sense?" "What will happen next?" and "Does this sound like language?" Moderately proficient readers do not make full and consistent use of the strategies of initiating and sampling, predicting and guessing, and correcting. Nonproficient readers use procedures that interrupt the reading process (e.g., focusing on small units of language such as letters, sounds, syllables, words), and they do not develop facility and flexibility with the integration of the reading strategies.

Reading Strategy Lessons

Reading strategy lessons encourage readers to use their prior experiences and knowledge, attend to the context of circumstances and situation, and use what they know about language (i.e., semantics, syntax, graphics, sound) in order to process written language; that is, to sample, predict, confirm, and construct meaning. Reading strategy lessons are authentic literacy events (Edelsky and Smith, 1984) in which the reader's strengths are used to minimize weaknesses.

Many strategy lessons involve the total class, but some activities are handled individually, or in a small group with students who have similar needs or interests. If a group is formed, the instructional time is typically brief, and the members of the group change regularly. Assigned reading groups based on general ability present a problem for students who are keenly aware that seven other children and a teacher may catch their *mistakes* (the term *miscue* is usually not used in such settings); this contributes to making reading seem a real chore—a fight for perfection. Betsy needs a real audience when she reads aloud, and members of assigned reading groups do not constitute a real audience; too often they are either waiting for mistakes or waiting for their turn. In addition, being assigned to a low, average, or high reading group categorizes and labels students. Too often these labels dictate the curriculum and direct students' attitudes about reading and about themselves. Betsy needs to gain confidence in herself as a reader; therefore, she must never be placed in a situation in which she perceives herself as a failure.

Talking About Reading and Writing

To see herself as a real reader and writer and consequently to bolster her self-confidence, Betsy needs to become aware of the role literacy plays in her life. To achieve this, Ms. Blau must find time to discuss with her and all students *the many uses* of reading and writing. She may develop a lesson with all the students about the literacy that surrounds them, or it may be done in small groups or as an individual conference.

Betsy needs to be consciously aware that reading and writing take place in countless settings, appear in a variety of genres, and serve numerous functions. Such awareness prevents students from assuming that only people who read novels are readers and only people who write stories are writers. Students come to realize that they are readers when they take a carton off the grocery shelf or follow the traffic signs when riding their bicycle, and that they are writers when they take down a phone number, leave a note, or write an entry in a diary.

As mentioned earlier, the Reading Interview reveals that many students express a subskills model of reading even though they are moderately proficient readers. The gap between what students think they should do and what they actually do when they are reading naturally often causes problems, especially when they come to difficult text. In order to get Betsy, when she is reading difficult text, to apply the strategies she uses very well when reading predictable text, she needs to know, for example, that it is permissible to substitute or even skip words; to continue reading even when she has some degree of uncertainty about concepts; and always to relate what she is reading to her past experiences and knowledge.

It is important to help students such as Betsy understand that the goal of reading is not to read accurately but to read for meaning. A good time to discuss this notion is when the teacher miscues or when a student produces a high-quality miscue. The teacher helps students see that for such miscues to occur, the reader had to be predicting and monitoring for meaning—the major goal in reading. Teachers such as D. Goodman (1987) help readers see themselves as detectives searching for clues to meaning; selecting some, discarding others, but always continuing on the trail to solve the reading detective game—seeking meaning in their reading.

Preview, Overview, Review

Many students such as Betsy often come to their reading without preparing themselves for it; that is, without searching their background for information that will help them construct meaning while reading. The activity of *brainstorming* helps students draw on what they know about a particular subject before they actually begin their study. For example, if students are to read a chapter in their science book about pollution, the teacher asks the students to mention everything they know about the subject. The students talk together in groups of two or three for three or four minutes, listing everything they know about the subject. Then they come together in a larger group to read their list to the class and to the teacher, who writes their ideas on the board. The teacher guides the students in organizing the information. Graphic displays on the chalkboard may simply categorize information by listing it under headings such as air pollution, noise pollution, and so on, or organize it, for example, by placing the word *pollution* in the center of the board and drawing lines out in spokes to subheadings. Some of the lines from the spokes may connect (for example, industrial pollution has to do with more than one kind of pollution), thus forming a web.

After this *preview,* the students quickly look at the materials to be studied. As they *overview* the materials, they add to the web or to the list. The teacher may want to add to the overview. The language of the subject matter is used in this supportive situation. The teacher encourages the students to use the web as a framework for their ideas, and to add to it as they read the material. If the idea frame is transferred to a large sheet of paper or the student's notebook, the class may return to it to amend, add, or delete ideas as they believe appropriate after they have read a portion of the text.

After reading the text, the students discuss the categorized lists or web in order to relate what they have learned to previously learned information. Such an activity will help students such as Betsy see how they can use their own knowledge and the information provided by classmates as a resource for reading, and how new information relates to and builds on old information.

Schema Story Strategy Lesson

Betsy has a strong sense of grammar at both the sentence and the story level (see her Grammatical Relations and Retelling scores). This sense of sentence and story helps her predict and construct semantically cohesive texts even when she does not feel completely secure in her own understanding of all the concepts in the passage. In this strategy lesson, the teacher divides a structurally and conceptually well-written story into several sections. The divisions are made at points in the story that are highly predictable, both syntactically and semantically. Each part of the story is pasted on a piece of construction paper, and one section is given to each member of a small group. The teacher asks the students to read their sections silently. It is crucial that the passages be of sufficient length to convey an idea or ideas; one or two paragraphs will usually be suitable. Good examples can be found in newspapers written for children or carefully selected chapters from science or social studies texts. The readers are then encouraged to think about what may have happened in the text before their section, and to predict what will happen next. The teacher asks the person who thinks he or she has the beginning of the story to read it. The students listen for clues and volunteer to read their passage when they think it is their turn. After the entire text is read, the students discuss how they made decisions about the position of their section in the total passage.

If this strategy is used individually, the student receives all the sections of the story, reads them, and then arranges them in an order that makes sense syntactically and semantically. This strategy and the discussion of what happens as students participate in it will help readers such as Betsy understand that they can make decisions based on their knowledge of the story's organizing structure and its semantic intent.

Selected Deletions Strategy Lesson

One means of encouraging Betsy to take risks by making predictions involves the careful deletion of words within a syntactically and conceptually well-constructed story. Ms. Blau may select a story suitable to Betsy's interests. After the first paragraph, words or phrases are deleted that are highly semantically and syntactically predictable. Only words or phrases that Betsy is sure to be able to fill in on her own are deleted. Betsy is not enough of a risk taker to attempt to fill in the blanks unless an acceptable response is ensured. For more confident readers, less predictable words may be deleted.

A single miscue does not provide enough information on which to make decisions about strategy lessons, but if in subsequent readings Ms. Blau finds other instances of Betsy's miscue involving a past perfect verb tense such as *has given* in line M0402, a strategy lesson may be constructed in which such verbs are deleted. Success with such a strategy lesson may indicate that miscues involving the past perfect tense, for example, have more to do with overattention to graphic information than with problems with syntax. In Betsy's case, it appears that this is a syntactic structure she has not previously met in print. If so, the selected deletion strategy lesson will allow her to become more familiar with the past perfect structure. It is a good idea to look through the *typescript* to determine whether a reader has miscued on any similar form or unit of language. In *The Man Who Kept House,* there is, unfortunately, no other instance of the past perfect verb tense.

A brief discussion concerning the strategy lesson procedure and how Betsy decided which word or phrase fit the slots will help her become more confident that she can fill in deletions because of what she is bringing to the passage; she and the author become partners in the construction of meaning.

Predicting Strategy Lessons

Betsy's miscues are often semantically acceptable (see her Meaning Construction score and Question 2 on her Coding Form). The strategies she uses to reflect her concern for meaning should be pointed out to her as strengths so that she will understand that they are aids to her reading. Betsy often "keeps going" in the text with a high degree of efficiency (e.g., the substitution of *day* for *morning* and *job* for *work*), but on occasion she is willing to accept nonsense (the substitution of the nonword *$gorun* for the text item *ground*). Because of her strong focus on meaning, it would be appropriate to encourage Betsy to move from nonword to meaningful substitutions, as she has already demonstrated that she is capable of doing. Because of her experience with a subskill reading program, Betsy needs to be assured that it is more important to make sense of the text than to sound out letters, syllables, and words. Betsy needs to develop confidence in the author and in herself to construct meaning.

One activity that encourages readers to predict involves using a selection that has an unfamiliar term in it. The term may be unfamiliar in three ways: (a) the concept is unknown, (b) the pronunciation is unknown, or (c) both the concept and the pronunciation are unknown. The students read the story individually, with a partner, or in a small group. When the readers come to a word they don't know, they think of all the possible words that could be substituted for the unknown word. The teacher may list these on the board, or the students may write them on a piece of paper. As the author provides more information and as the readers progress in the text, other substitutions are listed, and rejected suggestions are deleted from the list. By the end of the story, the students decide on their best substitution and explain what clues they used to make their decision.

The discussion following the activity will vary according to the readers. Betsy should be reminded that using letters and sounds is a way of confirming good guesses, but should not be used as the only cueing systems. Discussion might include all the ways of selecting cues that help readers predict the meaning of words and phrases. Some students may come to understand that all concepts are not equally important to all readers, and that readers must pursue the ones they believe to be most important, helpful, and interesting. It follows that, unless they are highly interested in the concepts of the text, it may not be necessary to learn how to pronounce the term or to learn about the concepts in depth. Discussion concerning the use of resources may be helpful; for example, *when* it is appropriate and efficient to use the dictionary, to go to other reference books, or to ask someone else for help.

The Selected Deletion and the Predicting Strategy lessons are both suitable for readers who are less proficient than Betsy. These strategies encourage readers to keep progressing in the text, to continue bringing their past experiences to the text, and to construct something that makes sense and sounds like language. Readers less proficient than Betsy may be advised to omit unknown words, say *blank* and go on reading, or put in a nonword place holder, as Betsy does with *$gorun* for *ground.*

Another predicting strategy lesson gets the reader involved in gaining cues from the entire text in order to make sense of unknown names. The Naming Strategy lesson encourages readers to continue reading, making acceptable substitutions for difficult-to-pronounce names of people, places, and things. The students are reminded that they must be concerned with gathering information about the character (Kokovinis in *The Great Brain*) or the place (Appalachian Mountain range) rather than in laboriously sounding out the name. In order to move along in the text, the substitution of *Koko* for *Kokovinis* and *the mountains* for *Appalachians* may be made. The pronunciation of the labels for the concepts can be determined through consulting a resource or by discussion at a more appropriate time.

You Become the Author

To help Betsy become more of a risk taker, to strengthen her proficiency in predicting, and to encourage her ability to confirm, she is invited to choose a book from five or six paperback books with interestingly illustrated covers. Betsy is asked not to peek inside the book, but on the basis of the title, cover picture, and cover print to predict what the book she chose will be about. Betsy can discuss her predictions, write them, or do both. She is then invited to become the second author and to write a book that she can compare with the professionally authored text. (Inevitably students think that their story surpasses the original.)

Less elaborate predictions can be made using headlines of news articles, titles of chapters, graphs, or illustrations. The students need not always write their predictions, but may discuss them, and after reading the text compare their guesses with the predictions of other students and with the actual text.

Discussion following the activity may lead Betsy to think about the information provided by the author and the information she adds in order to make a prediction. Students should ask themselves whether the reading is easier because of the anticipation of text that results from predicting.

Readers such as Brian (see Chapter 7) should be asked whether the prediction strategy helps them reach a goal Brian mentioned in the reading interview: to read *quicker*. The strategy lessons presented here, along with a discussion about what it is that causes slow reading, and when it is and is not appropriate to read slowly, are important and helpful. Betsy needs to be shown that the more she knows about a topic and the more interest she has in it, the faster and easier it will be to read about the topic. Ms. Blau may read to the students or ask them to read two passages, one of great interest and one of remote or no interest. A discussion of the two passages following the reading will help illustrate the point further.

Retrospective Miscue Analysis

At this point in her reading proficiency Betsy is quite likely her own best teacher. To build on her existing strengths, she may tape-record stories and then evaluate her own reading by listening to the tape and asking, "Am I making sense? Does my reading sound okay?" This kind of retrospective analysis of her own miscues should probably be done with the teacher first. After answering these questions, Betsy might talk with other students and the teacher about appropriate strategies to use to construct meaning.

Betsy needs to understand that her reading need not be free of miscues. A retrospective examination of her overcorrections and examples of her syntactically and semantically acceptable miscues may be discussed. Examples from other readers, including the teacher's miscues, may shed light on the discussion.

Students who appear not to be comprehending but who try to convince others and themselves that they have actually read, benefit from tape-recording and then critiquing their own reading. Recorded retellings of stories with or without the recorded readings help students consider their comprehension of the text.

Research being done in Retrospective Miscue Analysis (RMA) indicates a move toward more proficient reading as students who have participated in RMA instruction become aware of the strengths of their own reading strategies (Marek, in press; Weatherill, in press; Woodley and Miller, 1983)

Retelling Strategy Instruction

The retelling experience may be expanded into an instructional strategy lesson. When the aided retelling is completed, Ms. Blau may want to ask questions specific to Betsy's comprehension. For example, it may be useful to learn why readers use a particular reading strategy, or to learn about the influence of readers' background knowledge or of the influence of the text on comprehension. This is the opportune time to ask students why they did what they did as they read. If, for example, readers persistently substitute one word for another and then at a certain point in the text they self-correct, the teacher may ask what prompted the correction. The following questions may be asked following the aided retelling to provide insights into a reader's strategies.

Is there any (concept, idea, sentence, word) in the story that gave you trouble? (Offer the book to the reader to find the trouble spot.)
Why did you leave out this word?
You said (reader's word, nonword, or phrase) here. What do you think that means?
Have you ever heard this word before? What does it mean?
Did you know what this was before you began the story, or did you learn it as you read?
Where were the easiest and the hardest parts of this story? Explain.
Remember when you said (character named by reader) used a (nonword)? Can you explain that?
Did you understand the story from the very beginning?
Were there times when you didn't understand the story? Tell about those times. Find where they were in the story.
Did the pictures help or bother you? Explain.

Ms. Blau may have asked Betsy questions after the aided retelling of *The Man Who Kept House* in a dialogue such as the following:

T: Betsy, did you have any questions about the story? *(no response, Hands the book back to Betsy.)* Anything at all?

B: Uh uh *(no).*
T: Would you read this part again? *(turns to the second page of the story)*
B: "He began to make some butter. And he put the cream into the churn, he said . . ."
T: How did the woodman make butter?
B: He put the cream in a . . . churn.
T: What is a churn?
B: You can make butter in it I suppose. I never saw one. We made butter last year, but in a jar.
T: Well, you've got the right idea. You put the milk in a jar. A churn is a special kind of container for making butter. I'll see if I can find a churn or a picture of one to show you. Or if you are interested perhaps you can look in some of our reference books and find some information about one. Betsy, when the cow fell off the roof, you said she . . . uh . . . had the rope tied to her leg. Then what happened?
B: She was hanging on the roof.
T: *(sketches a house with a flat roof)* Betsy, will you draw . . . uh . . . where the cow was hanging?
B: *(Betsy draws the cow hanging between the roof and the ground.)*
T: Now, will you tell me where the cow was hanging?
B: The cow fell off the roof and the rope caught her and she was hanging between the roof and the ground.
T: *(points to the text)* Betsy, will you read this again?
B: "As for, as for the cow, she hang between the roof and the ground, and there she had to stay."
T: Betsy, would you like to read another story similar to the one you just read?
B: Yes, I liked it pretty good.
T: Well, Wanda Gag wrote a story called *Gone Is Gone.* Remember that she wrote *Millions of Cats?*
B: I know that book. We got it over there. I liked it.
T: *Gone Is Gone* is in the library. Ms. Bender *(librarian)* will help you find it and some other books Wanda Gág has written.

Ms. Blau might also suggest that Betsy look at other authors' versions of the folktale about a bragging husband who changes places with his wife for a day. David McKee's adaptation is *The Man Who Was Going to Mind the House;* William Wiesner's is *Turnabout.*

Cambourne (1986) suggests that written retellings be used to evaluate the developmental link between students' natural competence in oral language and their developing competence in written language. He offers a retelling strategy lesson that involves students in making predictions, reading for a variety of purposes, recalling literal and inferential information, sequencing, summarizing, paraphrasing, and evaluating. The strategy lesson would be suitable for Betsy as well as other readers of varied proficiency.

The teacher asks students in a small group to predict a story plot on the basis of a title only, and to write their predictions quickly (2 minutes maximum). The students then predict some words or phrases that a reader would expect to encounter in the text (2 minutes maximum). Students read and compare with others their plot and word predictions. Each student then makes one comment about one other group member's predictions; everyone listens. The students then read the text silently. The teacher may direct the students to read as if (a) they were going to tell the story to their best friend when finished, or (b) they were going to take a test over the material. After reading, the students write out the story as if they were writing it for someone who had not read it. In pairs, the students compare their retellings. They may ask each other:

What did I include/omit that you did not?
Why did you include/omit this?
Do you think I changed anything that alters the meaning?
Did I use any words/phrases that are not in the story, but are good substitutions?
If you could take a bit of my retelling and include it in yours, which part would you take? Why?

Strategy Lessons for Proficient Readers

Sometimes we like to say that the best way to help proficient readers is to stay out of their way. Certainly this is true to the extent that we must not impede readers by requiring them to fill out worksheets and workbooks, go through a programmed text, or read uninteresting and demeaning materials. The teacher makes the path smoother *for all readers* by coordinating a reading program that is rich in literature written by professional and student authors, and by encouraging students to select their own reading materials.

Through individual conferences and group discussions, teachers encourage readers to experience and respond to literature. They help students become acquainted with authors' styles and their ways of developing characters, themes, plots, and settings. Teachers help readers understand characterization when they invite students to investigate the ways in which authors reveal their characters. Do we come to know and love or hate a character through conversations, actions, reactions, and thoughts of the character, or through the narrative itself? Questions concerning the plot are not difficult for students to answer: Is there action or does the story drag? Is the story believable and is it original, or is it unbelievable and old hat? Is the reader prepared for events and is there a logical sequence of cause-and-effect happenings? Is there a climax, and do the events lead to the climax?

The teacher leads the students to think about themes that overpower the reader and those that emerge naturally from the text. Readers are encouraged to take responsibility for the discussions, and are urged to respond to the literature with honest comments and real questions.

Readers may be helped to look at human relationships such as those between children and parents. For example, readers may compare the relationship of parents and child in *The One-Eyed Cat* by Paula Fox with that of parent and children in *Homecoming* by Cynthia Voight. Readers may compare books on the same subject, or books written by the same author. They may collect folktales of one country and then present orally or in writing everything learned about that country including information about its geography, climate, people, beliefs, customs, products, and so on.

Students may study the characteristics, language, and style of one poet or illustrator. One student may want to present a poem in a variety of ways such as a tape recording with background music and sounds; and make slides, photographs, or a videotape. Students may be encouraged to look for stereotypes in their reading. They may select books dealing with a particular minority group and present a summary of findings after they have read the books. As students read more and more historical fiction, a recurring theme, such as the fight for freedom, may be found in books from different historical periods. Students may want to collect and write informational books and materials on a topic of interest (e.g., the solar system, transformers, computers, cooking, ecology), and then share these with other students including younger students.

The teacher's role is to establish a supportive environment in which students can with proficiency and eagerness discover their power with language.

Strategy Lessons for Nonproficient Readers

The reading strategies of sampling, predicting, and confirming are the same for all readers. Differences in proficiency lie in the way readers handle these strategies. Strategy lessons that focus on initiating, sampling, predicting, and confirming help nonproficient readers gain a better understanding and consequently a better control of the reading process.

As with all other readers, nonproficient readers need a whole language reading program. They need to be invited to do what proficient readers do; their attention drawn to the inferential aspect of reading. Many of the strategy lessons suggested for Betsy can be adapted for nonproficient readers.

There are other strategy lessons that are especially supportive for nonproficient readers. K. Hoskisson (1975) suggests that the teacher or a supportive proficient reader sit with the student and read the story *along with* the nonproficient reader. The *Assisted reading* should be in a natural voice and cadence. As readers come to a familiar repetitious word or phrase, they are encouraged to read it alone. Many troubled readers will not read, but will attend to the print, hum, or read an occasional word or phrase. This personal one-on-one setting is much like the setting of a parent and child reading together. There is no pressure, and the student begins to feel comfortable with the material and with the reading process.

Doake (1981) and Holdaway (1979) have helped popularize the *Big Book* concept, in which favorite picture books are enlarged so that a group of students can see, read, and discuss the text together. After reading with the teacher, children enjoy "playing school" with the Big Book as well as reading the standard-size book on their own. The language of Big Books is highly predictable. There are repetitious or cumulative words and phrases, and the concepts in the story are very familiar. Big Books are available from some publishing companies; teachers may make them; or students may make their own. Older students enjoy writing and illustrating Big Books for younger children.

In *Estimate, Read, Respond, Question* (Watson and Gilles, in press), students quickly look over the text (often content-area material) and estimate how far they can read with comprehension. Students make a check mark with a pencil in the margin at that spot. Each student then begins reading. In most cases the reading is silent, but it may be oral, or for readers who have major problems, *Assisted Reading* may be used. When the readers reach the check mark, they quickly respond to the text by telling what it reminds them of; giving a brief retelling; or giving their opinion of it. The student then *asks the teacher* a question about the text. The questions may be "real" ones in which the student seeks information and uses the teacher as a resource person, or the questions may be ones in which the information is actually in the text itself. After the student's questions, the teacher may or may not ask a question. The procedure is supposed to move quickly so that the reader does not get bogged down with responding or with the questioning procedure. The estimating procedure should not be omitted, as it gives the reader control of the situation. Discussion following the strategy has to do with what factors cause readers to make the estimations that they make, how readers in their responses relate the text to their lives, and what happens when readers ask rather than answer questions.

An Invitation

The reading strategy lessons suggested here do not by any means cover all the rich and supportive activities that help students become enthusiastic and proficient readers. A rich literacy community brings readers of *all* abilities together to participate in literacy events in which they become personally involved, learn from each other, and develop a lifelong and eager zest for reading and writing.

Within the past decade, educators referring to themselves as whole language teachers have pooled their knowledge and experiences to develop collections of strategy lessons and activities that are based on the theory, research, and view of reading explored in this book. We invite you to investigate these collections (see Bibliography) as well as to use your own knowledge of language, human development, and the reading process to organize a literate community for your classroom or clinic and to plan positive reading experiences for all your students.

Appendix A

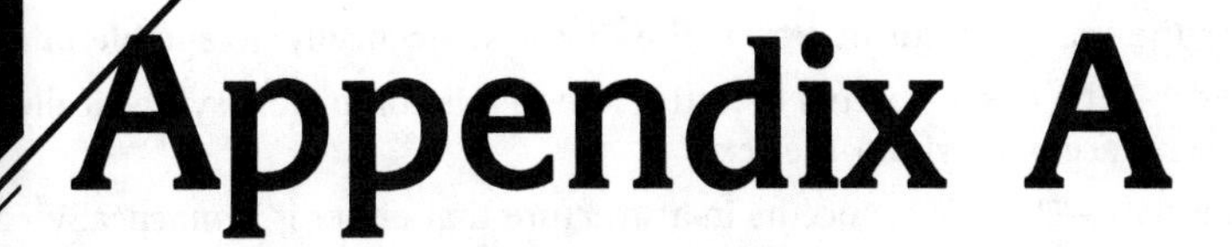

Summary of Procedures

Procedure I Questions
Procedure I Patterns
Procedure II Questions
Procedure III Questions
General Procedure for Marking Miscues

PROCEDURE I QUESTIONS

Question 1: *Syntactic acceptability*

Does the miscue occur in a structure that is syntactically acceptable *in the reader's dialect?*

Y (Yes)—The miscue occurs in a structure that is completely syntactically acceptable within the sentence and within the text.

P (Partial)—The miscue occurs in a structure that either is syntactically acceptable with the first part of the sentence or is syntactically acceptable with the last part of the sentence. Or, the miscue is syntactically acceptable within the sentence, but not within the complete text.

N (No)—The miscue occurs in a sentence that is not syntactically acceptable.

Question 2: *Semantic acceptability*

Does the miscue occur in a structure that is semantically acceptable *in the reader's dialect?* Semantic acceptability cannot be coded higher than syntactic acceptability..

Y (Yes)—The miscue occurs in a structure that is completely semantically acceptable within the sentence and within the text.

P (Partial)—The miscue occurs in a structure that is semantically acceptable with either the first part of the sentence or is semantically acceptable with the last part of the sentence. Or, the miscue is semantically acceptable within the sentence, but not within the complete text.

N (No)—The miscue occurs in a sentence that is not semantically acceptable.

Question 3: *Meaning change*

Does the miscue result in a change of meaning? This question is asked only if the miscues are both syntactically and semantically acceptable (Q1 = Y and Q2 = Y).

N (No)—Within the context of the entire passage no change in meaning is involved.

P (Partial)—There is inconsistency, loss, or meaning change of a minor idea, incident, character, fact, sequence, or concept.

Y (Yes)—There is inconsistency, loss, or meaning change of a major idea, incident, character, fact, sequence, or concept (see note below).

Question 4: *Correction*

Is the miscue corrected?

Y (Yes)—The miscue is corrected.

P (Partial)—There is either an unsuccessful attempt to correct, or the expected response is read and then abandoned.

N (No)—There is no attempt to correct.

Question 5: *Graphic similarity*

How much does the miscue look like the text?

H (High)—A high degree of graphic similarity exists between the miscue and the text.

S (Some)—Some degree of graphic similarity exists between the miscue and the text.

N (None)—No degree of graphic similarity exists between the miscue and the text.

Question 6: *Sound similarity*

How much does the miscue sound like the expected response?

H (High)—A high degree of sound similarity exists between the miscue and the text.

S (Some)—Some degree of sound similarity exists between the miscue and the text.

N (None)—No degree of sound similarity exists between the miscue and the text.

Note: Many have raised questions about the use of Y to equal loss in Question 3, while Y is equal to acceptability in Questions 1 and 2. This is a purposeful shift in order to cause coders to consider the quality of the miscue in relation to all the cueing systems and strategies automatically.

Procedure I Patterns

Patterns for Constructing Meaning

No Loss		*Partial Loss*		*Loss*
2 3 4	2 3 4	2 3 4	2 3 4	2 3 4
Y N Y	Y Y Y	Y P N	Y Y N	N – N
Y N N	P – Y	Y N P	Y P P	N – P
Y P Y	N – Y	Y Y P	P – P	P – N*
			P – N*	

*This pattern will be Loss except in a few cases. The criteria for Partial Loss needs to be considered carefully (see discusssion).

Patterns for Grammatical Relationship

Strength	*Partial Strength*	*Overcorrection*	*Weakness*
1 2 4	1 2 4	1 2 4	1 2 4
N N Y	Y N N	Y Y Y	N N N
P N Y	Y P N	Y Y P	P N N
Y N Y	Y N P		P P N
P P Y	Y P P		N N P
Y P Y			P N P
Y Y N			P P P

PROCEDURE II QUESTIONS

Question 1: *Syntactic Acceptability*

Is the sentence syntactically (grammatically) acceptable in the reader's dialect and within the context of the entire selection?

Y—The sentence, as finally produced by the reader, is syntactically acceptable.

N—The sentence, as finally produced by the reader, is not syntactically acceptable (partial acceptability is not considered in this procedure).

Question 2: *Semantic Acceptability*

Is the sentence semantically acceptable in the reader's dialect and within the context of the entire selection? (Question 2 cannot be coded Y if Question 1 has been coded N).

Y—The sentence, as finally produced by the reader, is semantically acceptable.

N—The sentence, as finally produced by the reader, is not semantically acceptable (partial acceptability is not considered in this procedure).

Question 3: *Meaning Change*

Does the sentence, as finally produced by the reader, change the meaning of the selection? (Question 3 is coded only if Questions 1 and 2 are coded Y).

N—There is no change in the meaning of the selection.

P—There is inconsistency, loss, or change of a *minor* idea, incident, character, fact, sequence, or concept in the selection.

Y—There is inconsistency, loss, or change of a *major* idea, incident, character, fact, sequence, or concept in the selection.

Question 4: *Graphic Similarity*

How much does the miscue look like the text item?

H—A high degree of graphic similarity exists between the miscue and the text.

S—Some degree of graphic similarity exists between the miscue and the text.

N—No degree of graphic similarity exists between the miscue and the text.

Question 5: *Sound Similarity*

How much does the miscue sound like the expected response (ER)?

H—A high degree of sound similarity exists between the miscue and the ER.

S—Some degree of sound similarity exists between the miscue and the ER.

N—No degree of sound similarity exists between the miscue and the ER.

PROCEDURE III QUESTIONS

Question 1: *Syntactic Acceptability*

Is the sentence syntactically acceptable in the reader's dialect and within the context of the entire selection?

Y—The sentence, as finally produced by the reader, is syntactically acceptable.

N—The sentence, as finally produced by the reader, is not syntactically acceptable (partial acceptability is not considered in this procedure).

Question 2: *Semantic Acceptability*

Is the sentence semantically acceptable in the reader's dialect and within the context of the entire selection? (Question 2 cannot be coded Y if Question 1 has been coded N.)

Y—The sentence, as finally produced by the reader, is semantically acceptable.

N—The sentence, as finally produced by the reader, is not semantically acceptable (partial acceptability is not considered in this procedure).

Question 3: *Meaning Change*

Does the sentence, as finally produced by the reader, change the meaning of the selection? (Question 3 is coded only if Questions 1 and 2 are coded Y.)

N—There is no change in the meaning of the selection.

P—There is inconsistency, loss, or change of a *minor* idea, incident, character, fact, sequence, or concept in the selection.

Y—There is inconsistency, loss, or change of a *major* idea, incident, character, fact, sequence, or concept in the selection.

Question 4: *Graphic Similarity*

How much does the miscue look like the text item?

H—A high degree of graphic similarity exists between the miscue and the text.

S—Some degree of graphic similarity exists between the miscue and the text.

N—No degree of graphic similarity exists between the miscue and the text.

General Procedure for Marking Miscues

Substitutions

Write the miscue above the appropriate text:

There
Where is Sven?

this is a
"No," said the voice.

Was something wrong with Papa?

Omissions

Circle the omitted text item:

We thought up different ways to jump.

Insertions

Write the OR above the caret ∧ used to mark the insertion:

B0321 First listen ∧

B0718 The other way

719 is ∧ to take care of your heart

Repetitions

Draw a line under the repeated text portion and up in front of the first word, ending in a circle. The letter in the circle shows the reason for regressing.

1. Anticipating and Reflecting

(R) The village where I grew up . . .

2. Repeating and Correcting

B0301 Blood (C) feels feeds

302 all the (C) c— cells and (C) oranges organs

3. Repeating and Abandoning a Correct Form

(AC) complaining
She was always comparing.

4. Repeating and Unsuccessfully Attempting to Correct

(UC) Clarida / Clarence
Her name was Clarible.

5. Repeating That Affects More Than One Miscue:

B0408-9 . . . the heart is (a) sensitive machine . . .
(C) sense (UC)

Additional Markings

1. Partials

(C) por-
M0405 The man left the porridge . . .

2. Nonword Substitutions:

$distroubles
If it bothers you to think of it as baby sitting . . .

3. Dialect, Misarticulations and Other Language Variations:

like(d)
. . . just about everybody likes babies.

$pecific
He had a specific place in mind.

$hangabers
They make hamburgers over the fire.

4. Intonation Shifts:

récord
He will record her voice.

6. Split Syllables:

The lit|tle girl yelled her head off.

7. Pauses:

23 sec.
M0105 do all day while I am away cutting wood?"

Appendix B

Gordon's Miscue Analysis: The Beat of My Heart

Marked Typescript
Retelling Script
Expository Retelling Guide
Procedure I Coding

MARKED TYPESCRIPT

Name *Gordon*

Date *May 23* Grade/Age *9 years*

Teacher *Mr. Murphy*

Reference *Beat of My Heart*

THE BEAT OF MY HEART

0101	Lub-dup . . .
0102	Lub-dup . . .
0103	Lub-dup . . .
0104	This strange sound
0105	is the sound
0106	of a wonderful machine
0107	inside your body.
0108	It is the sound
0109	of your heart beating.
0110	Your heart is a pump
0111	which will never
0112	stop working
0113	as long as you live,
0114	but it can rest
0115	even while it is working.
0116	Your heart
0117	is a hollow muscle
0118	divided into four parts.
0119	It is about the size

Handwritten miscue markings: 0101 *Lu-bump* RM (*Lu sounds like initial sounds in love.*); 0102 *Lu-bump* RM; 0103 *Lu-bump*; 0104 *8 sec.* before "strange", "sound" circled, 2; 0105 *$sound* 3; 0106 *8 sec.* before "wonderful", ⓒ *m- m-* on "machine"; 0108 ⓒ *It's* 4 over "It is", *6 sec.* before "sound"; 0109 *heartbeat* 5 over "heart beating", "ing" circled; 0110 *bump* 6; 0111 ⓒ *near* 7 over "will never stop"; 0114 ⓒ "rest" 8 insertion; 0115 *E* over "even"; 0117 *$mu-si'-cle* 9; 0118 ⓒ *in-* over "into"; 0119 Ⓡ "the size".

0120 of your fist. [R] [C] first[10]

0121 As you grow,

0122 it too will grow in size. [11]

0201 To find out

0202 where your heart is, [C] the[12]

0203 put your right hand

0204 in the middle [R]

0205 of the left side of your chest. [C] chests[13] ch-

0206 Now move your fingers around

0207 until you find

0208 the spot where

0209 the heartbeat is strongest. [8 sec.] strong[14] st-

0210 Your hand is now

0211 pointing to your heart.

0212 Listen to the heartbeat [your[15]]

0213 of a friend [R]

0214 by putting your ear

0215 to his chest. [on[16]]

0216 To hear the sound even better, [s[17]]

0217 hold an empty mailing tube [a[18]]

0218 or a rolled-up piece [C] roll-

0219 of heavy paper

0220 to your friend's heart. [C] [19]

0221 When the heart goes lub, [lump[20]] ← attempt by the author to represent a sound that doesn't have an equivalent English word. Based on miscue #1.

0222 it is drawing in blood.

0223 When it goes dup,

0224 it is pushing blood out

0225 to all parts of the body.

0226 Your heart has

0227 this most important job to do —

0228 pumping blood

0229 to all parts of your body.

0301 Blood feeds

0302 all the cells and organs

0303 of your body

0304 so that they can do

0305 their own special work

0306 to keep you physically fit.

0307 Your heart pumps blood

0308 from your head

0309 to your toes,

0310 to your liver

0311 and your lungs.

0312 Just as a wheel

0313 can turn slowly or fast,

0314 your heart can work

0315 at a slow or a fast pace.

0316 If you want to see

0317 how your heart changes quickly

0318 from working at a slow pace

0319 to working at a faster pace,

0320 try this.

0321 First listen

0322 to a friend's heartbeat

0323 and count the number of beats

0324 in a minute.

0325 Now ask your friend

0326 to run fast

0327 for about a minute.

0328 Then listen to his heart again.

0329 How many times a minute

0330 is his heart beating now?

0401 Count his heartbeats again

0402 after he has rested

0403 for a minute.

0404 By comparing the number

0405 of heartbeats

0406 under these different conditions,

0407 you will discover that

0408 the heart is

0409 a sensitive machine

0410 working inside the body.

0501 You can test this fact again
0502 by checking your own heartbeat.
0503 Place three fingertips
0504 of your right hand
0505 on the inside of your left wrist.
0506 You will feel the beat
0507 of your heart.
0508 This is called your pulse.
0509 Count the number of times
0510 your heart beats in a minute.

0601 Now, run for a minute
0602 and count the heartbeats
0603 in your pulse again.
0604 Lie down and rest for a minute,
0605 and then count once more.
0606 See how exercise makes
0607 your heart work
0608 harder and faster?
0609 Exercise helps your heart
0610 to become stronger
0611 and be able
0612 to do its work better.
0613 Your heart beats

0614 as long as you live.

0615 It rests for ⅙ of a second
0616 between every beat.

0617 When you are asleep or resting
0618 your heart beats

0619 at a slower rate.
0620 This rest gives your heart

0621 a chance to keep

0622 in good working condition

0623 as well as to grow

0624 bigger and stronger.

0701 Since you are becoming
0702 taller and heavier

0703 every school year,

0704 your heart must grow larger, too.

0705 Your bigger body needs
0706 a bigger motor to keep it
0707 in good working order.

0708 There are many ways
0709 to take care of your heart,

0710 but the two best ones are
0711 the easiest to do.

0712 One is to get lots of exercise

0713 by playing vigorous games

0714 out of doors.

0715 Play games that have lots

0716 of running and jumping,

0717 or hitting and kicking balls.

0718 The other way

0719 to take care of your heart

0720 is to be sure you get

0721 at least ten hours of sleep

0722 every night

0723 and do restful things

0724 from time to time

0725 throughout the day.

0726 On and on your heart beats—

0727 year in and year out.

0728 Lub-dup . . .

0729 Lub-dup . . .

0730 Lub-dup . . .

Retelling Script

Gordon's Combined Aided and Unaided Retelling

T: Thank you, Gordon. Now, if you'll close the book I'd like to ask you some questions. First, would you tell me what you remember about this selection?

G: Well, it was telling you about . . . about your body and how . . . how it works and . . . um . . . it tells you where . . . from what place . . . to what place your blood goes and . . . um . . . as you get bigger everything has to get bigger with it or else it stops. Ah, it was telling you how you can listen to your heart beat . . . um . . . and it tells you what to eat and . . . um . . . how to test out . . . *(20 seconds)*

T: Anything else?

G: Well, no.

T: You said it told how you can listen to your heartbeat. How did it say to do that?

G: It said that . . . ask your friend to run and then listen to his heartbeat. To count how many heartbeats and then you can lie down and then count again and . . . um . . . um . . . it said that you could listen to a friend's heartbeat and . . . um . . . you could do it by yourself. I can't think of anything else.

T: So, you said a couple of things. You said that it said this is how it works. Do you remember how it said it works?

G: Oh, not really.

T: Do you remember anything about how it works?

G: Well *(15 seconds),* you remember where the blood went?

T: Okay, tell me about it.

G: First it goes to your . . . goes to your . . . I forget where. I think it was your heart and then it goes to your toes and then it goes to your liver . . . ah . . . then it . . . it, I think it goes up again and it keeps on doing that and you can also put your finger on your heart to see how . . . to see where your heart beats the most . . . beats the heaviest.

T: Tell me about that beating the heaviest.

G: You put your fingertips on where your heart is and you try to find where it is the heaviest just with your fingers and then you count how many thumps you hear.

T: Have you ever done anything like that?

G: No.

T: So you said that you counted the thumps. Did it tell about what the heart sounded like at all?

G: Yeah, it said it was something like the bump.

T: Why do you think this selection was in a book? What do you think they wanted you to remember from reading?

G: Well, because in school you have to read things like that. You have to know all those things about your body. They told you a little bit about it so you could answer questions.

T: What was the main thing that this was about?

G: Your heartbeat.

T: Uh hum, so from reading this, what did you figure out was the most important thing?

G: That it beats.

T: And why is that important?

G: So you can stay alive.

T: So what does the blood do to help you stay alive?

G: It goes?

T: (10 seconds) Yes?

G: It goes from the heart. It goes down to your toes, it goes to your liver and it goes back down again . . . in a pattern.

T: You told me what you learned from reading this. Did you know anything about the heart before you began reading this?

G: Well, I knew blood went through your body, but I didn't know where it was going . . . what parts it was going to.

T: Okay, so the new information you got from this was what? Can you just sum that up?

G: That where the blood goes from place to place and um . . . um . . . ah . . . let's see . . . There were so many things, but I can't remember them all. I can't remember.

T: You said something about . . . that you could . . . um . . . test out? What was that part about?
G: I learned that you can . . . well . . . I knew that you could test some parts of your body. You could count how many heartbeats you had after you did certain things.
T: Like what?
G: Like running.
T: What happens when you run?
G: You get out of breath . . . uh . . . and your heart beats faster?
T: Is that . . . tell me about the heart beating faster.
G: It just does.
T: Did this selection tell you anything about what you should do for your heart?
G: Not really.
T: Do you know how you can take care of your heart?
G: You can take vitamin pills. You can drink milk and eat things that are good for you.

Gordon's Aided (Directly Cued) Retelling Continues

T: Gordon, the author told us something about the size of the heart. Can you remember what that was?
G: I think it gets bigger as you get bigger.
T: Do you remember the size of the heart?
G: It's one-six or something like that.
T: In this chapter the author tells us about certain . . . uh . . . experiments you can do to find out about the heart. You've mentioned asking your friend to run and then listening to his heartbeat. Can you tell me more about how you would do that?
G: You just listen.
T: How?
G: I don't know.
T: You also said you could put your finger on your heart to see where you heart beats the heaviest. Where exactly would you put your fingers?
G: On your chest.
T: Anywhere else?
G: Uh-uh *(no)*
T: Did the author compare the heart to anything?
G: Not that I can remember.
T: Gordon, would you draw a picture of the heart?
G: *(Draws a heart shape. Does not indicate the four parts as mentioned in the passage.)* Well, that's sorta like it, but not too much like the picture in the book.
T: I understand that.

Gordon's Retelling Specifically Related to the Reading Process

T: Gordon, did you think that story was easy or hard to read?
G: Kinda hard.
T: Why?
G: I didn't know a lot of the stuff.
T: *(hands the book back to Gordon)* Would you show me some part that you thought was hard?
G: *(spends 45 seconds looking at the story)* I think it was all hard.
T: Was any part easy?
G: It wasn't too bad, but not too easy.
T: What does this mean? *(points to "Lub-dup, Lub-dup . . .")*
G: That's the heartbeat.

T: Did you know that at the beginning of the story?
G: No. I found out and kinda guessed.
T: Gordon, can you remember what you were thinking as you read this? *(points to lines 0116–0118)* Will you read it?
G: "Your heart is a hollow . . ." I don't know that word (muscle) . . ."divided into four parts."
T: What are you thinking about.
G: I could divide my heart in four parts. *(divides his picture of a heart into four parts)*
T: You did divide it into four parts. Another question . . . how did you get this? *(points to* wrist *on line 0505)*
G: ". . . left wrist." I knew it wasn't right, but I got it when . . . *(reads silently ahead to line 0508)* . . . I read this about your pulse.
T: Is there anything you want to tell me about how you felt when you read that passage?
G: Um . . . no . . . it was kinda long.
T: Anything else?
G: Uh uh *(no)*
T: Gordon, thanks for reading. I enjoyed talking with you.

Reader: *Gordon* Date: *May 23*

Retelling Guide: The Beat of My Heart

Specific Information
(50 points) *18*

The Heart *(10)* *2*

Rests even while working *"tells how your body works"*
Is a hollow muscle
Divided into four parts *(Gets this on rereading)*
About the size of your fist
✓ Grows as you grow; needs to be bigger as body gets bigger

Blood *(8)* *4*

With one beat blood is drawn in; with the next beat blood is pushed out
Blood feeds cells and organs which is needed for the body to be physically fit
✓ Blood pumps to liver to lungs *goes in a pattern to toes*

Heartbeat *(8)* *2*

The heart can beat slow or fast (Analogy)
Heartbeat felt in your wrist is your pulse
Rests 1/6 second between beats
Beats at a slower rate when asleep or resting

Conditions *(8)* *5*

Exercise helps heart become stronger and do work better.
Two best ways of taking care of heart: vigorous games and at least 10 hours of sleep every night

Experiments Making Use of Specific Information: *(16)* *5*

✓ Find your heart by moving fingers around on the left side of your chest. Find where the beat is strongest. *(3) beats the heaviest* *2*

Listen to the heartbeat of a friend by putting your ear to his chest. Listen by using mailing tube or paper roll. *(3) you can listen to your heart* *0*

Learn how heart changes quickly from slow to fast pace by listening to a friend's heart. Count beats in a minute. Ask friend to run fast for a minute. Count beats in a minute. Count beats again after friend has rested for a minute. Compare number of beats. *(6)* *3*

Check own heartbeat by taking your pulse rate for a minute. Run for a minute and count again. *then count again* Lie down for a minute and count again. *(4)* *0*

Generalizations
(25 points) *6*

Heart is a machine inside the body
Heart has an important job to do
3 Exercise makes heart work harder and faster *partial*
3 Rest gives heart a chance to go slower *partial*

Major Concepts 3
(25 points)

Is a most important organ for life
There are ways we can find out about our hearts

Retelling

Specific Information	18
Generalizations	6
Major Concepts	3
Total Points	27

Inferences Did not appear to infer from text. After talking with the teacher about the heart (after retelling), drawing a picture of the heart, and rereading, Gordon divided his picture of the heart into four parts.

Comments Gordon shows very little interest in this article. He apparently did not bring much background information—"I didn't know a lot of that stuff." Learned a few things as he read: Lub-dup is a heartbeat.

Has bits of information but can't tie the pieces together.

MISCUE ANALYSIS PROCEDURE I CODING FORM

READER *Gordon* DATE *May 23*

TEACHER *Mr. Murphy* AGE/GRADE *9 yrs.* SCHOOL *M.L. King*

SELECTION *Beat of My Heart*

LINE No./MISCUE No.	READER	TEXT	1 SYNTACTIC ACCEPTABILITY	2 SEMANTIC ACCEPTABILITY	3 MEANING CHANGE	4 CORRECTION	See 2, 3, 4 MEANING CONSTRUCTION: No Loss	Partial Loss	Loss	See 1, 2, 4 GRAMMATICAL RELATIONSHIPS: Strength	Partial Strength	Overcorrection	Weakness	5 GRAPHIC SIMILARITY: H	S	N	6 SOUND SIMILARITY: H	S	N
1	Lu-bump	Lub-dup	Y	Y	N	N	✓			✓				✓			✓		
2	———	sound	N	N	—	N			✓				✓	—	—	—	—	—	—
3	$soud	sound	P	N	—	N			✓				✓	✓			✓		
4	It's	It is	Y	Y	N	Y	✓					✓		—	—	—	—	—	—
5	heartbeat	heart beating	Y	Y	N	N	✓			✓				✓			✓		
6	bump	pump	Y	N	—	N			✓		✓			✓			✓		
7	near	never	N	N	—	Y	✓			✓				✓			✓		
8	rest ^ Even	rest even	P	N	—	Y	✓			✓				—	—	—	—	—	—
9	$mu-si'-cle	muscle	Y	N	—	N			✓		✓			✓				✓	
10	first	fist	Y	P	—	Y	✓			✓				✓			✓		
11	———	too	Y	Y	N	N	✓			✓				—	—	—	—	—	—
12	the	your	Y	Y	N	Y	✓					✓				✓			✓
13	chests	chest	Y	N	—	Y	✓			✓				✓			✓		
14	strong	strongest	Y	Y	N	N	✓			✓				✓			✓		
15	your	the	P	P	—	N			✓				✓			✓			✓
16	on	to	P	P	—	N		✓					✓		✓				✓
17	sounds	sound	Y	Y	N	N	✓			✓				✓			✓		
18	a (d)	an	Y	Y	N	N	✓			✓				✓					✓
19	friend	friend's	P	N	—	Y	✓			✓				✓			✓		
20	lump	lub	Y	Y	N	N	✓			✓				✓			✓		
21	bump	dup	Y	Y	N	N	✓			✓				✓			✓		
22	feels	feeds	Y	P	—	Y	✓			✓				✓			✓		
23	oranges	organs	Y	N	—	Y	✓			✓				✓			✓		
24	———	physically	Y	P	—	N		✓			✓			—	—	—	—	—	—
25	fit	fat	Y	N	—	N			✓		✓			✓			✓		
			COLUMN TOTAL																
			PATTERN TOTAL																
			PERCENTAGE																

a. TOTAL MISCUES ____

b. TOTAL WORDS ____

a ÷ b × 100 = MPHW ____

(Goodman, Watson, Burke)

MISCUE ANALYSIS PROCEDURE I CODING FORM

READER Gordon DATE May 23

TEACHER Mr. Murphy AGE/GRADE 9 yrs. SCHOOL M.L. King

SELECTION Beat of My Heart

LINE No./MISCUE No.	READER	TEXT	1 SYNTACTIC ACCEPTABILITY	2 SEMANTIC ACCEPTABILITY	3 MEANING CHANGE	4 CORRECTION	See 2, 3, 4 MEANING CONSTRUCTION: No Loss	Partial Loss	Loss	See 1, 2, 4 GRAMMATICAL RELATIONSHIPS: Strength	Partial Strength	Overcorrection	Weakness	5 GRAPHIC SIMILARITY: H	S	N	6 SOUND SIMILARITY: H	S	N
26	$liver (sounds like diver)	liver	Y	N	—	Y	✓			✓				✓			✓		
27	if	a	P	P	—	Y	✓			✓						✓			✓
28	the (ə)	a (ā)	P	P	—	N							✓			✓			✓
29	rate	pace	N	N	—	Y	✓			✓				✓				✓	
30	chances	changes	Y	P	—	Y	✓			✓				✓			✓		
31	quick Ⓓ	quickly	Y	Y	N	Y	✓					✓		✓			✓		
32	place	pace	Y	P	—	Y	✓			✓				✓			✓		
33	listen ‸ To	listen to	P	P	—	Y	✓			✓				—	—	—	—	—	—
34	a few minutes.	a minute.	Y	Y	P	N		✓		✓				—	—	—	—	—	—
35	the	his	Y	Y	N	N	✓			✓					✓				✓
36	beat	heart	Y	Y	N	N	✓			✓				✓				✓	
37	Now	How	N	N	—	Y	✓			✓				✓			✓		
38	yet	now	Y	Y	P	N		✓		✓						✓			✓
39	finished	has rested	Y	Y	P	Y	✓					✓		—	—	—	—	—	—
40	$coopering	comparing	Y	N	—	N			✓		✓			✓			✓		
41	———	a	N	N	—	Y	✓			✓				—	—	—	—	—	—
42	sense	sensitive	Y	N	—	P			✓		✓			✓				✓	
43	face	fact	Y	P	—	Y	✓			✓				✓				✓	
44	then	three	N	N	—	Y	✓			✓				✓					✓
45	fingers	fingertips	P	P	—	N		✓			✓			✓			✓		
46	side	inside	P	P	—	N		✓			✓			✓			✓		
47	$wist	wrist	Y	N	—	P			✓		✓			✓			✓		
48	find	feel	Y	Y	N	N	✓			✓					✓			✓	
49	Then	This	N	N	—	P			✓				✓	✓				✓	
50	you	your	P	P	—	Y	✓			✓				✓			✓		
			COLUMN TOTAL																
			PATTERN TOTAL																
			PERCENTAGE																

a. TOTAL MISCUES ____

b. TOTAL WORDS ____

a ÷ b × 100 = MPHW ____

(Goodman, Watson, Burke)

MISCUE ANALYSIS PROCEDURE I CODING FORM

READER GORDON DATE MAY 23

TEACHER MR. MURPHY AGE/GRADE 9 YRS. SCHOOL M.L. KING

SELECTION BEAT OF MY HEART

LINE No./MISCUE No.	READER	TEXT	1 SYNTACTIC ACCEPTABILITY	2 SEMANTIC ACCEPTABILITY	3 MEANING CHANGE	4 CORRECTION	See 2, 3, 4 MEANING CONSTRUCTION: No Loss	Partial Loss	Loss	See 1, 2, 4 GRAMMATICAL RELATIONSHIPS: Strength	Partial Strength	Overcorrection	Weakness	5 GRAPHIC SIMILARITY: H	S	N	6 SOUND SIMILARITY: H	S	N
51	one	once	Y	P	—	N			✓		✓			✓			✓		
52	——	to	Y	Y	N	N	✓			✓				—	—	—	—	—	—
53	a	as	P	P	—	Y	✓			✓				✓					✓
54	1–6 (one-six)	1/6	N	N	—	N			✓				✓	✓			✓		
55	minute	second	P	P	—	N			✓				✓			✓			✓
56	on	or	P	P	—	Y	✓			✓				✓					✓
57	rest	resting	P	P	—	Y	✓			✓				✓			✓		
58	that	at	P	P	—	Y	✓			✓				✓			✓		
59	a	in	P	P	—	N			✓				✓			✓			✓
60	work	working	P	P	—	Y	✓			✓				✓			✓		
61	you	to	P	P	—	N			✓				✓		✓		✓		
62	big	bigger	P	P	—	N		✓					✓	✓			✓		
63	strong	stronger	N	N	—	N			✓				✓	✓			✓		
64	——	school	Y	Y	N	N	✓			✓				—	—	—	—	—	—
65	large	larger	Y	Y	N	Y	✓					✓		✓			✓		
66	Then	There	N	N	—	Y	✓			✓				✓				✓	
67	best two	two best	Y	Y	N	N	✓			✓				—	—	—	—	—	—
68	ways	ones	Y	Y	N	N	✓			✓					✓		✓		
69	a lot	lots	Y	Y	N	N	✓			✓				—	—	—	—	—	—
70	——	vigorous	Y	Y	P	N		✓		✓				—	—	—	—	—	—
71	is	——	P	P	—	N			✓					—	—	—	—	—	—
72	for	from	N	N	—	Y	✓			✓				✓				✓	
73	——	in	Y	N	—	Y	✓			✓				—	—	—	—	—	—
						COLUMN TOTAL	47	9	17	45	10	5	13	45	5	7	35	9	13
						PATTERN TOTAL	73			73				57			57		
						PERCENTAGE	64%	12%	23%	62%	14%	7%	18%	79%	9%	12%	61%	16%	23%

a. TOTAL MISCUES 73

b. TOTAL WORDS 635

a ÷ b × 100 = MPHW 11.5

(Goodman, Watson, Burke)

Appendix C

Blank Forms

Procedure I Coding Form
Procedure I Reader Profile
Procedure II Coding Form
Procedure II Reader Profile
Procedure II Retelling Summary
Procedure IV Conference Form
Man Who Kept House Typescript
Narrative Retelling Guide
Beat of My Heart Typescript
Expository Retelling Guide
Reading Interview

MISCUE ANALYSIS PROCEDURE I CODING FORM

READER ____ DATE ____

TEACHER ____ AGE/GRADE ____ SCHOOL ____

SELECTION ____

			1	2	3	4	See 2, 3, 4			See 1, 2, 4				5			6		
			SYNTACTIC ACCEPTABILITY	SEMANTIC ACCEPTABILITY	MEANING CHANGE	CORRECTION	MEANING CONSTRUCTION			GRAMMATICAL RELATIONSHIPS				GRAPHIC SIMILARITY			SOUND SIMILARITY		
LINE No./MISCUE No.	READER	TEXT					No Loss	Partial Loss	Loss	Strength	Partial Strength	Overcorrection	Weakness	H	S	N	H	S	N
a. TOTAL MISCUES ____ b. TOTAL WORDS ____ a ÷ b × 100 = MPHW ____			COLUMN TOTAL																
			PATTERN TOTAL																
			PERCENTAGE																

(Goodman, Watson, Burke)

MISCUE ANALYSIS PROCEDURE I READER PROFILE

	%	%
MEANING CONSTRUCTION		
No Loss		
Partial Loss		
Loss		
GRAMMATICAL RELATIONS		
Strength		
Partial Strength		
Overcorrection		
Weakness		
GRAPHIC/SOUND RELATIONS		
Graphic		
High		
Some		
None		
Sound		
High		
Some		
None		
RETELLING		
Characters		
Events		
Total		
Holistic Score		

MPHW ____ TIME ____

READER DATE

TEACHER AGE/GRADE SCHOOL

SELECTION

REPEATED MISCUES ACROSS TEXT

LINE	READER	TEXT	COMMENTS (place in text, correction, etc.)

COMMENTS

(Goodman, Watson, Burke)

MISCUE ANALYSIS PROCEDURE II CODING FORM

LANGUAGE SENSE

SENTENCE NO.	No. MISCUES IN SENTENCE	1 SYNTACTIC ACCEPTABILITY	2 SEMANTIC ACCEPTABILITY	3 MEANING CHANGE	PATTERN (See 1,2,3) Strength YYN	Partial Strength YYY YYP	Weakness NN_ YN_
	COLUMN TOTAL						
	PATTERN TOTAL						
	PERCENTAGE						

READER | DATE

TEACHER | AGE/ GRADE | SCHOOL

SELECTION

WORD SUBSTITUTION IN CONTEXT

SENTENCE No.	MISCUE NO.	READER Dialect ⓓ	TEXT	4 GRAPHIC H	S	N	5 SOUND H	S	N
			COLUMN TOTAL						
			TOTAL MISCUES						
			PERCENTAGE						

a. TOTAL MISCUES ____
b. TOTAL WORDS ____
a ÷ b × 100 = MPHW ____

(Goodman, Watson, Burke)

MISCUE ANALYSIS PROCEDURE II READER PROFILE

	%	%
LANGUAGE SENSE		
Strength		
Partial Strength		____
Weakness		
GRAPHIC/SOUND RELATIONS		
Graphic		
High		
Some		____
None		
Sound		
High		
Some		____
None		
RETELLING		
Holistic Score		
or Comments		

MPHW ____ TIME ____

READER DATE

TEACHER AGE/GRADE SCHOOL

SELECTION

REPEATED MISCUES ACROSS TEXT

LINE	READER	TEXT	COMMENTS (place in text, correction, etc.)

COMMENTS

(Goodman, Watson, Burke)

MISCUE ANALYSIS PROCEDURE II RETELLING SUMMARY

READER ______________________________

DATE ______________________________

SELECTION ______________________________

Holistic Retelling Score (optional): ______________________________

Plot Statements

Theme Statements

Inferences

Misconceptions

Comments

(Goodman, Watson, Burke)

MISCUE ANALYSIS PROCEDURE IV INDIVIDUAL CONFERENCE FORM

READER ______________________________ DATE ______________

TEACHER ______________ AGE/GRADE ______________________

SELECTION ____

Does the sentence, as the reader left it, make sense within the context of the story?

Yes ______________________________ Total ______________

No ______________________________ Total ______________

Number of Sentences ______________ Comprehending Score ______________

Divide total Yes by Total number of sentences for Comprehending Score

Retelling Information

Comments

(Goodman, Watson, Burke)

Name ____________________

Date ____________________ Grade/Age ____________________

Teacher ____________________

Reference ____________________

THE MAN WHO KEPT HOUSE

0101 Once upon a time there was a woodman

0102 who thought that no one worked as hard as

0103 he did. One evening when he came home

0104 from work, he said to his wife, "What do you

0105 do all day while I am away cutting wood?"

0106 "I keep house," replied the wife, "and

0107 keeping house is hard work."

0108 "Hard work!" said the husband. "You don't

0109 know what hard work is! You should try

0110 cutting wood!"

0111 "I'd be glad to," said the wife.

0112 "Why don't you do my work some day? I'll

0113 stay home and keep house," said the woodman.

0114 "If you stay home to do my work, you'll

0115 have to make butter, carry water from the

0116 well, wash the clothes, clean the house, and

0117 look after the baby," said the wife.

0118 "I can do all that," replied the husband.

0119 "We'll do it tomorrow!"

0201 So the next morning the wife went off to

0202 the forest. The husband stayed home and

0203 began to do his wife's work.

0204 He began to make some butter. As he put

0205 the cream into the churn, he said, "This is

0206 not going to be hard work. All I have to do

0207 is sit here and move this stick up and down.

0208 Soon the cream will turn into butter."

0209 Just then the woodman heard the baby

0210 crying. He looked around, but he could not

0211 see her. She was not in the house. Quickly,

0212 he ran outside to look for her. He found the

0213 baby at the far end of the garden and

0214 brought her back to the house.

0301 In his hurry, the woodman had left the

0302 door open behind him. When he got back to

0303 the house, he saw a big pig inside with its

0304 nose in the churn. "Get out! Get out!"

0305 shouted the woodman at the top of his voice.

0306 The big pig ran around and around the

0307	room. It bumped into the churn, knocking it
0308	over. The cream splashed all over the room.
0309	Out the door went the pig.
0310	"Now I've got more work to do," said the
0311	man. "I'll have to wash everything in this
0312	room. Perhaps keeping house is harder work
0313	than I thought." He took a bucket and went
0314	to the well for some water. When he came
0315	back, the baby was crying.
0316	"Poor baby, you must be hungry," said the
0317	woodman. "I'll make some porridge for you.
0318	I'll light a fire in the fireplace, and the
0319	porridge will be ready in a few minutes."
0320	Just as the husband was putting the
0321	water into the big pot, he heard the cow
0401	mooing outside the door. "I guess the cow is
0402	hungry, too," he thought. "No one has given
0403	her any grass to eat or any water to drink
0404	today."
0405	The man left the porridge to cook on the
0406	fire and hurried outside. He gave the cow
0407	some water.

0408 "I haven't time to find any grass for you
0409 now," he said to the cow. "I'll put you up
0410 on the roof. You'll find something to eat
0411 up there."
0412 The man put the cow on top of the house.
0413 Then he was afraid that she would fall off
0414 the roof and hurt herself. So he put one
0415 end of a rope around the cow's neck. He
0416 dropped the other end down the chimney.

0501 Then he climbed down from the roof and
0502 went into the house. He pulled the end of the
0503 rope out of the fireplace and put it around
0504 his left leg.
0505 "Now I can finish making this porridge,"
0506 said the woodman, "and the cow will
0507 be safe."
0508 But the man spoke too soon, for just then
0509 the cow fell off the roof. She pulled him up
0510 the chimney by the rope. There he hung,
0511 upside down over the poridge pot. As for the
0512 cow, she hung between the roof and the
0513 ground, and there she had to stay.

0514 It was not very long before woodman's

0515 wife came home. As she came near the

0516 house, she could hear the cow mooing, the

0601 baby crying, and her husband shouting for

0602 help. She hurried up the path. She cut the

0603 rope from the cow's neck. As she did so,

0604 the cow fell down to the ground, and the

0605 husband dropped head first down the chimney.

0606 When the wife went into the house, she

0607 saw her husband with his legs up the

0608 chimney and his head in the porridge pot.

0609 From that day on, the husband went into

0610 the forest every day to cut wood. The wife

0611 stayed home to keep house and to look

0612 after their child.

0613 Never again did the woodman say to his

0614 wife, "What did you do all day?" Never

0615 again did he tell his wife that he would

0616 stay home and keep house.

Reader: ______________________ Date: ______________________

Retelling Guide: Procedure I

The Man Who Kept House

Character Analysis:
(40 points)

Recall (20 points)
9 – Man (husband)
9 – Woman (wife)
2 – Baby

Development (20 points)
Husband
2 – Woodman
3 – Thought he worked very hard
5 – Changed attitude over time
Housewife
5 – Worked Hard
5 – Accepted challenges

Events:
(60 points)

Woodman thinks he works very hard. He comes home and asks his wife what she does all day. Wife responds that she keeps house and keeping house is hard work. (10 points) ____

The husband challenges the wife to change places. The wife agrees and tells husband what he has to do. The husband says they will change places the next day. (10 points) ____

The wife goes off to the forest and the husband stays home. (5 points) ____

The husband is involved in a number of events that cause problems: (15 points) ____

Butter making.

Baby cries and woodman goes to find her. He leaves the door open.

Pig gets into the house, the woodman chases it and the pig spills the cream.

Woodman starts to clean up the mess.

The baby cries again and the woodman prepares to feed the baby.

The cow's mooing interrupts the woodman who realizes that the cow needs to be fed. He puts the cow on the roof to feed. He is afraid the cow might fall off the roof so he throws the rope from the cow's neck down the chimney. When he gets into the house he ties the rope to his own leg.

As he thinks again about the porridge, the cow falls off the roof pulling the woodman up the chimney. Cow and woodman are hanging, one in the house and one outside.

As the wife returns home she hears the commotion. She cuts the cow down and then finds her husband upside down with his head in the porridge pot. (10 points) ____

Every day after that the husband goes to his work and the wife to hers. The husband never again asks the wife what she does every day nor says he will do her work. (10 points) ____

Points – character analysis ____

Points – events ____

Total Points ____

Plot

The old man believes his work is harder than his wife's. When he trades places with her he discovers her work is more complicated and harder than he thought.

Theme

Things aren't always as easy as they appear to be. Keeping house is demanding work. A woman's job is just as hard as a man's. The grass is always greener on the other side of the fence.

Name ______________________________

Date ______________________ Grade/Age ______________________

Teacher ______________________________

Reference ______________________________

THE BEAT OF MY HEART

0101 Lub-dup . . .

0102 Lub-dup . . .

0103 Lub-dup . . .

0104 This strange sound

0105 is the sound

0106 of a wonderful machine

0107 inside your body.

0108 It is the sound

0109 of your heart beating.

0110 Your heart is a pump

0111 which will never

0112 stop working

0113 as long as you live,

0114 but it can rest

0115 even while it is working.

0116 Your heart

0117 is a hollow muscle

0118 divided into four parts.

0119	It is about the size
0120	of your fist.
0121	As you grow,
0122	it too will grow in size.

0201	To find out
0202	where your heart is,
0203	put your right hand
0204	in the middle
0205	of the left side of your chest.
0206	Now move your fingers around
0207	until you find
0208	the spot where
0209	the heartbeat is strongest.
0210	Your hand is now
0211	pointing to your heart.
0212	Listen to the heartbeat
0213	of a friend
0214	by putting your ear
0215	to his chest.
0216	To hear the sound even better,
0217	hold an empty mailing tube
0218	or a rolled-up piece

0219	of heavy paper
0220	to your friend's heart.
0221	When the heart goes lub,
0222	it is drawing in blood.
0223	When it goes dup,
0224	it is pushing blood out
0225	to all parts of the body.
0226	Your heart has
0227	this most important job to do —
0228	pumping blood
0229	to all parts of your body.

0301	Blood feeds
0302	all the cells and organs
0303	of your body
0304	so that they can do
0305	their own special work
0306	to keep you physically fit.
0307	Your heart pumps blood
0308	from your head
0309	to your toes,
0310	to your liver
0311	and your lungs.

0312	Just as a wheel
0313	can turn slowly or fast,
0314	your heart can work
0315	at a slow or a fast pace.
0316	If you want to see
0317	how your heart changes quickly
0318	from working at a slow pace
0319	to working at a faster pace,
0320	try this.
0321	First listen
0322	to a friend's heartbeat
0323	and count the number of beats
0324	in a minute.
0325	Now ask your friend
0326	to run fast
0327	for about a minute.
0328	Then listen to his heart again.
0329	How many times a minute
0330	is his heart beating now?

0401	Count his heartbeats again
0402	after he has rested
0403	for a minute.

0404	By comparing the number
0405	of heartbeats
0406	under these different conditions,
0407	you will discover that
0408	the heart is
0409	a sensitive machine
0410	working inside the body.

0501	You can test this fact again
0502	by checking your own heartbeat.
0503	Place three fingertips
0504	of your right hand
0505	on the inside of your left wrist.
0506	You will feel the beat
0507	of your heart.
0508	This is called your pulse.
0509	Count the number of times
0510	your heart beats in a minute.

0601	Now, run for a minute
0602	and count the heartbeats
0603	in your pulse again.
0604	Lie down and rest for a minute,
0605	and then count once more.

0606	See how exercise makes
0607	your heart work
0608	harder and faster?
0609	Exercise helps your heart
0610	to become stronger
0611	and be able
0612	to do its work better.
0613	Your heart beats
0614	as long as you live.
0615	It rests for 1/6 of a second
0616	between every beat.
0617	When you are asleep or resting,
0618	your heart beats
0619	at a slower rate.
0620	This rest gives your heart
0621	a chance to keep
0622	in good working condition
0623	as well as to grow
0624	bigger and stronger.

0701	Since you are becoming
0702	taller and heavier
0703	every school year,

0704 your heart must grow larger, too.

0705 Your bigger body needs

0706 a bigger motor to keep it

0707 in good working order.

0708 There are many ways

0709 to take care of your heart,

0710 but the two best ones are

0711 the easiest to do.

0712 One is to get lots of exercise

0713 by playing vigorous games

0714 out of doors.

0715 Play games that have lots

0716 of running and jumping,

0717 or hitting and kicking balls.

0718 The other way

0719 to take care of your heart

0720 is to be sure you get

0721 at least ten hours of sleep

0722 every night

0723 and do restful things

0724 from time to time

0725 throughout the day.

0726 On and on your heart beats—

0727 year in and year out.

0728 Lub-dup . . .

0729 Lub-dup . . .

0730 Lub-dup . . .

Reader: ______________________ Date: ______________________

Retelling Guide: The Beat of My Heart

Specific Information
(50 points) ____

The Heart *(10)* ____

Rests even while working
Is a hollow muscle
Divided into four parts
About the size of your fist
Grows as you grow; needs to be bigger as body gets bigger

Blood *(8)* ____

With one beat blood is drawn in; with the next beat blood is pushed out
Blood feeds cells and organs which is needed for the body to be physically fit
Blood pumps to liver to lungs

Heartbeat *(8)* ____

The heart can beat slow or fast (Analogy)
Heartbeat felt in your wrist is your pulse
Rests 1/6 second between beats
Beats at a slower rate when asleep or resting

Conditions *(8)* ____

Exercise helps heart become stronger and do work better.
Two best ways of taking care of heart: vigorous games and at least 10 hours of sleep every night

Experiments Making Use of Specific Information: *(16)* ____
Find your heart by moving fingers around on the left side of your chest. Find where the beat is strongest. *(3)* ____

Listen to the heartbeat of a friend by putting your ear to his chest. Listen by using mailing tube or paper roll. *(3)* ____

Learn how heart changes quickly from slow to fast pace by listening to a friend's heart. Count beats in a minute. Ask friend to run fast for a minute. Count beats in a minute. Count beats again after friend has rested for a minute. Compare number of beats. *(6)* ____

Check own heartbeat by taking your pulse rate for a minute. Run for a minute and count again. Lie down for a minute and count again. *(4)* ____

Generalizations
(25 points) ____

Heart is a machine inside the body
Heart has an important job to do
Exercise makes heart work harder and faster
Rest gives heart a chance to go slower

Major Concepts ____
(25 points)

Is a most important organ for life
There are ways we can find out about our hearts

Retelling

Specific Information ____

Generalizations ____

Major Concepts ____

Total Points ____

Inferences

Comments

READING INTERVIEW

Name ______________________ Age ________ Date ______________________

Occupation ______________________ Educational Level ______________________

Sex ________ Interview Setting ______________________

1. When you are reading and come to something you don't know, what do you do?

   Do you ever do anything else?

2. Who is a good reader you know?

3. What makes _____ a good reader?

4. Do you think _____ ever comes to something she/he doesn't know?

5. "Yes" When _____ does come to something she/he doesn't know, what do you think he/she does?

"No" Suppose _____ comes to something she/he doesn't know. What do you think she/he would do?

6. If you knew someone was having trouble reading how would you help that person?

7. What would a/your teacher do to help that person?

8. How did you learn to read?

9. What would you like to do better as a reader?

10. Do you think you are a good reader? Why?

Appendix D

Previous Miscue Analysis Formats

1. Original Reading Miscue Inventory Questions
2. Goodman Taxonomy of Reading Miscues

Original Reading Miscue Inventory Questions

Question 1: *DIALECT. Is a Dialect Variation Involved in the Miscue?*

If a variation is involved, the appropriate box is marked "Y" for yes. If no dialect variation is involved, the box is left blank.

Question 2: *INTONATION. Is a Shift in Intonation Involved in the Miscue?*

If a shift is involved, the appropriate box is marked "Y" for yes. If there is no variation involved, the box is left blank.

Question 3: *GRAPHIC SIMILARITY. How Much Does the Miscue Look Like What Was Expected?**

Y—A high degree of graphic similarity exists between the miscue and the text.

P—Some degree of graphic similarity exists between the miscue and the text.

N—A graphic similarity does not exist between the miscue and the text.

Question 4: *SOUND SIMILARITY. How Much Does the Miscue Sound Like What Was Expected?**

Y—A high degree of sound similarity exists between the miscue and what was expected.

P—Some degree of sound similaity exists between the miscue and what was expected.

N—A sound similarity does not exist between the miscue and what was expected.

Question 5: *GRAMMATICAL FUNCTION. Is the Grammatical Function of the Miscue the Same as the Grammatical Function of the Word in the Text?**

Y—The grammatical functions of the two are identical.

P—It is not possible to determine the grammatical function.

N—The grammatical functions of the two differ.

Question 6: *CORRECTION. Is the Miscue Corrected?*

Y—The miscue is corrected.

P—There is an unsuccessful attempt at correction. Or a correct response is abandoned.

N—There has been no attempt at correction.

Question 7: *GRAMMATICAL ACCEPTABILITY. Does the Miscue Occur in a Structure that is Grammatically Acceptable?*

Y—The miscue occurs in a sentence that is grammatically acceptable and is acceptable in relation to prior and subsequent sentences in the text.

P—The miscue occurs in a sentence that is grammatically acceptable but is not acceptable in relation to prior and subsequent sentences in the text. Or the miscue is grammatically acceptable only with the sentence portion that comes before or after it.

N—The miscue occurs in a sentence that is not grammatically acceptable.

Question 8: *SEMANTIC ACCEPTABILITY. Does the Miscue Occur in a Structure that is Semantically Acceptable?*

Y—The miscue occurs in a sentence that is semantically acceptable and is acceptable in relation to prior and subsequent sentences in the text.

P—The miscue occurs in a sentence that is semantically acceptable but is not acceptable in relation to prior and subsequent sentences in the text. Or the miscue is semantically acceptable only with the sentence portion that comes before or after it.

*If the miscue is an omission or insertion, this category is not marked. If the miscue involves more than one word, this category is not marked. If the miscue involves intonation only, this category is not marked.

N—The miscue occurs in a sentence that is not semantically acceptable.

Question 9: *MEANING CHANGE. Does the Miscue Result in a Change of Meaning?*

Y—An extensive change in meaning is involved.
P—A minimal change in meaning is involved.
N—No change in meaning is involved.

Goodman Taxonomy of Reading Miscues*

Correction
0. No attempt at correction is made.
1. The miscue is corrected.
2. An original correct response is abandoned in favor of an incorrect one.
3. An unsuccessful attempt is made at correcting the miscue.

Dialect
0. Dialect is not involved in the miscue.
1. Dialect is involved in the miscue.
2. Idiolect is involved in the miscue.
3. A supercorrection is involved in the miscue.
4. There is a secondary dialect involved in the miscue.
5. A foreign language influence is involved in the miscue.
9. Dialect Involvement is doubtful.

Graphic Proximity
0. There is no graphic similarity between ER and the OR.
1. The ER and the OR have a key letter or letters in common.
2. The middle portions of the ER and OR are similar.
3. The end portions of the ER and OR are similar.
4. The beginning portions of the ER and OR are similar.
5. The beginning and middle portions of the ER and OR are similar.
6. The beginning and end portions of the ER and OR are similar.
7. The beginning, middle and end portions of the ER and OR are similar.
8. There is a single grapheme difference between the ER and the OR, or a reversal involving two letters.
9. The ER and the OR are homographs.

Phonemic Proximity
0. There is no phonemic similarity between the ER and the OR.
1. The ER and the OR have a key sound or sounds in common.
2. The middle portion of the ER and the OR are similar.
3. The ER and OR have the end portions in common.
4. The ER and OR have the beginning portion in common.
5. The ER and OR have common beginning and middle portions.
6. The ER and OR have common beginning and end portions.
7. The beginning, middle and end portions of the ER and OR are similar.

*Adapted from Gollasch, F (1982), *The Selected Writings of Kenneth S. Goodman* (Vol. 1). London: Routledge & Kegan Paul.

8. The ER and OR differ by a single vowel or consonant or vowel cluster.
9. The ER and OR are homophones.

Allologs

0. An allolog is not involved in the miscue.
1. The OR is a contracted form of the ER.
2. The OR is a full form of the ER contraction.
3. The OR is a contraction which is not represented in print.
4. The OR is either a long or short form of the ER.
5. The OR involves a shift to idiomatic form.
6. The OR involves a shift from idiomatic form.
7. The OR involves a misarticulation.

Syntactic Acceptability

0. The miscue results in a structure which is completely syntactically unacceptable.
1. The miscue results in a structure which is syntactically acceptable only with the prior portion of the sentence.
2. The miscue results in a structure which is syntactically acceptable only with the following portion of the sentence.
3. The miscue results in a structure which is syntactically acceptable only within the sentence.
4. The miscue results in a structure which is syntactically acceptable within the total passage.
5. The miscue results in a structure which is syntactically acceptable within the sentence except for other unacceptable miscues.
6. The miscue results in a structure which is syntactically acceptable within the total passage except for other unacceptable miscues in the sentence.

Semantic Acceptability

0. The miscue results in a structure which is completely semantically unacceptable.
1. The miscues results in a structure which is semantically acceptable only with the prior portion of the sentence.
2. The miscue results in a structure which is semantically acceptable only with the following portion of the sentence.
3. The miscue results in a structure which is semantically acceptable only within the sentence.
4. The miscue results in a structure which is semantically acceptable within the total passage.
5. The miscue results in a structure which is semantically acceptable within the sentence except for other unacceptable miscues.
6. The miscue results in a structure which is semantically acceptable within the total passage except for other unacceptable miscues in the sentence.

Transformation

0. A grammatical transformation is not involved.
1. A transformation occurs which involves a difference in deep structure between the ER and OR.
2. A transformation occurs in which the deep structure of the ER and the OR remains the same while the surface structure of the OR is generated by a different set of compulsory rules.
3. A transformation occurs in which the deep structure of the ER and the OR remains the same while the surface structure of the OR is generated by alternate available rules.

4. The deep structure has been lost or garbled.
5. There is some question of whether or not a transformation is involved in the miscue.

Syntactic Change

0. The syntax of the OR and the ER are unrelated.
1. The syntax of the OR and the ER have a single element in common.
2. The syntax of the OR has a key element which retains the syntactic function of the ER.
3. There is a major change in the syntax of the OR.
4. There is a minor change in the syntax of the OR.
5. There is a major change within the structure of the phrase.
6. There is a minor change within the structure of the phrase.
7. There is a change in person, tense, number or gender of the OR.
8. There is a change in choice of function word or another minor shift in the OR.
9. The syntax of the OR is unchanged from the syntax of the ER.

Semantic Change

0. The OR is completely anomalous to the rest of the story.
1. There is a change or loss affecting the plot in a basic sense or creating major anomalies.
2. There is a change or loss involving key aspects of the story or seriously interfering with subplots.
3. There is a change or loss resulting in inconsistency concerning a major incident, major character or major sequence.
4. There is a change or loss resulting in inconsistency concerning a minor incident, minor character or minor aspect of sequence.
5. There is a change or loss of aspect which is significant but does not create inconsistencies within the story.
6. There is a change or loss of an unimportant detail of this story.
7. There is a change in person, tense, number, comparative, etc. which is noncritical to the story.
8. There is a slight change in connotation.
9. No change has occurred involving story meaning.

Intonation

1. An intonation shift within a word is involved.
2. An intonation shift is involved between words within one phrase structure of the sentence.
3. Intonation is involved which is relative to the phrase or clause structure of the sentence.
4. A shift in terminal sentence intonation is involved.
5. The intonation change involves a substitution of a conjunction for terminal punctuation or the reverse.
6. The intonation change involves direct quotes.

Submorphemic Language Level

0. The submorphemic level is not involved.
1. There is a substitution of phonemes.
2. There is an insertion of a phoneme(s).
3. There is an omission of a phoneme(s).
4. There is a reversal of phonemes.
5. There are multiple minor phonemic variations.

Bound and Combined Morpheme Level

1. The miscue involves an inflectional suffix.
2. The miscue involves a noninflected form.
3. The miscue involves a contractional suffix.
4. The miscue involves a derivational suffix.
5. The miscue involves a prefix.
6. The miscue crosses affix types.
7. The miscue involves the base. There is some confusion over what constitutes the root word.

Word and Free Morpheme Level

1. The ER and/or the OR involve a multiple morpheme word.
2. The ER and/or the OR involve a single morpheme word.
3. The ER is a single morpheme word and the OR is a multiple morpheme word.
4. The ER is a multiple morpheme word and the OR is a single morpheme word.
5. The miscue involves a free morpheme within a longer word.
6. The miscue involves one or both of the free morphemes in a compound or hyphenated word.
7. The OR is a nonword.
8. The OR is a phonemic or morphophonemic dialect alternate of the ER.

Phrase

1. A substitution is involved at the phrase level.
2. An insertion is involved at the phrase level.
3. An omission is involved at the phrase level.
4. A reversal is involved at the phrase level.

Clause

1. A substitution is involved at the clause level.
2. An insertion is involved at the clause level.
3. An omission is involved at the clause level.
4. A reversal is involved at the clause level.
5. Clause dependency is altered within the sentence. Only one ER sentence should be involved in the miscue.
6. Clause dependency is altered across sentences. Two ER sentences should be involved in the miscue.

Grammatical Category and Surface Structure of Observed Response

1. Noun Category
2. Verb Category
3. Noun Modifier
4. Verb Modifier
5. Function Word Category
6. Indeterminate Category
7. Contraction Category

Observed Response in Visual Periphery

0. The visual periphery is not involved in the miscue.
1. The OR can be found in the near visual periphery.
2. The OR can be found in the extended visual periphery.
9. It is doubtful whether the visual periphery was inolved in the miscue.

Bibliography and References

The bibliography that follows includes not only the references from the text but selected readings for teacher/researchers who want more information.

I. Strategy Lessons and Whole Language Instruction

The references in this section include discussions of ideas and concepts closely related to the application of miscue analysis to classroom and clinical settings.

Bridge, C. (1979). Predictable materials for beginning readers. *Language Arts, 56*(5)503–507

Buchanan, E. (Ed.). (1980). *For the Love of Reading.* Winnepeg: Cel Group.

Burke, C. L. (1980). The Reading Interview: 1977. In B. P. Farr and D. J. Strickler (Eds.), *Reading Comprehension: Resource Guide.* Bloomington, IN: School of Education, Indiana University.

Cambourne, B. (1987). Retelling as a learning strategy. In D. Watson (Ed.), *Ideas with Insights: Language Arts for Elementary Children.* Urbana, IL: National Council of Teachers of English.

Cochrane, O., Cochrane, D., Scalena, S., and Buchanan, E. (1984). *Reading, Writing and Caring.* Winnipeg: Whole Language Consultants; New York: Richard C. Owen.

Disinger, J. (1987). Language detectives. In D. Watson (Ed.), *Ideas with Insights: Language Arts for Elementary Children.* Urbana, IL: National Council of Teachers of English.

Edelsky, C., and Smith, K. (1984). Is that writing—or are those marks just a figment of your curriculum? *Language Arts, 61*(1)24–32.

Gilles, C., Bixby, M., Crowley, P., Crenshaw, S., Henrichs, M., Reynolds, F., Pyle, D. (In press). *Whole Language Strategies for Secondary Students.* New York: Richard C. Owen.

Goodman, D. (1987). Learning and learning to read and write. In D. Watson (Ed.) *Ideas with Insights: Language Arts for Elementary Children.* Urbana, IL: National Council of Teachers of English.

Goodman, D. (1987). What have you read (written) today? In D. Watson (Ed.), *Ideas with Insights: Language Arts for Elementary Children.* Urbana, IL: National Council of Teachers of English.

Goodman, Y. (1970). Using children's miscues for teaching reading strategies. *Reading Teacher, 23*(3)455–459.

Goodman, Y. (1975). Reading comprehension: A redundant phrase. *The Michigan Reading Journal, 9*(2)27–31.

Goodman, Y. (1975). Reading strategy lessons: Expanding reading effectiveness. In W. D. Page (Ed.), *Help for the Reading Teacher: New Directions in Research* (pp. 34–41). Urbana, IL: National Conference on Research in English.

Goodman, Y. (1976). Strategies for comprehension. In P. Allen and D. Watson (Eds.), *Findings of Research in Miscue Analysis: Classroom Implications* (pp. 94–102). Urbana, IL: ERIC Clearinghouse on Reading and Communication Skills and National Council of Teachers of English.

Goodman, Y. (1978). Kidwatching: An alternative to testing. *Journal of National Elementary Principals, 57*(4)41–45.

Goodman, Y. (1982). Retellings of literature and the comprehension process. *Theory into Practice, 21*(4)301–307.

Goodman, Y., and Burke, C. (1969). Do they read what they speak? *Grade Teacher, 26*(7)144–150.

Goodman, Y., and Burke, C. (1972). *RMI Manual. Procedures for Diagnosis and Evaluation.* New York: Richard C. Owen.

Goodman, Y., and Burke, C. (1980). *Reading Strategies: Focus on Comprehension.* New York: Richard C. Owen.

Goodman, Y., and Watson, D. (1977). A reading program to live with: Focus on comprehension. *Language Arts, 54*(8)868–879.

Harste, J., and Carey, R. (1979). Comprehension as spelling. In J. Harste and R. Carey (Eds.), *New Perspection on Comprehension* (Monographs in Teaching and Learning). Bloomington, IN: School of Education, Indiana University.

Harste, J., Woodward, V., and Burke, C. (1984). *Language Stories and Literacy Lessons.* Exeter, NH: Heinemann Educational Books.

Holdaway, D. (1979). *Foundations of Literacy.* Sydney, Australia: Ashton Scholastic.

Hoskisson, K. (1975). The many facets of assisted reading. *Elementary English, 52*(3)312–315.

Kalmbach, J. (1986). Getting at the point of retelling. *Journal of Reading, 29*(4)326–33.

Menosky, D., and Goodman K. (1971). Unlocking the program. *Instructor, 80*(7)44–46.

Newman, J. (1986). *Whole Language: Translating Theory into Practice.* Exeter, NH: Heinemann Books.

Reed, L. (Ed.), (1982). *Basic skills issues and choices: Issues in basic skills planning and instruction.* St. Louis, MO: CEMREL.

Rhodes, L. (Ed.). (1981). *Children's Literature: Activities and Ideas.* Denver, CO: University of Colorado.

Rhodes, L. (1981). I can read! Predictable books as resources for reading and writing instruction. *Reading Teacher, 34*(5)511–518.

Smith, E., Goodman, K., and Meredith, R. (1978). *Language and Thinking in the Elementary School* (2nd ed.). New York: Holt, Rinehart and Winston.

Smith, F. (1973). *Psycholinguistics and Reading.* New York: Holt, Rinehart and Winston.

Smith, F. (1983). Reading like a writer. *Language Arts, 60*(5)558–567.

Smith, J. (1987). The literacy olympics. In D. Watson (Ed.), *Ideas with Insights: Language Arts for Elementary Children.* Urbana, IL: National Council of Teachers of English.

Spitzer, R. (1975). Taking the pressure off. *Journal of Reading, 19*(3)198–200.

Tompkins, G. E., and Webeler, M. (1983). What will happen next? Using predictable books with young children. *Reading Teacher, 36*(6)498–502.

Watson, D. (1976). Helping the reader: From miscue analysis to strategy lessons. In K. Goodman (Ed.), *Miscue Analysis: Applications to Reading Instruction.* Urbana, IL: ERIC Clearinghouse on Reading and Communication Skills and National Council of Teachers of English.

Watson, D. (1982). Reading and writing: Making and breaking the connection. *The Missouri Reader, 7*(2)8–9.

Watson, D. (1982). What is a whole-language reading program? *The Missouri Reader,* 7(1)8–10.

Watson, D. (Ed.), (1987). *Ideas with Insights: Language Arts for Elementary Children.* Urbana, IL: National Council of Teachers of English.

Watson, D., Gilles, C. (1987). E.R.R.Q. In D. Watson (Ed.), *Ideas with Insights: Language Arts for Elementary Children.* Urbana, IL: National Council of Teachers of English.

Woodley, J., and Miller, L. D. (1983). Retrospective miscue analysis: Procedures for research and instruction (Research on Reading in Secondary Schools Monographs Nos. 10 & 11, pp. 53–67). Tucson, AZ: University of Arizona, Reading Department.

II. Background Information, Theory, and Research

This section includes writings in the fields of reading, linguistics, psycholinguistics and sociolinguistics that provide teacher/researchers with knowledge about the principles underlying the Reading Miscue Inventory. In addition, in-depth discussions about miscue research and theory are also included. Many of the research reports used the Goodman Taxonomy of Reading Miscues or the original Reading Miscue Inventory for analysis of data.

Allen, P. D. (1969). *A Psycholinguistic Analysis of the Substitution Miscues of Selected Oral Readers in Grades Two, Four, and Six and the Relationship of These Miscues to the Reading Process: A Descriptive Study.* Unpublished doctoral dissertation, Wayne State University, Detroit, MI.

Allen, D., and Watson, D. (Eds.). (1976). *Research Findings in Miscue Analysis.* Urbana, IL: National Council of Teachers of English.

Altwerger, B., and Goodman, K. (1981). *Studying Text Difficulty Through Miscue Analysis: A Research Report* (Occasional Paper No. 3). Tucson, AZ: University of Arizona, College of Education, Program in Language and Literacy.

Anders, P. L. (In press). *Theory Related to Practice: Implications for Elementary Reading Instruction.* New York: Allyn and Bacon.

Burke, C. L. (1969). *A Psycholinguistic Description of Grammatical Restructurings in the Oral Reading of a Selected Group of Middle School Children.* Unpublished doctoral dissertation, Wayne State University, Detroit, MI.

Carlson, K. L. (1970). *A Psycholinguistic Description of Selected Fourth Grade Children Reading a Variety of Contextual Materials.* Unpublished doctoral dissertation, Wayne State University, Detroit, MI.

Christian, D. (1979). *Language Arts and Dialect Differences* (Dialects and Educational Equity Series). Arlington, VA: Center for Applied Linguistics.

Christian, D., and Wolfram, W. (1979). *Exploring Dialects* (Dialects and Educational Equity Series). Arlington, VA: Center for Applied Linguistics.

Coles, R. E. (1981). *The Reading Strategies of Selected Junior High School Students in the Content Areas.* Unpublished doctoral dissertation, University of Arizona, Tucson.

DeFord, D. (1981). Reading, writing and other essentials. *Language Arts, 58*(6)652–658.

Doake, D. (1981). *Book Experience and Emergent Reading in Preschool Children.* Unpublished doctoral dissertation, University of Alberta, Edmonton.

Ewoldt, C. (1977). *A Psycholinguistic Description of Selected Deaf Children Reading Sign Language.* Unpublished doctoral dissertation, Wayne State University, Detroit.

Gollasch, F. W. (1980). *Readers' Perception in Detecting and Processing Embedded Errors in Meaningful Text.* Unpublished dissertation, University of Arizona, Tucson.

Gollasch, F. W. (Ed.). (1982). *Language and Literacy: The Selected Writings of Kenneth S. Goodman* (Vols. 1 and 2). Boston: Routledge and Kegan Paul.

Goodman, K. (1965). Dialect barriers to reading comprehension. *Elementary English, 42,* 853–860.

Goodman, K. (1968). Study of Children's Behavior While Reading Orally (Contract No. OE-6-10-136). Washington, DC: Department of Health, Education and Welfare.

Goodman, K. (1969). Analysis of reading miscues: applied psycholinguistics, *Reading Research Quarterly, 5*(1)652–658.

Goodman, K. S. (1970). Behind the eye: what happens in reading. In K. S. Goodman and O. Niles (Eds.), *Reading Process and Program.* Urbana, IL: National Council of Teachers of English.

Goodman, K. (1973). Miscue Analysis: Applications to Reading Instruction. Urbana, IL: ERIC Clearinghouse on Reading and Communication Skills and National Council of Teachers of English.

Goodman, K. S. (1973b). Miscues: windows on the reading process. In K. S. Goodman (Ed.), *Miscue Analysis: Applications to Reading Instruction* (pp. 3–14). Urbana, IL: ERIC Clearinghouse on Reading and Communication Skills and the National Council of Teachers of English.

Goodman, K. (1983). *Text Features as They Relate to Miscues: Determiners, the and a/an* (Occasional Paper No. 8). Tucson, AZ: University of Arizona, College of Education, Program in Language and Literacy.

Goodman, K. (1984). Unity in reading. In A. C. Purves and O. Niles (Eds.), *Becoming Readers in a Complex Society.* Chicago: University of Chicago Press.

Goodman, K. S. (1985). *What's Whole in Whole Language.* Toronto, Ontario: Scholastic Books.

Goodman, K. S. (1986). *Revaluing Readers and Reading* (Occasional Paper No. 15). Tucson, AZ: University of Arizona, College of Education, Program in Language and Literacy.

Goodman, K. S., and Buck, C. (1973). Dialect barriers to reading comprehension revisited. *Reading Teacher, 27*(1)6–12.

Goodman, K. S., and Burke, C. L. (1969). *A Study of Oral Reading Miscues That Result in Grammatical Retransformations* (Contract No. OEG-0-8-070219-2806 (0101)). Washington, D.C.: U.S. Department of Health, Education and Welfare.

Goodman, K. S., and Burke, C. L. (1970). When a child reads: a psycholinguistic analysis. *Elementary English, 47*(1)121–129.

Goodman, K. S. and Burke, C. L. (1973). *Theoretically Based Studies of Patterns of Miscues in Oral Reading Performance* (Grant No OEG-0-9-320375-4269). Washington, D.C.: U.S. Department of Health, Education and Welfare.

Goodman, K., and Gespass, S. (1983). *Text Features as They Relate to Miscue Pronouns* (Occasional Paper No. 7). Tucson, AZ: University of Arizona, College of Education, Program in Language and Literacy.

Goodman, K., and Goodman, Y. (1978). *Reading of American Children Whose Language is a Stable Rural Dialect of English or a Language Other Than English* (Contract No. NIE-C-00-3-0087). Washington, D.C.: National Institute of Education.

Goodman, K., and Goodman, Y. (1981). *A Whole Language Comprehension Centered View of Reading: A Position Paper* (Occasional Paper NO. 1). Tucson, AZ: University of Arizona, College of Education, Program in Language and Literacy.

Goodman, K., Goodman, Y., and Flores, F. (1979). *Reading in the Bilingual Classroom: Literacy and Biliteracy.* Arlington, VA: National Clearinghouse for Bilingual Education.

Goodman, Y. M. (1967). *A Psycholinguistic Description of Observed Oral Reading Phenomena in Selected Young Beginning Readers.* Unpublished doctoral dissertation, Wayne State University, Detroit, MI.

Goodman, Y. M. (1971). *Longitudinal Study of Chidren's Oral Reading Behavior* (Contract No. OEG-5-9-325062-0046). Washington, D.C.: U.S. Department of Health, Education, and Welfare.

Gruber, H. E., and VonEche, J. J. (1977). *The Essential Piaget.* New York: Basic Books.

Gutknecht, B. A. (1971). *A Psycholinguistic Analysis of the Oral Reading Behavior of Selected Children Identified as Perceptually Handicapped.* Unpublished doctoral dissertation. Wayne State University, Detroit, MI.

Halliday, M. A. K. (1975). *Learning How to Mean: Explorations in the Development of Language.* London: Edward Arnold.

Harste, J., and Burke, C. (1977). A new hypothesis for reading teacher research: both the teaching and learning of reading are theoretically based. In P. D. Pearson (Ed.), *Reading: Research, Theory and Practice. Twenty-sixth Yearbook-NRC.* Minneapolis, MN: Mason Publishing.

Horn, E. (1929). The child's early experience with little a. *Journal of Educational Psychology, 20*(3)161–168.

Hunt, K. (1965). *Grammatical Structures Written at Three Grade Levels.* Champaign, IL: National Council of Teachers of English.

Irwin, P. and Mitchell, J. (1983). A procedure for assessing the richness of retellings. *Journal of Reading, 26*(5) 391–396.

Lee, S. and Sadoski, M. Holistic Evaluation of Plot and Theme (Unpublished manuscript, 1986).

Lincoln, Y., and Guba, E. (1985). *Naturalistic Inquiry.* Beverly Hills, CA: Sage Publications.

Long, P. C. (1985). *The Effectiveness of Reading Miscue Instruments—A Research Report* (Occasional Paper No. 13). Tucson, AZ: University of Arizona, College of Education, Program in Language and Literacy.

Marek, A. (dissertation in process). *Retrospective Miscue Analysis as an Instructional Strategy with Adult Readers.* University of Arizona, Tucson.

Marek, A., Goodman, K. S., and Babcock, P. (1985). *Annotated Miscue Analysis Bibliography* (Occasional Paper No. 16). Tucson, AZ: University of Arizona, College of Education, Program in Language and Literacy.

Menosky, D. M. (1971). *A Psycholinguistic Description of Oral Reading Miscues Generated During the Reading of Varying Positions of Text by Selected Readers from Grades Two, Four, Six and Eight.* Unpublished doctoral dissertation, Wayne State University, Detroit, MI.

Neisser, U. (1976). *Cognition and Reality.* San Francisco: Freeman and Company.

Page, W. D. (1970). *A Psycholinguistic Description of Patterns of Miscues Generated by a Proficient Reader in Second Grade, and an Average Reader in Sixth Grade Encountering Ten Basal Reader Selections Ranging from Pre-Primer to Sixth Grade.* Unpublished doctoral dissertation, Wayne State University, Detroit, MI.

Psycholinguistic Approach to Reading (PAR). (1974). El Cajon, CA: Cajon Valley Union School District. (ERIC Document Reproduction Service No. ED 108 150)

Robinson, H. (1971). *Coordinating Reading Instruction.* Glenview, IL: Scott, Foresman and Company.

Rosenblatt, L. (1978). *The Reader, the Text, the Poem,* Carbondale, IL: Southern Illinois University Press.

Sadoski, M. C., and Page, W. D. (1984). Miscue combination scores and reading comprehension: analysis and comparison. *Reading World, 24*(October)45–53.

Shuy, R. (1967). *Discovering American Dialects.* Champaign, IL: National Council of Teachers of English.

Siegel, M. (1984). *Reading as Signification.* Unpublished doctoral dissertation, Indiana University, Bloomington.

Smith, F. (1971). *Understanding Reading: A Psycholinguistic Analysis of Reading and Learning to Read.* New York: Holt, Rinehart and Winston.

Smith, L. A., and Lindberg, M. (1979). Building instructional materials. In K. S. Goodman (Ed.), *Miscue Analysis: Applications to Reading Instruction* (pp. 77–90). Urbana, IL: ERIC Clearinghouse on Reading and Communication Skills and National Council of Teachers of English.

Tierney, R. J., Bridge, C. A., and Cera, M. J. (1979). The discourse processing operations of children. *Reading Research Quarterly, 14*(4)539–573.

Weatherill, D. W. (1983). *The Reading Strategies Average Upper-Elementary Students Observed Through Miscue Analysis.* Unpublished Dissertation Proposal, University of Arizona, Tucson.

Wolfram, W., Potter, L., Yanofsky, N. M., and Shuy, R. (1979). *Reading and Dialect Differences* (Dialects and Educational Equity Series). Arlington, VA: Center for Applied Linguistics.

Woodley, J. W. (1983). *Perceptions of Tachistoscopically Presented Lines of Print.* Unpublished doctoral dissertation, University of Arizona, Tucson.

Yaden, D. B., and Templeton, S. (1986). Introduction: metalinguistic awareness—an etymology. In D. B. Yaden and S. Templeton (Eds.), *Metalinguistic Awareness and Beginning Literacy: Conceptualizing What It Means to Read and Write* (pp. 3–10). Portsmouth, NH: Heinemann.

III. Books for Children and Young Adults

The following resources include books for children and adolescents. These resources may be used to begin a classroom library or to select books related to thematic units or students' interests. Children's books mentioned in the text are also listed.

National Council of Teachers of English, 1111 Kenyon Rd., Urbana, IL 01801

Journals: Language Arts, English Journal
Books: Reading Ladders, NCTE to You

International Reading Association, 800 Barksdale Rd., P.O. Box 8139, Newark, DE 19714–8139.

The Reading Teacher
The Journal of Reading

Children's Choices:
In addition to the titles listed below, note should be made of *Reading Unlimited* and *Reading Systems* (Glenview, IL: Scott Foresman).

Covernton, J. (Compiler). (1985). *Putrid Poems.* Adelaide, Australia: Omnibus Books.
Fitzgerald, J. D. (1967). *The Great Brain.* New York: Dell Publishing Company.
Fox, P. (1984). *The One Eyed Cat,* New York: Bradbury Press.
Martin, Jr. B. (1983). *Brown Bear, Brown Bear, What Do You See?* New York: Holt, Rinehart and Winston.
McKee, D. (1973). *The Man Who Was Going to Mind the House.* New York: Abelard-Schuman.
Paterson, K. (1978). *The Great Gilly Hopkins.* New York: Thomas Y. Crowell.
Richler, M. (1975). *Jacob Two-Two Meets the Hooded Fang.* New York: Alfred A. Knopf.
Rosen, M. (1981). *You Can't Catch Me.* Harmondsworth, Middlesex, England: Puffin Books, Penguin Books Ltd.
Smith, D. (1973). *A Taste of Blackberries.* New York: Thomas Y. Crowell.
Tolstoy, A. (1971). *The Great Big Enormous Turnip.* Glenview, IL: Scott Foresman and Company.
Voight, C. (1981). *Homecoming.* New York: Ballantine Books.
Wiesner, W. (1972). *Turnabout.* New York: The Seabury Press.
Wigginton, E. (1972–1980). *Foxfire* (Books 1–6). Garden City, NY: Anchor Press.

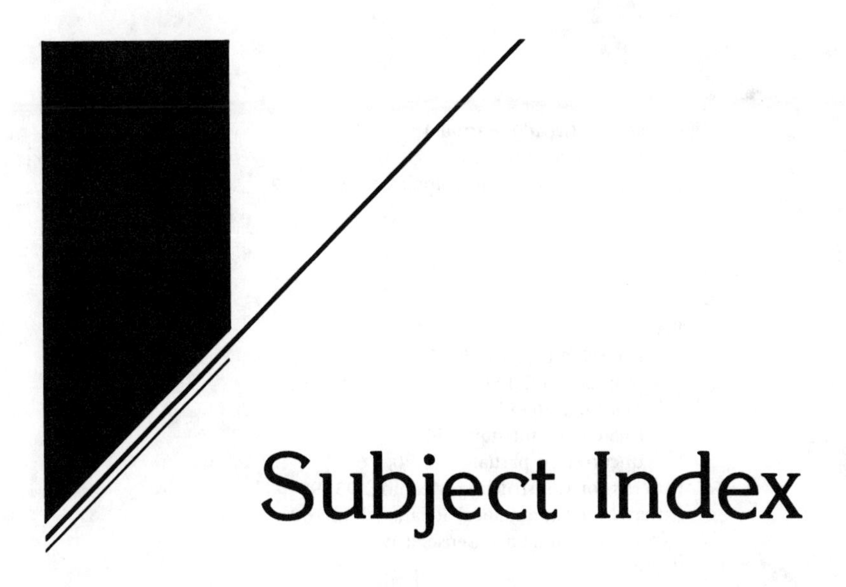

Subject Index

Author Index

About the Authors

Yetta M. Goodman is Professor of Education at the University of Arizona, Tucson, Arizona.

Dorothy J. Watson is Professor of Education at the University of Missouri—Columbia, Columbia, Missouri.

Carolyn L. Burke is Professor of Education at Indiana University, Bloomington, Indiana.

DATE DUE
CEIVED APR 1 4 1993